Praise for *Guiding Readers – Layers* ...

'If you want to run effective, inspired and engaging guided reading ___ ___ ... your school with junior-aged learners then look no further– just buy this book. It distils the principles, offers practical examples, and recommends rich texts (fiction and non-fiction) in a thoroughly accessible and inviting manner. This is a super book - a great buy. A must buy.'
Professor Teresa Cremin, The Open University

'Extremely informative in how to get the most from my guided reading sessions in class. I now feel much more confident in understanding how children go through the complex process of comprehending a text and what I can do to help them. The authors clearly have a lot of experience and expertise in this area, resulting in clear, practical advice that will benefit any teacher of reading. It has improved my classroom practice and I recommend it to trainee and qualified teachers alike.' *Luke Craig, Year 6 teacher, Britannia Village Primary School, London Borough of Newham*

'This very welcome publication is an invaluable resource and a must-read for training and practising teachers, English subject leaders and teacher educators. The authors provide an authoritative and comprehensive synthesis of research into reading comprehension with practical exemplars of practice in classrooms and further guidance for staff development.'
Mary Anne Wolpert, Primary PGCE Deputy Course Manager, Faculty of Education, University of Cambridge

'The book makes essential reading for all teachers attempting to unpick the complex but vital process of teaching text comprehension skills. It features "plain English" references to theory and research, a teacher-friendly frame for mapping the potential of guided reading texts, and a selection of case studies that teachers can read, digest, try and then apply. The book offers busy practitioners an efficient, on-the-ground tool for auditing practice, text selection, and scaffolding sessions – all essential skills – along with suggestions for staff professional development. A very comprehensive but accessible book. I read the majority in one sitting and will certainly be having a go with some of the ideas before the end of term!' *Gill Evans, Head Teacher, Holcombe Brook Primary School*

'This handbook is a very rich resource for teachers and schools, demonstrating why and how thoughtfully planned guided reading can be so valuable in the classroom. The case studies illuminate some of the many ways in which a teacher's choice of high-quality texts can give rise to fascinating dialogic discussions, enhancing the children's pleasure and deepening their understanding.' *Dr Gabrielle Cliff Hodges, Senior Lecturer in Education, Faculty of Education, University of Cambridge*

'An essential tool for new and experienced teachers of guided reading, it simplifies the concept and process behind the subject while providing a wealth of practical resources and examples for everyday classroom use.' *Lauren Huntley, Class teacher and Reading Coordinator, Parsloes Primary School, London Borough of Barking and Dagenham*

'This book weaves together pedagogy, research and real classroom case studies in an incredibly accessible way. It will inspire and equip teachers and librarians to adopt a rich, effective and enjoyable approach for guiding their pupils to develop as readers.' *Fiona Evans, Head of School Programmes, National Literacy Trust.*

Guiding Readers – Layers of meaning

A handbook for teaching reading comprehension to 7–11 year olds

Wayne Tennent
David Reedy
Angela Hobsbaum
Nikki Gamble

First published in 2016 by the UCL Institute of Education Press,
University College London, 20 Bedford Way, London WC1H 0AL

www.ucl-ioe-press.com

© Wayne Tennent, David Reedy, Angela Hobsbaum, Nikki Gamble 2016

British Library Cataloguing in Publication Data:

A catalogue record for this publication is available from the British Library

ISBNs

978-1-78277-182-1 (paperback)

978-1-78277-183-8 (PDF eBook)

The authors and publishers would like to thank the following for permission to reproduce
copyright material. **p. 59**: Reproduced by permission of Whale and Dolphin Conservation
(NB: this advertisement has since been amended); **p. 60**: Reproduced by permission of
Immediate Media Co. Ltd.; **p. 72**: Cover image for *The Lost Thing* © Shaun Tan, 2000.
First Published in Australia and New Zealand by Lothian Children's Books, an imprint of
Hachette Australia Pty Ltd. US Edition published by Arthur A. Levine Books, an Imprint
of Scholastic Inc.; **p. 87**: 'Maggie Dooley' from *I Had a Little Cat: Collected poems for
children* by Charles Causley, originally published by Macmillan Children's Books. Printed
by kind permission of David Higham Associates; **p. 97**: 'The Malfeasance' by Alan Bold.
Reproduced by kind permission of Alice Bold. Copyright © Alan Bold to Alice Bold;
pp. 114–15 and 120–1: From *True Stories: The Story Behind Chocolate* by permission of
Capstone Global Library Ltd. Photo on source p. 17 ©Tyler Hicks/Getty. Photo on source
p. 21 ©Tim Platt/Getty; **pp. 116–17 and 122–3**: From *Espresso Ideas Box: Chocolate* by
Jillian Powell, first published in the UK by Franklin Watts, an imprint of Hachette Children's
Books, Carmelite House, 50 Victoria Embankment, London EC4Y 0DZ. Photo on source
p. 4 © Danita Delimont/Alamy. Photo on source p. 5 © BrazilPhotos/Alamy. Photo on
source p. 20 © Richard Semik/Shutterstock; **pp. 141–3**: *The Wildman* reproduced by
permission of The Agency (London) Ltd, © Kevin Crossley-Holland, 1976; First published
by André Deutsch; All rights reserved and enquiries to The Agency (London) Ltd, 24
Pottery Lane, London W11 4LZ, fax: 020 7727 9037; **pp. 152–3**: 'The Flowers' © Alice
Walker. Reproduced by permission of The Joy Harris Literary Agency and Houghton Mifflin
Harcourt; **p. 160**: Cover image of *Tadpole's Promise* by Jeanne Willis, illustrated by Tony
Ross, reproduced by permission of Andersen Press; **p. 161**: Cover image for *The Fairy
Stories of Oscar Wilde* © Harold Jones Estate. Reproduced by permission; **p. 176**:
Cover image for *Memorial*, © Gary Crew and Shaun Tan, 1999. First Published in Australia
and New Zealand by Lothian Children's Books, an imprint of Hachette Australia Pty Ltd.;
p. 188: Reproduced with permission of Curtis Brown Group Ltd, London, on behalf of
Grace Nichols. Copyright © Grace Nichols 1996.

Every effort has been made to trace copyright holders and to obtain their permission
for the use of copyright material. The publisher apologizes for any errors or omissions
and would be grateful if notified of any corrections that should be incorporated in future
reprints or editions of this book.

The opinions expressed in this publication are those of the authors and do not necessarily
reflect the views of the UCL Institute of Education, University College London.

Cover and text designed and set by emc design ltd; cover image © photoslb com/
Shutterstock

Printed by CPI Group (UK) Ltd, Croydon, CR0 4YY

Contents

About the authors

Nikki Gamble is Director of Just Imagine, a creative centre for teachers that puts children's literature at the centre of learning. Formerly Head of English in the Faculty of Education at Anglia Ruskin University, Nikki has worked extensively with teachers in classrooms across the UK and internationally. Most recently she has managed the Developing Excellence in Reading project for the London Schools Excellence Fund. Recent publications include *Exploring Children's Literature* (3rd edition, 2013) and *4XR: A Five Step Framework for Teaching Reading 7–13* (2016).

Angela Hobsbaum worked at the UCL Institute of Education on MA and doctoral programmes and latterly as a national director for Reading Recovery, during which time she learned to appreciate the importance of giving children access to high-quality literacy and the effectiveness of scaffolded instruction.

David Reedy is General Secretary and Immediate Past President of the United Kingdom Literacy Association (UKLA) and Co-Director of the Cambridge Primary Review Trust (CPRT). Until 2014 he was Principal Adviser for primary schools in the London Borough of Barking and Dagenham. Recent publications include contributions to *Teaching English Creatively* (2nd Edition, 2015, ed. Teresa Cremin), *Teaching Grammar Effectively in Key Stage 1* (UKLA, 2016) with Eve Bearne and Rebecca Kennedy, and *Teaching Grammar Effectively in the Primary Classroom* (UKLA, 2014) with Eve Bearne.

Wayne Tennent worked for many years as a primary teacher in London and also spent a number of years teaching overseas. He is a Senior Lecturer in Education at the University of East London. He teaches on MA Education and doctoral programmes. His particular area of interest is literacy, and specifically the reading comprehension process. He has worked for a number of years with schools – both primary and secondary – developing pedagogical practices to support the teaching of reading comprehension. His book *Understanding Reading Comprehension* was published in 2015.

Introduction

Being able to read effectively, efficiently, and with enjoyment is a skill every child needs. For more than 15 years, since guided reading was first introduced to England through the National Literacy Strategy (DfEE, 1998), this approach has been advocated as the accepted teaching method to foster good reading with pupils aged 4–11 and beyond. But using guided reading is a complex task. While there has been ample advice on using this approach with early readers who are just attaining fluency, little support has been available on how best to use it with older pupils who have mastered the basics and are now ready to tackle short chapter books and more demanding texts. This book aims to help teachers of 7–11 year olds make better use of guided reading in their English lessons, and it may also be useful for teachers working with 12 year olds too. It presents alternative approaches to what has become the conventional, 'traditional' method of guiding readers that we have observed in schools.

How this book can help teachers

This book starts by describing the complex cognitive processes involved in understanding a text and going beyond the words on the page to explore deeper layers of meaning. It shows how teachers can select worthwhile texts and how they can design effective guided reading lessons. Through case studies drawn from classrooms today, it provides examples of guided reading lessons, from 7 year olds who are just becoming fluent readers to more challenging lessons for high attainers at the top of the primary school or 12 year olds in their first year of secondary school. It concludes with suggestions for a sequence of professional development sessions, which can be followed by the school's English subject leader or senior teacher with responsibility for literacy to improve practice across the school. It also provides suggestions on choosing texts – picture books, short stories, poetry, and non-fiction – recommended for pupils in these age groups; the lists of texts will be updated regularly on our website: www.guidingreaders.com.

Guided reading

'Guided reading' is a commonly used term across the English-speaking world to describe the teaching of reading in small groups. The approach originated in the 1960s in New Zealand (Simpson, 1966) to accompany a newly published set of early reading books. It subsequently spread to Australia, where it was advocated by Don Holdaway in the 1970s (Holdaway, 1979). At this time it was used specifically with beginning and early readers. The practice later became widespread in the United States, due in large part to the work of Fountas and Pinnell (1998), who advocated its use with older developing readers. It was introduced to England in 1998 through the National Literacy Strategy, and became a recognized feature of literacy lessons throughout primary school.

Guiding readers

From its inception, the purpose of guided reading has been to show young readers how to gain meaning from text. The role of the teacher is to guide the young reader through this process. By guiding reading, we mean the *deliberate and explicit teaching of reading strategies that support the comprehension of text.* However, it is obvious that the nature of this guidance will change across the 4–11 age range and beyond. As noted above, guided reading has its roots in the teaching of early readers and it has been clearly described for children aged 4–6. However, the differentiation in approach needed for more competent readers aged over 7, who are beyond the early stages of literacy learning, has never been adequately described. Children who are able to read, understand, and appreciate books at an appropriate level, and who are ready to encounter more challenging and varied texts, will need more sophisticated teaching to explore deeper layers of meaning. Guiding readers in the 7–11 age range will not necessarily include the cueing strategies required when guiding younger readers. For these older pupils, the teacher will need to use strategies that help readers to attain an accurate, literal comprehension and also to engage with text at a deeper level, appropriate for this age range. Strategies to support text comprehension include predicting, questioning, summarizing, thinking aloud, and visualizing; these are described more fully later, indicating how they can be taught as part of guided reading lessons.

The strategies do not include inference-making, synthesizing, analysing, and critiquing. These are outcome skills that can be achieved through the effective use of the reading strategies. For example, inference-making skills can be developed by ensuring the reader asks appropriate questions of the text: the strategy of questioning helps to develop the skill of inference-making.

What this book doesn't do – book banding and the readability trap

Teachers sometimes want books for guided reading to be organized into bands, according to their reading level, much like Book Bands for guided reading in Key Stage 1 (Bodman and Franklin, 2014). There are also programs that claim to be able to assign a difficulty level to a text using software that utilizes a readability formula. These programs can be seductive for busy teachers, but unfortunately they can also be misleading. To illustrate, we can compare two texts: first, the popular *Diary of a Wimpy Kid*, which has undoubtedly been successful in engaging some of the most unwilling readers. Secondly,

Kevin Crossley-Holland's *The Seeing Stone*, which might be regarded as a more literary story. Some of the *Wimpy Kid*'s appeal may be due to the ease with which the reader can access the text through cartoon stickman-style drawing and schoolboy humour. *The Seeing Stone* is a historical fantasy, woven around Arthurian legend, in very short chapters.

But which is the more challenging? A simple readability formula would suggest that *Wimpy Kid* requires a higher reading level. Renaissance Learning's Accelerated Reader program assigns this book a level of 5.2; *The Seeing Stone* has a book level of just 4.3. But a knowledgeable teacher will recognize that the demands made on the reader in terms of context, historical understanding, and literary language are far greater in *The Seeing Stone*. Counting the length of words and sentences is not sufficient to make a judgement about the challenge a text will present.

Another example of the fallibility of text level is its inadequacy in assigning a reading level to a picture book, where the meaning is created by the interplay of text and image. Formulae that use only the linguistic features of the text cannot take account of the rich meanings in the illustrations. Using the same formula, Anthony Browne's subtle picture book *The Tunnel* is assigned a book level of 2.7, whereas another hugely popular but far more straightforward story, Claire Freedman's *Aliens in Underpants Save the World*, has a book level of 3.2. But understanding *The Tunnel* requires more than being able to read the words.

So, in thinking about the accessibility and challenge of a text, a number of factors have to be taken into consideration before making a judgement. This is why we do not offer a 'banding' approach to texts for guided reading at this level. Instead, in Chapter 2 we offer a different way to evaluate text.

Part 1: How we read and what to read

Chapter 1, Making sense of texts: reading in the moment and reflecting on reading, describes the mental processes involved in comprehension. As skilled readers we are largely unaware of what's happening in our heads when we try to understand text. So why do teachers have to know about this? Teachers need to be aware of these processes in order to know what they have to consider *before* teaching, when thinking about the text to be used. Then they need to be aware of what is happening *as* the text is read to enable the pupil to get a generalized understanding and *after* the text is read to ensure this understanding is deepened; finally, at a *later* reflective stage, such factors as appreciation and evaluation become important.

Chapter 2, Text potential: selecting quality texts for guided reading, describes how teachers can decide on the merits of a text and the possibilities it holds for teaching. The teacher needs to know what the text offers in terms of its language and the way ideas are conveyed. Then the teacher must decide on the specific goals to be addressed when working with this text in the context of a particular guided reading group. For example, should the focus be on acquiring a literal comprehension of the text? Or is it related to developing more evaluative and appreciative responses to the text? Is the proposed text 'fit for purpose' given the group of children to be taught and the learning intentions to be addressed?

Part 2: What to teach and how to teach it

Chapter 3, Strategies for teaching comprehension, discusses the teacher's role in helping pupils to explore texts in more depth, by describing a number of useful strategies. One of the key strategies is questioning and in this chapter a sequence of questions is described that the teacher can incorporate when planning the lesson, each tapping a deeper layer of meaning.

Chapter 4, Scaffolding learning through dialogue, explains how teachers can facilitate the kind of learning conversations that will enable pupils to ask questions, to explore meanings tentatively, and to build their understanding collectively. In such conversations, teachers must relinquish authority and give up the role of arbiters; they have to ask authentic questions and learn the skill of dialogic talk.

Part 3: Case studies of guided reading: lessons from the classroom

Having covered the processes involved in understanding text and the decisions a teacher must make in deciding which text to use, Part 3 will consider how all of this translates into practice in the classroom through case study examples. These case studies show how teachers in real classrooms have designed lessons or series of lessons to guide readers effectively.

Chapter 5, Introduction to the case studies, explains how the case studies are presented.

Chapter 6, Examples of guiding reading for 7–9 year olds (Years 3 and 4), includes three case studies: a sequence of lessons based on advertisements, a picture book, and a poem.

Chapter 7, Examples of guiding reading for 9–11 year olds (Years 5 and 6), includes four case studies including a poem, a non-fiction text, a film clip, and a fiction text.

Chapter 8, Examples of more challenging reading lessons for 10–12 year olds, offers three fiction topics – a short story, a classic short story, and a picture book – and a poem.

Part 4: Developing guided reading through the school

Chapter 9, Building a reading school: opportunities for professional development, provides guidance for senior leaders and literacy coordinators on how a consistent guided reading programme can be rolled out for pupils over 7. A suggested programme of professional development is provided, together with advice on resourcing in order to build a reading school. These sessions enable schools to examine their resources and to support teachers when planning their guided reading lessons, emphasizing the importance of encouraging learning dialogue with the pupils. Measuring reading skills, beyond the decoding of words, is notoriously difficult, because no clear developmental trajectory for comprehension has been mapped; some ways in which teachers can collect evidence of pupils' learning are described.

Chapter 10, Planning for provision across a year group, suggests how teachers can select a balanced variety and range of material over the whole year and provides an introduction to the lists of texts, which are available on the website. From these, teachers can make a selection, taking account of the interests of the class or group and the reading skills that need to be developed.

Additional material, lists of books, interviews with authors, videos of classroom practice and more are all available at www.guidingreaders.com

References

Bodman, S. and Franklin, G. (eds) (2014) *Which Book and Why: Using book bands and book levels for guided reading in Key Stage 1*. London: Institute of Education Press.

Department for Education and Employment (DfEE) (1998) *National Literacy Strategy: Framework for teaching*. London: Department for Education and Employment.

Fountas, I.C. and Pinnell, G.S. (1998) *Guided Reading: Good first teaching for all children*. Portsmouth, NH: Heinemann.

Holdaway, D. (1979) *The Foundations of Literacy*. Gossford, Australia: Ashton-Scholastic.

Simpson, M. (1966) *Suggestions for Teaching Reading in Infant Classes*. London: Methuen Educational.

Part 1

How we read and what to read

Chapter 1: Making sense of texts: reading in the moment and reflecting on reading

Chapter 2: Text potential: selecting quality texts for guided reading

1 Making sense of texts: reading in the moment and reflecting on reading

What's going on in our heads when we try to make sense of a text? As fluent readers, we tend to be unaware of what's happening, unless the process is interrupted in some way, for example, by an unknown word, an unusual construction, or a difficult idea. For young readers, such interruptions are likely to be more frequent. That is why teachers of reading need to recognize the source of any difficulty, in order to know how young readers have made sense of the text or what difficulties they may have encountered. One way of understanding this is to think about the reading process at two points in time: first, we need to be aware of the key underlying skills at work *as we read* the text, and secondly we need to consider any analysis or personal response made *after* the text has been read. This chapter focuses on (i) the key underlying skills that occur *in the moment* of reading; and (ii) the analysis and responses we make *afterwards*, through reading reflections.

Reading in the moment

Reading in the moment requires the reader to make sense of text as it is being read. In doing so, the reader builds up a literal understanding of the text, by dealing with the surface layer of meaning. In fact, this is what you are doing now, but as skilled readers this is something of which you are probably almost unaware. If we break this process down, we can see that attaining a literal understanding can actually present numerous challenges for children who are still developing their reading skills, even if we assume that they are competent at word recognition.

The reason for this is that comprehension is not a single process, but is made up of a number of components (Duke, 2005) that work interactively and interdependently as the text is read. The act of text comprehension requires numerous processes to take place in our heads. Irwin (1991) describes these processes as a series of levels; unpacking these levels of processing exposes the components of comprehension.

The microprocesses level

To comprehend written text we have to understand what the words on the page mean. While this seems obvious, it is not as straightforward as it might appear. The word 'breeze', for example, could refer to a type of gentle wind, as in the following sentence:

> There was a gentle breeze blowing across the lake.

However, it might also refer to something that is very easy to do, as in:

> The test was a breeze and I finished it in 20 minutes.

In order to understand what a word means, the reader must link the word to the right context in which it is used (Aitchison, 2003), and we cannot assume a child reader, whose oral vocabulary is still developing, will have experienced this word in the relevant context. This is further complicated by the fact that about 70 per cent of commonly used English words have more than one meaning (Bromley, 2007). In fact, you can probably think of a few meanings for the word 'mean': one of these might relate to its mathematical or statistical sense. To show how we learn words in context and the way in which words can have more than one meaning, we can take examples from the study of mathematics. For example, words such as 'odd', 'even', 'times', and 'table' (to name but a few – there are many more) have very different meanings in their mathematical context when compared to their everyday usage. As well as single words, readers also have to make sense of groups of words. This can become complicated because of such things as phrasal verbs, idioms, and figurative language. In the earlier example, the word 'breeze' described a type of wind. Of course, 'wind' can be pronounced in another way, which totally changes its meaning, e.g. 'wind the clock'. Turning this pronunciation of 'wind' into a verb shows how many different meanings can stem from the same word. For example, it is possible to generate the following phrasal verbs:

> wind up – wind down – wind back

So, at the end of a teaching career, you might want to wind down and relax, wind back the clock, and remember all the children who used to wind you up.

One way to think about the words and groups of words in a text is to think of them as a series of concepts. The more concepts there are, the more difficult it is to keep track of the piece overall, regardless of such things as sentence complexity. Robert Nye's (1997) story *Lord Fox* provides an example of this. The story opens with the following five sentences:

> There was once a <u>young woman</u> called <u>Lady Mary</u> who had two <u>brothers</u> called <u>Forbes</u> and <u>Edward</u>.
>
> They lived together in the <u>wild border country</u> between <u>England</u> and <u>Scotland</u>, in a <u>fine house</u> which <u>stood</u> on a <u>cliff</u> overlooking <u>the sea</u>.
>
> Lady Mary was <u>beautiful</u>, and she had more <u>men</u> wanting to <u>marry</u> her than she could <u>count on the fingers of both hands</u>.
>
> Forbes and Edward were very <u>proud</u> and very <u>fond</u> of their lovely <u>sister</u>, and <u>anxious</u> that she should <u>choose</u> well amongst her <u>suitors</u>.
>
> Now among her suitors was a <u>certain</u> <u>Lord Fox</u>.

Conservatively, there are 24 different concepts raised in the first five sentences of this story; these have been underlined. This raises a number of issues for the reader attempting to comprehend this text at even a literal level. To begin with, the reader has to assign meaning to each of them. As we have seen, many words in English have more than one meaning and this text provides several examples of this. The reader has to assign the correct meaning to 'country' and 'fine'. The reader also has to make sense of what is meant by a 'certain' Lord Fox (as opposed to an uncertain one?). Some words might be entirely new and are perhaps unknown, such as 'anxious' and 'suitors'. Also, even if concepts are known, we can't assume that all readers will assign the same meaning to them; for instance, does 'wild' mean the same thing to everyone?

To help with the process of assigning meaning to these concepts, readers have to apply their background knowledge to the text. In this instance, the reader will need a concept of 'England' and 'Scotland' as nations separated by a 'wild border country'. Without this background knowledge it will be much more difficult to make sense of the text.

The reader also has to make sense of the idiom of counting on the fingers of both hands. As skilled readers with extensive knowledge of the English language, we know that this means Lady Mary has lots of admirers rather than that she is actually counting them on her fingers. In this way, readers bring their knowledge of language usage to the process of comprehending text.

A further point to consider is that there are a lot of words and phrases to remember. Indeed, it is unlikely that you will be able to remember them all without rereading the text. You will probably not be able to recall the text itself word-for-word. When we read text, we use both our long- and short-term memory. Our long-term memory is involved in storing and retrieving background knowledge information. Our short-term, or working, memory enables us to maintain sense when we encounter new pieces of information as we read. We are not able to handle large amounts of information as we read because our working memory has a limited capacity, so when we encounter new concepts we have to integrate them with those already stored in our long-term memory. The individual's comprehension at this level of processing is also affected by familiarity with the content, the level of interest, and awareness of the language or literary style used. This leads us on to the next level of processing.

The integrative processes level

When we read written text, we usually have to engage with a series of sentences. The integrative processes level is where readers make links between the words and sentences they have read in order to achieve some sort of coherence. This is achieved by making inferences to fill in any gaps in understanding. This may come as a surprise, because as teachers of reading we might think of inference-making in relation to 'bigger' issues such as character motivation. However, we also make inferences to link statements within and between sentences. For example, let's look again at one of the sentences introduced earlier and add a second one:

> The test was a breeze and I finished it in 20 minutes.
> I went home early.

Here, the reader might make the link that the person went home early *because* she/he finished the test in 20 minutes. This is not stated explicitly; the reader infers it.

These inferences are really important because texts are very rarely ever completely explicit. In the text above, for example, it is not stated what the test is actually about or how long it was meant to take. We might make more inferences about these aspects later, but, as the text is being read, the reader is trying to find and make links to explain the relation between the test being easy and going home early. It is by making these links that the reader is able to integrate the sentences into a coherent whole.

Taking the *Lord Fox* example, we can see how the reader might integrate each sentence with the previous one as new information is encountered:

> There was once a young woman called **Lady Mary** who had two brothers called **Forbes** and **Edward**.
> **They** lived together in the wild border country between England and Scotland, in a fine house which stood on a cliff overlooking the sea.
> Lady Mary was **beautiful**, and she had more **men wanting to marry her** than she could count on the fingers of both hands.
> Forbes and Edward were very proud and very fond of their lovely sister, and anxious that she should choose well amongst her **suitors**.
> Now among her suitors was a certain Lord Fox.

Examples of integration in this text include having to resolve the pronoun 'they' at the beginning of the second sentence. The reader has to link this back to the characters introduced in the first sentence: Lady Mary, Forbes, and Edward. This requires an inference to be made. If this link is not made, the reader will not know who 'they' are. The reader may also make links within sentences, such as in the third one, where the reader may infer that people wanted to marry Lady Mary *because* she was beautiful. Links may also be made across sentences. For example, if the reader does not know what 'suitors' are, it may be possible to infer its meaning by making a link to the previous sentence, where it is stated that many men wanted to marry her.

The macroprocesses level

The process of integrating the words and phrases across a series of sentences into a coherent whole takes us to what Irwin (1991) describes as the macroprocesses level. At this point, readers organize their understanding of the text they are reading into a mental model (Johnson-Laird, 1983). This involves creating a general understanding of the text – a picture in your head, if you like, although, as Johnson-Laird notes, the mental model isn't necessarily a visual representation. A key element of this is the creation of a situation model (van Dijk and Kintsch, 1983), which involves relating the text that has been read to a context. For the *Lord Fox* story, this might mean that the reader understands that Lady Mary and her two brothers live in an isolated area. Lady Mary is very beautiful and many men want to marry her, including Lord Fox. Different readers might produce a slightly different mental representation if asked to describe one, although it might have similar elements. However, it is important to note that the mental representation described here is not the same as the text as it appeared in the story. This is because we don't remember the text word-for-word. The creation of a mental model allows the reader to engage with further text and to incorporate this too. The comprehension of the text is constantly being adjusted in the light of new information as it is processed.

The elaborative processes level

Having constructed a mental representation, the reader is then likely to elaborate or develop it by making further inferences. For example, in the *Lord Fox* story, the reader might situate the narrative in the past because of the style of the writing ('There was once a young woman called Lady Mary'), the use of particular vocabulary ('suitors'), and perhaps because of previous reading experiences that locate lords and ladies as characters from a different era. There is no other indication from the narrative so far that this is the case. The reader might also infer the size of Lady Mary's house, given that they are a titled family, and also begin to visualize what Lady Mary might actually look like. Elaborations of this kind are likely to take place as we read and can be developed further through discussion afterwards.

The metacognitive processes level

When Irwin talks of the metacognitive processes, she is referring to comprehension monitoring. This is an important component of skilled reading, and involves readers tracking their understanding of the text as they read. Relating this to the *Lord Fox* story, a reader might pause for thought if, hypothetically, the next sentence after Lord Fox is introduced reads, 'Lord Fox pulled up in his red Ferrari and did a wheel spin on the gravel driveway.' This of course is plausible, but if readers have developed a mental representation of the text whereby it is set in the past – the nineteenth century, for example – it would require them either to change their mental representation, or to check whether they have misinterpreted something they had encountered previously.

The components of comprehension exposed

Irwin's levels of processing reveal a number of components of comprehension that the teacher needs to consider when guiding reading; problems in any one of these will affect the reader's understanding. They include:

- vocabulary
- grammatical understanding
- memory
- inference-making
- comprehension monitoring
- background knowledge.

When reading in the moment, the reader processes the text using all of these components, to a greater or lesser extent, with the initial purpose of gaining a literal understanding of the text. Of course, these components, although separated into a discrete list here, work in an interactive manner. As was shown above when reading the *Lord Fox* story, readers might apply their knowledge of vocabulary and know that 'country' can have more than one meaning, but using the context of the story they can infer that here it doesn't relate to some sort of nation-state but rather to a rural landscape. The important point to remember is that *it cannot be assumed that all children will process the text in the same way*. This is because each reader comes to each text with a unique profile in terms of ability to utilize these components. Their oral vocabularies will be different as will their working memory capacities; they may well have different inference-making skills; they may not be aware that text needs to be monitored as it is read, and each reader will bring to the text different background knowledge based on different life experiences. It is for these reasons that different readers comprehend text in different ways.

Reading reflections

Reflecting on one's reading takes place *after* the text has been read. This involves the reader engaging with the deeper layers of meaning in the text. These reflections might require the reader to search the text for clues, make judgements about characters, consider the text's language features, evaluate its literary merits, or begin to form a personal opinion. The quality of these reflections will depend on the sense the reader has made of the text when reading in the moment; this, as we have seen, is a complex process in itself. Reading reflections build on the surface layer of meaning. If the understanding of the surface layer of the text is not well developed, the reader is less likely to be able to reflect upon her/his reading to good effect. Added to this, we know that the literal comprehension developed from a piece of text is likely to vary from reader to reader, so their reading reflections are also likely to be different.

When readers reflect on their reading, they process the text in a slightly different way from reading in the moment, because they have time to consider their understanding. However, they will still make use of the components of comprehension outlined earlier when reflecting on their reading, but now in a more elaborate way. The most important component for supporting reading reflection is inference-making.

When reflecting on their reading, readers are likely to make different kinds of inferences. When reading *in the moment*, they tend to make connective inferences that knit the sentences together, and anaphoric inferences where they resolve pronouns, such as working out who *they* are in the second sentence in the *Lord Fox* story. When *reflecting on their reading*, readers will make deductive and inductive inferences (Tennent, 2015). Deductive inferences are those that are 100 per cent certain, and inductive inferences are those that are logically plausible. Deductive inferences are those made by analysing the text for evidence; inductive inferences require readers to apply background knowledge as part of their reflection. Deduction has its roots in mathematics and logic, and Tennent questions the extent to which we actually make deductive inferences when we reflect on a text; we can use the evidence in the text, but the answer may still not be 100 per cent certain. However, we can see how these inferences may be made when we look back to the *Lord Fox* text.

When reflecting on our reading, we can refer back to evidence in the text, such as the fact that Lady Mary had a title (she was not only a woman but held the title 'Lady'), together with the fact that she lived in a 'fine house', and come to the conclusion that she was rich (although of course she may not be). We may not have arrived at this conclusion during the course of reading the text, but, by using the evidence in the text, our understanding of it will have developed. Similarly, we may reflect on the fact that nobody knew much about Lord Fox, and conclude that there is something suspicious about him. Again, by reflecting on the text through the use of evidence, we are developing another layer of meaning.

Similarly, we may apply further background knowledge during our reflection. For example, we may question whether it is right for Mary's brothers to want to see her married and whether Mary should accept this. From our modern perspective, this may seem sexist; we may also question whether it is acceptable that men want to marry Mary just because she is beautiful. Indeed, we might even want to question what it means to be beautiful. So, by applying background knowledge to support the making of inductive inferences, the reader is able to develop another layer of meaning.

In these examples, inference-making helps to deepen our understanding of the text by using available evidence and by applying our background knowledge to the linguistic aspects of the text; this type of reading reflection allows us to make judgements about characters and to develop our opinions.

What we haven't touched on yet are the literary aspects. These would include reflection on such things as the author's intent and choice of words. This adds another layer of meaning for the reader to consider because, as Zwaan (1996: 241) notes, literary texts are often 'inconsiderate'. By this he means that writers do not necessarily make everything straightforward for the reader; they do not always use simple words and sentences. Indeed, Zwaan considers this to be the hallmark of what might be considered 'good' literature:

> A successful author presumably uses literary devices in a manner that creates aesthetic effects (e.g. suspense), thereby making it appealing for the reader to overcome any processing difficulties created by the devices. In other words good literary texts are inconsiderate in an interesting way.
>
> (Zwaan, 1996: 243)

Or, as Dr Johnson said, 'What is written without effort is in general read without pleasure.'

Now, bearing in mind that we aim to expose children to 'good' or high-quality literature, it is inevitable that they will encounter texts that are 'inconsiderate' – texts that are by design ambiguous or difficult, or which challenge the way we expect to read. We need only look at Anthony Browne's picture books to see this, or consider *The Iron Man* by Ted Hughes.

This is a book to which children in the United Kingdom are commonly exposed in primary school. At the opening of the story we see an enormous and mysterious iron man standing on the top of a cliff. Swaying in the wind, he eventually falls into the sea. Hughes describes his fall as follows:

CRRRAAAASSSSSSH!

Down the cliff the Iron Man came toppling, head over heels.

CRASH!

CRASH!

CRASH!

From rock to rock, snag to snag, tumbling slowly.

And as he crashed and crashed and crashed

His iron legs fell off.

His iron arms broke off, and the hands broke off the arms.

His great iron ears fell off and his eyes fell out.

His great iron head fell off.

All the separate pieces tumbled, scattered, crashing, bumping, clanging, down on to the rocky beach far below.

A few rocks tumbled with him.

Then

Silence.

This text is likely to challenge young readers in a number of ways. For a start, we cannot presume that they have developed meaning at the surface layer adequately. Their literal understanding is not likely to be as well developed as with a less literary text. When reflecting on their reading, they may note that the text presents challenges in terms of its layout. Hughes organizes the lines of the text to replicate the Iron Man's fall. Also, the ending presents a challenge upon which the reader may wish to reflect:

Then

Silence.

Here we have an incomplete sentence: 'Then silence.' Grammatically this would be considered incorrect because it is incomplete (and no doubt any child writing such a sentence would be told as much). Here, Hughes is being inconsiderate and it is up to the reader to make sense of this.

What we have described in this section on reading reflections is the same underlying skill – inference-making – being applied to two very different contexts: a largely linguistic one in the *Lord Fox* story (although there are literary aspects that can be drawn from this) and a literary one in *The Iron Man* example. What these examples show is that helping children to understand is not simply about guiding them to develop the component processes involved in text comprehension; we must also consider the text itself in terms of its challenges and what it has to offer. This brings us to the issue of *text potential*, as it is not possible to separate the child's ability to comprehend from the text they are being asked to read, and this will be considered more fully in the next chapter.

Further factors to consider

There are other factors that teachers need to keep in mind when guiding readers.

Reading goals

The ability to apply these components to the comprehension process may be compromised if there is a lack of awareness of the importance of reading goals. The pupil needs to understand what is to be achieved by reading a particular text. Some pupils may believe that reading is about decoding words rather than seeking meaning (Myers and Paris, 1978). Yuill and Oakhill (1988) suggest that some children don't make inferences because they don't know when it is appropriate to do so.

Indeed, Cain and Oakhill (1999) suggest that it is precisely those struggling with comprehension who need to be made aware of the aims and purposes of reading. Palincsar and Brown (1984) also stress the importance of clarifying the purpose of the reading task. The case studies presented later in this book show how to make reading goals explicit when guiding readers. In some of the case studies the teachers present the pupils with questions prior to reading, to give them a focus for their reading.

Motivation

Perfetti *et al.* (1996) state that lack of motivation may lead to general comprehension failure. To improve motivation and to stimulate interest, the text itself needs to be interesting. Singer (1994) regards this as a factor that affects inference-processing, citing a number of studies that demonstrate this point.

Age

A further factor could be age. Taking a developmental path, it has been found that young readers are less likely to make inferences, and that inference-making ability is likely to increase with age (Casteel and Simpson, 1991). This should come as no surprise, particularly when we consider that world knowledge and vocabulary knowledge also increase with age. This is further complicated by the fact that all readers, including adult readers, have limited processing capacity with which to engage with text. As we read, our brains can do only a certain amount of work. For younger readers, more of this brain work is likely to be spent on decoding the text, leaving less capacity available to work on the task of comprehension.

Conclusion

When we ask developing readers to make sense of text, we are asking them to undertake a cognitively complex process. They have to be able to understand words and phrases, and integrate them across a series of sentences. They then have to link this to their background knowledge and fill in any gaps in understanding by way of inference-making. It is for this reason that achieving even a literal understanding is not necessarily going to be straightforward. To guide readers effectively, it is essential to understand how they have made sense of what they have been reading (their reading in the moment) and to use this to inform how this understanding of the text can be deepened (through reading reflections). The most obvious way to do this is by asking them; developing effective dialogic interactions is therefore important, as will be shown in the case studies later in this book, where the interaction between the teacher and the pupils is examined. However, there is another interaction that needs to be considered, and that is the interaction between the reader and the text. This interaction is considered in the next chapter.

References

Aitchison, J. (2003) *Words in the Mind: An introduction to mental lexicon* (3rd edition). Oxford: Blackwell.

Bromley, K. (2007) 'Nine things every teacher should know about words and vocabulary instruction'. *Journal of Adolescent and Adult Literacy*, 50 (7), 528–37.

Cain, K. and Oakhill, J.V. (1999) 'Inference making and its relation to comprehension failure'. *Reading and Writing*, 11, 489–503.

Casteel, M.A. and Simpson, G.B. (1991) 'Textual coherence and the development of inferential generation skills'. *Journal of Research in Reading*, 14, 116–30.

Duke, N.K. (2005) 'Comprehension of what for what: Comprehension as a non-unitary construct'. In S. Paris and S. Stahl (eds) *Current Issues in Reading Comprehension and Assessment*. Mahwah, NJ: Lawrence Erlbaum, 93–104.

Irwin, J.W. (1991) *Teaching Reading Comprehension Processes* (2nd edition). Boston: Allyn and Bacon.

Johnson-Laird, P. (1983) *Mental Models: Towards a cognitive science of language, inference, and consciousness*. Harvard: Harvard University Press.

Myers, M. and Paris, S.G. (1978) 'Children's metacognitive knowledge about reading'. *Journal of Educational Psychology*, 70, 680–90.

Palincsar, A.S. and Brown, A.L. (1984) 'Reciprocal teaching of comprehension-fostering and comprehension-monitoring activities'. *Cognition and Instruction*, 1, 117–75.

Perfetti, C.A., Marron, M.A., and Foltz, P.W. (1996) 'Sources of comprehension failure: Theoretical perspectives and case studies'. In C. Cornoldi and J. Oakhill (eds) *Reading Comprehension Difficulties: Processes and intervention*. Mahwah, NJ: Lawrence Erlbaum, 137–65.

Singer, M. (1994) 'Discourse inference processes'. In M.A. Gernsbacher (ed.) *Handbook of Psycholinguistics*. San Diego, CA: Academic Press.

Tennent, W. (2015) *Understanding Reading Comprehension: Processes and practices*. London: Sage.

Van Dijk, T.A. and Kintsch, W. (1983) *Strategies of Discourse Comprehension*. New York: Academic Press.

Yuill, N. and Oakhill, J. (1988) 'Effects of inference awareness training on poor reading comprehension'. *Applied Cognitive Psychology*, 2 (1), 33–45.

Zwaan, R.A. (1996) 'Towards a model of literary comprehension'. In B. Britton and A.C. Graesser (eds) *Models of Understanding Text*. Mahwah, NJ: Lawrence Erlbaum, 241–56.

Children's texts

Hughes, T. (1968) *The Iron Man*. London: Faber and Faber.

Nye. R. (1997) *Lord Fox and Other Spine-Chilling Tales*. London: Orion.

2 Text potential: selecting quality texts for guided reading

A principal aim in teaching reading is to develop independent readers, who are capable of dealing with sophisticated texts and able to make informed reading choices for both academic and personal reading. To achieve this, pupils need to experience engaging, well-written, thoughtfully designed, expertly illustrated books and other resources. This chapter aims to help primary teachers select the best books for this purpose.

How to evaluate texts: some underlying principles

'Reading for pleasure' is not an 'add-on'

A principle that underpins the texts selected for our case studies and book lists is that 'reading for pleasure' is not an 'add-on' to which we turn our attention once children have learnt to decode; rather, it is the context in which all reading should take place. Motivation, independence, and emotional involvement serve to create readers who will want to continue reading beyond the acquisition of a basic proficiency. So it is fundamental that when texts for teaching are selected, we bear in mind children's reading and recreational interests and choose material that has the capacity to appeal to them, while also considering the quality of language and illustration and the variety of authors and genres.

Being familiar with texts is essential

One of the issues raised most often by teachers wishing to develop reading in their schools concerns the quality and appropriateness of the texts they use. In our observations, the reading lesson sometimes fails because the text chosen does not allow for sufficiently challenging teaching and learning. *There is no short cut to teaching reading well; you have to know the texts you are using.* Before teaching a text, the teacher must have read and evaluated its suitability, and the text potential tool (see p. 32) is one way to do this, as illustrated in all of our case studies.

The ability to assess the quality of a text is developed through extensive reading. Searching for the right text can be time-consuming, so building up a personal knowledge bank of novels, stories, poems, and non-fiction is essential. Over time, a reading teacher acquires a library she/he can dip into with increasing confidence. In this chapter we offer guidance on choosing books for guided reading.

Some schools have mechanisms for sharing knowledge, such as a termly staff meeting to talk about new books or a staff reading club. The professional development activities included in Chapter 9 offer a route to do this. Finding the right text is important, but it takes time to keep up-to-date with recently published books. We have included a curated list of books for different age groups, which we will continue to update online at www.guidingreaders.com.

Texts should be chosen for the potential they offer

As the resourcing of reading is a substantial financial commitment and one that requires a budget to be allocated on an ongoing basis, it is essential that purchasing decisions are made wisely. In terms of judging cost-effectiveness, it is important to look at the potential of the text. Can it be used with more than one group in different ways? A rich text can support teaching over several lessons. A book that is slight in its scope may be cheaper, but possibly provide less value for money. Ways to review the school's reading resources are suggested in Chapter 9.

Choosing the text: potential and challenges

Once children are able to read or decode the words, the question of text difficulty requires different considerations. Assessing whether readers can decode enough words to be able to access the meaning of the text is no longer the most important factor. Of course, there may be residual issues with longer, more complex words, technical vocabulary, or words that are taken from other languages, but other aspects of the text affect the level of challenge and accessibility. However, these challenges also provide possibilities for learning and potential foci for teaching.

The challenges of texts

The challenges and potential posed by texts are influenced by a number of aspects:

- subject – what is the text about?
- text-type, purpose, and intended readership – is it written to amuse, persuade, inform, or warn? Is it a balanced view?
- theme – the deeper meaning
- narrative features – from whose perspective is it written? Where is it set?
- literary features – particular stylistic devices
- language features
- grammar, syntax, sentence structure
- vocabulary
- historical, social, and cultural context – where is it set and who is represented?
- coherence
- visual features – design of material
- making links to background knowledge.

These aspects will be discussed in more detail below and each one features in the text potential diagram (see p. 32).

Subject

To assess the appropriateness and difficulty of the subject, teachers need to know their pupils' interests and experience. The challenge presented by a text varies according to the readers' prior knowledge of a subject. When the content is well within the readers' experience, they may be able to tackle a text that is linguistically and structurally more challenging. This explains the anecdotal reports of teachers who have been surprised to find 'struggling readers' successfully tackling material such as a Haynes car manual at home even though they appear unable to read beyond the most basic texts in school.

Texts will vary in conceptual difficulty, but reading will be easier if:

- pupils have some understanding of the concepts
- their prior understanding is activated, perhaps through paired talk
- the subject of the text is one that interests them
- sufficient context is provided prior to reading.

Some subjects incorporate specialized vocabulary and may have particular ways of presenting ideas, for instance, using maps, diagrams, tables, or graphs. The difficulties posed by subject-specific material will depend on prior experience.

Some questions to consider:

- Is the subject matter familiar or will it extend the knowledge of the class or group? Is the topic unusual?
- Is the content likely to be of interest to the class or group?
- Are there opportunities for integrating the reading sessions with other aspects of the curriculum?
- Are issues thoughtfully presented?
- Does the text appeal to you and is it likely to appeal to the pupils?

Text-type, purpose, and intended readership

As well as conveying the content, texts are often written with a particular purpose, for example, to inform, persuade, or amuse. Even an information book will be influenced by the author's values, which may be explicitly or implicitly expressed. Being able to recognize bias and subjectivity requires an ability to decentre, to see another person's point of view. Being able to detect authorial bias demonstrates a more sophisticated appreciation of the text. All books are written from a particular standpoint and no presentation of facts is value-free. Some texts are explicitly persuasive – advertisements, political manifestos – or instructive, such as recipes or manuals, and their effectiveness can be examined.

Some questions to consider:

- Why was this text written and who is it aimed at?
- What value judgements are implied by the text?
- Can these judgements be explored with the group?

Theme

While the subject of a text refers to the text's content, to what is immediately evident, 'theme' is the term used to describe the unifying ideas that lie below the surface of the text. For example, the subject of Nicky Singer's *Feather Boy* is a young boy who visits an old lady in a care home and tries to fulfil a promise to help her make a coat of feathers, so that she can exorcise the ghost of her dead son. But the dominant themes of this story are the value of intergenerational relationships, growth and self-belief, the therapeutic effects of oral storytelling and history, and overcoming fears.

Books with deceptively simple plots may have profound themes. An example is Eric Carle's *Draw Me a Star*, which is about an artist who paints animals, flowers, the rain, a rainbow, and a star. However, responses to this text demonstrate varied interpretations of the themes, which have been variously described as 'creation-myth', 'life-cycle', 'covenant of hope', and 'afterlife'. The goal of sensitive teaching is to open up possibilities for interpretation rather than leading towards a predetermined answer. Such different interpretations show that a response at a thematic level is highly personal. Picture books that appear to be straightforward in terms of plot and language can often have complex themes.

The themes in fiction are one of the ways in which readers relate stories to their own lives and are able to move from the specific to more general understandings.

Some questions to consider:

- What themes can I identify in this text?
- Can I anticipate which of these may be easily identified and understood by the pupils?
- Does the text present interesting ways of describing human experience and exploring the world?

Narrative features

Narrative is composed of several elements: plot, narration, setting, and character. The plot comprises the main events that make up a story. At its simplest level, the plot is linear and moves chronologically through the events. However, stories are not always told in this way. A writer might choose to begin at the end, to employ flashbacks, or tell the story episodically, non-sequentially. Stories might also include sub-plots, which may provide additional challenges for readers as they have to hold more than one strand in their heads, sometimes with large sections of intervening narrative.

As well as the sequence of events, the narration (that is, the process of narrating or telling the story) influences the reader's understanding. This may be something as straightforward as telling the story in the first person as an observer or a character from the story (using the pronouns 'I', 'we', 'me'). One of the constraints of a first-person narration is that it limits the events that can be written about and, to be credible, a consistent point of view needs to be employed. A third-person narration ('he', 'she', 'they') might follow the lives of all the characters in the story (the omniscient narrator) or might be focalized through the eyes of one of the characters. In the latter, a reader might feel as though she/he is reading a first-person narration, even though the story is actually written in the third person.

Sometimes dual narration will be used so that two or more points of view are presented. These points of view might be first person or a mix of first and third person. Picture-book texts may also vary in narrative complexity. Anthony Browne's recent version of the Goldilocks story, *Me and You*, has a dual narrative presented on two facing pages, which requires the reader to understand that these events are happening simultaneously.

Stories take place in a setting: the time and place where the story is set. Time can be present, past, or future and is often genre-specific. So science fiction is frequently set in the future. Historical fiction is set in the past. Time-slip or time-travel novels juxtapose one time frame against another. This might have the effect of revealing something about the values of contemporary society or be used to take the protagonist on a journey of self-discovery. The other aspect of setting is place, which may be familiar or unfamiliar to the reader. Unfamiliar settings allow readers to experience vicariously places beyond their current experience. They might offer a contrast to the reader's life or show similarities that transcend time and place.

The importance of the setting to the story varies. Some stories are highly dependent on the setting; this is true for otherworld fantasy and for most historical fiction. In answer to the question, 'Could this story be set somewhere else?' the answer would be 'No'. However, in some stories the setting is less important.

There are no stories without characters. At the very least, a story must have one character. Characters have relationships with each other: they can be in conflict or support, they can be heroes or anti-heroes, protagonists or antagonists.

Some questions to consider:

- Is there anything interesting about the way this story is narrated?
- Is the setting important and how is it realized?
- How are the characters rendered? Are they believable? Are they similar to characters in other stories?

Literary features

Different text-types have their own distinctive features. Stories, poems, advertisements – all use language in different ways, enhancing or embellishing it for impact.

While the simplest kind of narrative is a linear, chronological recount written in the third-person past tense, writers may use different methods to draw the reader into the story. For instance, the present tense might be employed as a device to signal a shift in time, to create a dream sequence, or take the reader into the thoughts of a character.

Poetic language may include imagery and metaphor, alliteration, rhyme, and metre and is not restricted to poems; fine fiction writing may be poetic. Figurative language, such as *'The road was a ribbon of moonlight over the purple moor'*, or personification, *'Forest letting her hair down to the teeming creeping of her forest ground'*, make comprehension more difficult. Younger children might find metaphor hard to grasp, and allusions are contingent upon recognizing original sources. For instance, a reader unfamiliar with the biblical account of the crucifixion would not recognize this reference in the death of Aslan in C.S. Lewis's *The Lion, The Witch and the Wardrobe*. This doesn't necessarily mean that they cannot understand the significance of that episode or that their appreciation will be lessened; it just means they will not have the specific cultural referent to draw upon when reading it.

Non-fiction texts may include comparison and contrast, problems and solutions, causes and effects. These relationships may not be immediately understood by novice readers.

Some questions to consider:

- Are there particular literary features with which pupils will not be familiar and that will need to be taught?
- Is the text structured in unfamiliar ways?
- Is the language vivid or powerful; is word choice apposite?
- Is the writer's voice distinctive?

Language features

The language used by a writer may not always be Standard English; some writers use Non-Standard English and some characters speak in dialect. Texts will also differ in their register, from the very formal register of a legal document to the informal speech between friends, or the dialogue in a play script where everything is conveyed through speech and a different intonation can change the meaning.

Dialogue may be presented in ways that challenge readers. Direct tagged speech – 'What do you want?' **asked Tom** – is easier than an exchange of untagged speech, which requires readers to follow closely in order to identify which character is speaking. However, the untagged speech requires the reader to 'fill the gap' and interpret the manner in which something is said as well as to identify who is speaking, so may be a subtler way of representing dialogue.

Some questions to consider:

- Is the language contemporary or old-fashioned; what are the clues?
- How familiar are the pupils with the register of this text?
- Is the text written in Standard English or in dialect? Are there any dialect words that are likely to be unknown?
- Does the dialogue sound authentic and are characters distinguishable by the way they speak?

Grammar and syntax

Short, simple sentences are generally easier to read than complex sentences with embedded subordinate clauses. Punctuation acts as a guide to pronunciation, and reading aloud helps to develop an implicit understanding of the grammar of the sentence.

However, simple sentences do not necessarily make a text easy to understand. Sometimes writing that has been deliberately simplified may not convey concepts successfully, hindering rather than aiding reading. For instance, in *The Tale of Peter Rabbit*, Beatrix Potter writes, '*I am sorry to say that Peter was not very well during the evening. His mother put him to bed, and made him some chamomile tea; and she gave a dose of it to Peter.*' The Ladybird 'Read it Yourself' edition (2013) simply states, '*Peter Rabbit was not very well. Mrs. Rabbit put him to bed and made him some tea.*' The words are simpler but what is made unclear is why Mrs Rabbit would give tea to an unwell Rabbit. In Potter's original it is clear from the word 'dose' that chamomile tea is to be given as a medicine.

Furthermore, the overuse of short sentences can make the writing appear stilted, leading to staccato reading as readers struggle to find the rhythm of the text. But sometimes short sentences may be used for deliberate effect: '"*I have a golden bedroom," he said to himself, and he prepared to go to sleep; but just as he was putting his head under his wing, a large drop of water fell on him. Then another drop fell.*' (Jane Ray, 1994, *The Happy Prince*)

Ellipsis also makes demands on the reader. '*The youngest sister was both kind and beautiful, the older had a dark, jealous heart.*' The omission of 'sister' (the older sister) may not be immediately apparent to all readers.

Some questions to consider:

- Does the sentence structure follow the patterns of oral language or is this disrupted for literary effect?
- Are sentences long and will children need help to be able to follow the meaning?
- Are constructions active or passive? Is the writer's meaning obscured by the choice of voice?

Vocabulary

It is often assumed that word choice makes the text hard to understand. While it may generally be true that polysyllabic words are harder to read than monosyllabic words, there are other factors to take into account. The 'pterodactyl phenomenon' describes the ease with which a beginner reader will read complex words such as 'pterodactyl' or 'tyrannosaurus', because of enthusiasm for the subject matter. In the same way, lexical words like 'aeroplane' and 'elephant' might be easily recognized from the context, while grammatical words such as 'however' or 'eventually' may prove more difficult.

A text where the vocabulary has been kept artificially simple is likely to be unrewarding to read. One of the delights of reading is encountering new words that help us to distinguish finer nuances of meaning. For example, what is the difference between 'sobbed', 'wept', and 'cried'? What would be lost if a book for young readers used only 'cried' because 'wept' and 'sobbed' were considered less familiar?

A further point to make about vocabulary is that most English words have several meanings, as was described in Chapter 1 (see p. 29). Dictionaries may give us partial or incomplete definitions and it is only by working with both contextual and dictionary definitions that we can start to arrive at a more complete understanding.

In the case studies, you will find examples of teachers using this knowledge to plan lessons in which they anticipate that vocabulary will need to be explicitly taught. (See Case study 3, 'Maggie Dooley'; Case study 4, 'The Malfeasance'; Case study 5, Chocolate; Case study 11, 'For Forest'.)

Some questions to consider are:

- Does the text include a lot of technical vocabulary that will need to be explained before reading?
- Are there words from other languages?
- Does the word choice elicit an emotional response?

Historical, social, and cultural context

All texts are set in a context: fiction may be contemporary, imaginary, or historical; non-fiction texts may show current or past events, in familiar or strange places. It is useful to consider whether the characters portrayed in fiction are likely to be ones to which the children can relate, and, in non-fiction text, whose perspective is presented and who is missing from the account.

Some questions to consider:

- Is the historical, social, and cultural context recognizable to the children or does the text take them into new worlds? Will they need a bridge to enable them to access the world of the text?
- How can the pupils be helped to make connections to their own lives?

Coherence

It is difficult for any text to be completely explicit. If we read the sentence 'I went to the beach', there is still information missing: we don't know if it is a pebble beach or a sandy one. If we add the next sentence 'I took my bucket and spade', we might presume it is a sandy beach (although even then we don't know the colour of the sand; on volcanic islands such as Tenerife many of the sandy beaches are black). Readers seek to find coherence within sentences and between sentences so that the text makes sense. In Chapter 1, when we analysed the opening to *Lord Fox* by Robert Nye (1997), we saw how making coherence can be affected by the number of concepts the reader has to hold in the memory while reading, and how easily information between sentences can be integrated by inference-making (such as resolving pronouns and inferring causal links). Longer sentences can make this integration more difficult.

<u>Some questions to consider</u>:

- How easy it to fill in the 'gaps' in the text?
- How easy is it to integrate information between sentences?
- How accessible are the concepts to the reader? If the concepts relate to phenomena beyond the reader's knowledge and experience then it becomes more difficult for them to access and to integrate.

Sophisticated visual features, design, and book production

Visual features of a text affect the meaning it conveys. A visual language includes colour, shapes, texture, and line. A palette of sepia tones may indicate that a story is set in the past, as it does in Paul Fleischman's *The Matchbox Diary*, or a world in which the imagination is not allowed to flourish, which lacks colour, as in Faye Hanson's *The Wonder*. A broken line may give an image a dynamic feel or express movement, as it does in Quentin Blake's masterful drawings, while a bold black outline may give a feeling of stasis as it does in Dick Bruna's *Miffy* stories.

The medium used can also help to convey the meaning of the text. For example, Jeannie Baker's collaged picture books use natural materials such as seeds and grasses to express her ecological message.

The framing of illustrations is also important. In Anthony Browne's *Voices in the Park*, four voices tell the same story from their various points of view. For each story a different frame is used. In Charles's story the framing around the illustrations is a metaphor for his captivity. The illustrations in Smudge's story bleed to the edge of the page, reflecting her free spirit.

Aspects of typography such as font size, type, and layout affect the way we respond to a text. The tone of a text can be changed completely by font choice. Sans serif, rounded fonts such as Arial have a friendly look and feel, while Times New Roman looks serious and formal.

Designers also play with typography to emphasize meaning. In Jan Oke's *Naughty Bus*, words playfully mirror the actions of the toy bus. Typography is a key feature of Lauren Child's books. Emboldened text may indicate when a character is shouting and a trail of text around a page may indicate that a character is going on a journey. Designs that some readers find intriguing may be off-putting for others. Some may find it difficult to follow text that isn't presented in a clear, left-to-right linear layout or be able to decipher the letters of a highly decorative font.

Visual texts also have a grammar that may not be readily understood; novice graphic novel readers might find splash pages (where a single panel is used on one page, often with a lot of detail and action) difficult to interpret.

Comic texts have their own conventions that regular readers will know well, but these will not necessarily be readily understood by readers new to the genre. They may be perplexed by the order in which to read the frames or may not understand the use of speech bubbles for dialogue and thought bubbles for unspoken ideas.

Some questions to consider:

- How do colour, line, pattern, the arrangement of shapes, and the use of light and dark affect the meaning of this text?
- Can you tell how the images have been made and how this affects the meaning?
- How do text and images work together? Do they mean something different when read together or separately?
- Does this text have any interesting design features? Do any of the design features require the text to be read in a particular way?

Making links to background knowledge and experiences

When readers make sense of text, they do so by making links or connections to what they already know. Keene and Zimmerman (1997) note three different kinds of connections:

- text to self – highly personal connections between a text and the reader's own life experiences
- text to text – connections readers make when they are reminded of another text that they have read
- text to world – wider connections readers make to the reading event by accessing other knowledge that might have been gained through television, movies, and visits.

Some questions to consider:

- Does this text invite readers to make connections to their personal experience?
- Does it remind readers of similar texts – similar in plot or style?
- Can readers relate this text to some other information they know?

The potential of the text

Prior to teaching, it is essential to get to know the text and understand what it has to offer the reader. The prompts above offer some guidance. The text potential diagram (see below) represents this visually and is a useful planning tool. The diagram is intended as an aid when planning your teaching; it is not a checklist. There is no need to write something in each box for every text.

In the case studies, we demonstrate how the text potential diagram can be used. Any planning must take into account the particular group of pupils for whom you are planning the work. For example, in the case studies, the text potential diagram for 'For Forest' (planned as a more challenging text for able pupils in Year 6) is different from that for 'The Malfeasance', which was designed for Year 5 pupils. The text potential diagrams reflect this; some boxes have been left empty because they don't apply to those pupils. It isn't necessary to complete each box; focus on what is most relevant to this group of pupils.

Exploring what the text offers

Vocabulary
- unknown words
- technical vocabulary
- multiple meanings
- slang
- unusual words

Narrative features
- plot
- character
- setting

Historical, social, and cultural context

All texts have a context e.g. Southern States of USA in 1930s, etc.

Making links to background knowledge:

Possible connections to personal experience, world knowledge, and familiarity with other texts.

Mapping Text Potential

The challenges in the text and the opportunities for teaching presented by the text

Language features

e.g.:
- speech: direct and indirect
- Standard and non-standard English
- register – level of formality

Grammar; Syntax

Sentence structure

Theme

Deeper meaning, e.g. loss, triumph over adversity, redemption, friendship, loyalty, overcoming problems, justice, fairness, etc.

Visual features

Illustration, colour, shape, layout, medium, line, composition, typography, point of view

Literary features
- narration
- voice
- imagery
- metaphor
- simile
- alliteration
- pun, etc.

Coherence

How easy is it to follow the text when reading?

How are sentences linked? Check that readers are able to follow.

Subject

What is the text about? e.g. First World War, a lost dog, the circus, food.

Text type, purpose, and intended readership

Including bias, values, etc.

Conclusion: the value of choosing a text with potential for learning and teaching

In what they read, children should be exposed to a full range of emotions, from joy to anger, curiosity, or sadness. The characters and situations they meet in print should present a range of social situations and family structures, a variety of ethnicities, sexualities, and disabilities, representing not merely the contexts familiar to them but extending their experience vicariously.

They are entitled to read books where the writer crafts language to engage the reader, by expressing ideas clearly and concisely or by making the reader take a new perspective. They should also encounter books where care has been taken to provide appropriate illustrations, which, in the case of non-fiction, are accurate and informative, or, in the case of literature and poetry, allow space for the reader to develop an imaginative response and an aesthetic appreciation, unconstrained by marketing, branding, and packaging.

Reading (both fiction and non-fiction) offers the opportunity to learn about life, reflecting readers' lives and offering opportunities to understand the world through the eyes of others. Through the teaching of reading, teachers model how to be a discerning reader and how to find and appreciate quality texts.

Reference

Keene, E.K. and Zimmerman, S. (1997) *Mosaic of Thought: Teaching comprehension in a reading workshop*. Portsmouth, NH: Heinemann.

Children's texts

Browne, A. (1999) *Voices in the Park*. Picture Corgi.

— (2011) *Me and You*. Picture Corgi.

Bruna, D. (2004) *Miffy Goes Swimming*. Big Tent Entertainment.

Carle, E. (1995) *Draw Me a Star*. Picture Puffin.

Fleischman, P. (2013) *The Matchbox Diary*. Walker Books.

Hanson, F. (2013) *The Wonder*. Templar/Candlewick.

Ladybird (2013) *The Tale of Peter Rabbit*. Read it Yourself with Ladybird. Frederick Warne.

Lewis, C.S. (2001) *The Lion, the Witch and the Wardrobe*. HarperCollins.

Nye, R. (1997) *Lord Fox and Other Spine-Chilling Tales*. Orion.

Oke, J. (2004) *Naughty Bus*. Little Knowall Publishing.

Potter, B. (1902) *The Tale of Peter Rabbit*. Frederick Warne.

Ray, J. (1994) *The Happy Prince*. Orchard.

Singer, N. (2002) *Feather Boy*. HarperCollins.

Part 2

What to teach and how to teach it

Chapter 3: Strategies for teaching comprehension

Chapter 4: Scaffolding learning through dialogue

3 Strategies for teaching comprehension

When guiding readers through the process of text comprehension, teachers will have to consider *what* to teach and *how* to teach it.

The question of *what* to teach will be informed by factors described in the first two chapters of this book. Chapter 1 covered the largely invisible mental processes involved in understanding a text. It was noted that comprehension is not a single process but is rather composed of different components. Decoding ability is one important component, but understanding is not simply about this alone. The teacher of reading must also consider how easily the readers will be able to access a piece of text in terms of such factors as their background knowledge, the depth and breadth of their vocabulary, and the ease with which they are likely to keep track of (or monitor) what they are reading. As such, *the starting point is to consider the readers themselves and what they are likely to bring to a particular text.*

Once this initial relation between the reader and the text has been considered, the teacher then needs to decide what this text offers – what we have called in Chapter 2 its text potential. For example, the text may offer the opportunity to focus closely on characterization or settings or how the language is used purposefully by the author. Crucially, *the focus of teaching will be influenced by the teacher's knowledge of the readers' needs*.

Having located the text to be used and decided what the focus of the teaching should be, the teacher then needs to consider *how* to teach it. And it is at this point that we would like to make explicit our pedagogical stance. We believe that guiding readers is not about the teacher telling the readers what they *should* understand from the text. In that scenario, everything comes from inside the teacher's head and the reader is little more than an 'empty bucket' to be filled with information. If you want to go down this road, then it is easier to tell the reader the 'correct' answer; in other words, you may as well tell them *what* to comprehend.

But the reason why the kind of teaching advocated here is called *guiding* reading is to stress that what is important is the *reader's* understanding, not the teacher's. The teacher may want to *share* her/his understanding of the text at some point, but this is not the same thing as presenting it as the 'correct' version. As Tennent (2015) notes, what is in the teacher's head is largely irrelevant; ultimately, the teacher needs to know what's in the reader's head.

The teacher's task is to deepen the reader's understanding of the text by initially ascertaining what sense the reader has made of the text just after having read it: the child's reading 'in the moment'. This will give an indication of the reader's literal understanding. Once the teacher has established this, she/he is in a position to focus on the more reflective aspects of reading, or reading reflections as they have been described in Chapter 1, and attention can turn to deepening this understanding, by making links to the reader's background knowledge and inviting an emotional or evaluative response to the text.

In this scenario, the teaching and learning interactions are very different from those where the teacher is working from her/his own understanding of the text. This is because the teacher is not focusing on *what* needs to be understood but rather *how* to develop the reader's understanding.

This brings us back to the point that *we don't teach comprehension* because comprehension is an outcome; rather, *we teach strategies to support comprehension*. So what are these strategies?

Strategies to support the development of comprehension

To support the text comprehension of developing readers as they read in the moment and also in their reading reflections, teachers can use a number of strategies when guiding reading. Duke and Pearson (2002) outline some of these and present a rationale for using them. Most of the following analysis is based on their thoughts. The first four of these strategies are used in the **Reciprocal Teaching** approach to guided reading (Palincsar and Brown, 1984) and feature in a number of the case studies included later. These strategies are summarized in Table 3.1 and then explored in more detail below, with examples.

Table 3.1: Strategies that can be used when guiding readers

STRATEGIES	WHAT THE STRATEGY INVOLVES
Predicting	Making a logically plausible guess as to what will happen next.
Questioning	Asking questions about the text to expose different layers of meaning.
Clarifying	Checking how specific words and phrases have been understood.
Summarizing	Stating the main events, actions, or ideas in the text.
Thinking aloud	Reading a few sentences or a paragraph and verbalizing what has been understood. Then repeating this activity across a text.
Noting the text structure	Highlighting the main linguistic features of a specific text-type.
Visualizing	Developing a visual image of written text.

Predicting

Duke and Pearson (2002) cite numerous studies that show how encouraging developing readers to predict the action and events of upcoming text supports their comprehension. Encouraging prediction can also support the development of inference-making skills (Palincsar and Brown, 1984). In its simplest form, prediction can be described as guessing what might happen next in a text. However, there is more to it than that. When readers make a prediction, they need to activate their prior knowledge and anticipate the upcoming text in the light of this.

An example of this can be seen in the following transcript. This features some 10–11-year-old pupils in a guided reading lesson making predictions about *The Strap Box Flyer* by Paul Jennings. In this short story set in rural Australia, a trickster called Giffen is selling glue for $10 a tube; he claims that this glue is very strong. Giffen proves this by dabbing it onto a piece of rope, sticking the rope onto a car roof, then lifting the car off the ground with a small crane.

However, Giffen does not tell anyone that the glue lasts for only four hours. Miss Tibbs, an old lady, uses the glue to put up some shelves. She places her precious china collection on the shelves – including her favourite china horse. After four hours the shelf collapses, smashing the china. When asked to make a prediction about what will happen next, the following interaction occurred:

Child A: I think he's going to go to another town, and ... erm, sell some more. And Miss Tibbs, yeah? She will go after him and catch him.

Teacher: Really?

Child A: Yeah, and she'll, and she'll ... get her money.

Child B: Yeah and Giffen might go to jail.

Teacher: (looking at Child C) What do you think?

Child C: I don't think he will.

Teacher: No?

Child C: No, he's, he's greedy. All he wants is money. He won't give the money back. And also, also, Miss Tibbs is an old lady – she won't be able to go to find him.

Teacher: So what *will* happen then?

Child C: Erm ... I think he'll hide ... Yeah, Australia is a big country too, so I don't think they'll find him.

Teacher: You think he'll hide.

Child C: Yeah, and then he'll sell some more glue somewhere else.

In this interaction we see all three readers making predictions based on their prior knowledge. This prior knowledge comes from the previously read text (Giffen won't give the money back because he is greedy) and from knowledge of the world (criminals get sent to prison; Australia is a big country).

Questioning

The types of questions that readers are asked about text can help them to access different layers of meaning. For this reason, asking questions that require inferential responses supports the development of inference-making skills. Duke and Pearson (2002) note that it is particularly important to get developing readers themselves to ask questions of the text as they read. They point to the work of Raphael and her colleagues (Raphael and McKinney, 1983; Raphael and Pearson, 1985; Raphael and Wonnacott, 1985), who have identified three types of questions that support comprehension:

1. Right there – the answer is explicit in the text.
2. Think and search – the answer can be found in the text but some level of inference-making will be required.
3. On my own – the reader is encouraged to bring her/his background knowledge to the text.

An adapted version of these question-types can be seen in some of the case studies featured later in this book, where they are described as 'looking' questions, 'clue' questions, and 'thinking' questions. The aim of these questions is to encourage readers to reach different layers of meaning in texts.

It is interesting to note that these layers can be applied to the real world; for example, take a look out of the window, and answer these questions:

- What colour is the sky? (Looking – literally.)
- Do you think it is going to rain? (How do you know? What's your evidence? What clues did you use?)
- Is it good that it rains? (Can you think of yes and no answers to this question and justify your thinking?)

In relation to *The Strap Box Flyer* story explored with the group of 10–11-year-old readers described above, the three questions linked to the opening of the story outlined above were as follows:

- What was Miss Tibbs searching for? ('looking')
- Does Giffen like his customers? ('clue')
- Why do you think people trusted Giffen? ('thinking')

The first of these questions allows the teacher to assess the children's literal comprehension. The answer is that Miss Tibbs was looking for the china horse that fell from the shelf. However, the teacher would take the opportunity to follow up this question with others that would allow the group to show their literal understanding of the text as a whole. The second question aims to help the reader to make inferences using evidence available in the text. In this way, different parts of the text become connected as links are made. The third question allows the readers to make links to their background knowledge and encourages them to evaluate, justify, and speculate. The second and third question-types have an explicit aim of deepening the reader's understanding. As with the first question, they are not ends in themselves; rather, they are jumping-off points for dialogue.

Clarifying

Clarification is a strategy highlighted by Palincsar and Brown (1984). Here the reader has the opportunity to ask for clarification about the meaning of unknown words or phrases. This encourages readers to monitor their understanding to ensure that the text is consistent. It also allows the teacher to check whether there are any gaps in understanding. In *The Strap Box Flyer* there would appear to be very little need for clarification. It is not a particularly difficult text to decode and there seems to be little in the way of challenging vocabulary. However, in the guided reading lesson described here, some clarification was necessary in the next part of the story. Here, a boy called Scott ignores his father's wishes to throw away his broken canoe and instead fixes it with Giffen's glue (and you can probably work out the implications of this).

Teacher:	So there are no words that need clarifying then? [Silence from the children.] Mmm, I'm not sure of one word … Scott's father told him to take the broken canoe to the 'tip'. What's a 'tip'?
Child B:	It's … It's … erm … Is it? It's the pointy … erm…
Teacher:	Pointy?
Child C:	It's the front … the front of the canoe.
Child B:	Yeah! That's it!
Teacher:	How do you mean?
Child C:	You know a canoe? It has a pointy bit at the front.
Teacher:	So that's the tip?
Child C:	Yeah.
Teacher:	Yeah, but that's doesn't make sense, does it? Scott has to take his canoe to the pointy bit at the front. That doesn't make sense.

After some further discussion, guided by the teacher, the group worked out that a tip was a place where rubbish is taken. They decided it was a word more obviously related to Australia because none of them used it. They talked in terms of a 'rubbish dump'. The point to make here is that, although they had a good idea of the narrative, clarifying this one simple word enhanced their understanding.

Summarizing

Summarizing encourages readers to focus on the main content of the text and this in turn supports the process of comprehension monitoring (Palincsar and Brown, 1984). It involves the reader distinguishing between important and unimportant information in a text and then synthesizing the key points briefly. Of course, what one reader might consider to be important information, another may not. There is an example of this in the guided reading session on *The Strap-Box Flyer*, when readers were summarizing the section where Scott's canoe broke.

Child D: Scott got some glue from Giffen … erm … He wanted to fix his canoe … He fixed it and … went to the lake and he was enjoying himself … erm … He forgot the time and the boat broke and he drowned.

Teacher: I think you got most of the main points there. What do you think?

Child A: Errrr … I think it's important when his parents … His parents called the police … it's important to say that.

Child B: The life jacket! What about the life jacket?

Teacher: What about the life jacket?

Child B: Well, Scott … He … he forgot to put it on.

Teacher: Is that important?

Child B: Yeah, he wouldn't have drowned otherwise.

Child D: Yeah we should add that.

Here we see that the children are working to co-construct the main points of the text.

Thinking aloud

As the term suggests, thinking aloud involves making one's thoughts audible while the text is being read. In this situation, the reader pauses after reading some text and makes her/his thoughts explicit. There are two types of think-alouds: teacher think-alouds and pupil think-alouds. Teacher think-alouds model the process for the pupils so that they know what to do. Pupil think-alouds are believed to lead to more thoughtful and strategic reading.

As an example, a teacher used think-alouds to locate the reading difficulties experienced by two lower-attaining pupils; he gave them a text that he believed they could decode. He asked them to read it and stop every two or three sentences and say what they were thinking. He found that both pupils had difficulty in understanding some of the vocabulary in the text, as they both 'filled in' gaps in their understanding by making inferences (which of course is positive as they are using a useful strategy), but the inferences they made were not always correct. As a consequence, they had only a limited understanding of the text. The teacher then used clarification to identify the unknown words.

Noting the text structure

Teaching pupils how texts are structured, whether they are narrative or informational, helps with text comprehension. This is because knowledge of how the text is organized is transferred to similar texts when these are next encountered.

The non-fiction case study presented later in the book (Case study 5, Chocolate, in Chapter 7) provides an example of this. In this case study, which tied in with the class topic of chocolate, the teacher found examples from two non-fiction texts that covered the same content but in different ways. Using labelled cards with words such as 'Headline', 'Sub-heading', 'Glossary', etc., the pupils had to locate the same features in both texts. The teacher even created a label that was a 'red herring' and was not a feature of these types of text. The teacher felt this activity helped the pupils to understand the generic characteristics of non-fiction texts.

Visualizing the text

Encouraging children to represent the text in visual form (as in a story map) after the text has been read supports the comprehension process. It allows the elements of the text to be captured and makes it more memorable.

An example of a story map can be found in the short story case study using Alice Walker's 'The Flowers', Case study 8 in Chapter 8. Here we can see how the children have made sense of the text in terms of plot and characterization.

Teaching the strategies through scaffolded learning

Teachers of reading have a range of strategies at their disposal. The challenge is how best to bring them into the teaching and learning interaction of a guided reading lesson. Strategies need to be introduced to pupils explicitly; the children should then be encouraged to practise using them. Scaffolded learning provides the most effective approach in terms of helping pupils master these strategies themselves.

The metaphor of scaffolding was first introduced by Wood, Bruner, and Ross (1976). Linked closely to Vygotsky's (1978) idea of the 'more knowledgeable other', scaffolding works on the principle that learners will be able to 'solve a problem, carry out a task or achieve a goal' (Wood et al., 1976: 90), which they would not ordinarily be able to do by themselves, with the support of an adult or more expert other, such as a teacher. The scaffolding provided by the teacher is gradually dismantled as the pupil gains mastery. The teacher should provide no more support than is necessary to enable the learner to complete the task.

There are two features of scaffolding that are particularly important when viewed in the context of guiding readers through the text comprehension process. The first of these relates to how the adult controls 'elements of the task' (Wood et al., 1976: 90). By controlling some elements of the task, the adult can provide support, and focus on specific aspects that the learner is likely to encounter within the task. So, for example, the teacher of reading might decide to use a text that is easily decodable (thereby reducing the text difficulty) in order to focus on developing the reader's inference-making ability. A text that is more difficult to decode might hamper the intended focus of the learning.

How the teacher controls the elements of a task leads us to what Wood *et al.* (1976: 98) describe as the 'scaffolding functions'. These functions are aspects of the task that the teacher needs to consider both before and during the interaction. There are six functions, and in Table 3.2 below these are linked explicitly to the process of guiding readers. As we can see from the table, the scaffolding functions affect the guiding of readers both prior to, and during, the interaction. In the table the term 'tutor' is used as this is the one used by Wood *et al.*

Table 3.2: Linking the scaffolding functions to the guiding of readers

SCAFFOLDING FUNCTIONS (FROM WOOD *ET AL.*, 1976: 98)	USING THE SCAFFOLDING FUNCTION TO GUIDE READERS
Recruitment 'Enlist the problem-solver's interest in and adherence to the requirements of the task.'	It is easier to get readers reading if the text is interesting. When planning the teaching and learning interaction, texts must be chosen carefully to ensure that they will interest the pupils.
Reduction in degrees of freedom 'This involves simplifying the task by reducing the number of constituent acts required to reach a solution. In effect, the "scaffolding" tutor fills in the rest and lets the learner perfect the component sub-routines that he can manage.'	This will occur before the lesson, through the choice of texts and the learning focus. For example, if the focus is on developing inference-making, then it would not be appropriate to choose a text that is difficult to decode. If the teacher really wants to use a text that is difficult to decode, the teacher should read it to the pupils, to simplify the task.
Direction maintenance 'Learners lag and regress to other aims, given limits in their interests and capacities. The tutor has the role of keeping them in pursuit of a particular objective. Partly it involves keeping the child "in the field" and partly a deployment of zest and sympathy to keep him motivated. The effective tutor also maintains direction by making it worthwhile for the learner to risk a next step.'	This scaffolding function occurs during the course of the lesson. The teacher can keep the reader's attention on the task by using a variety of strategies, especially through careful questioning.

Marking critical features 'A tutor, by a variety of means, marks or accentuates certain features of the task that are relevant.'	This scaffolding function occurs both before and during the course of the interaction. The teacher will have considered the text potential before teaching and noted points appropriate for investigation. These points – or critical features – will be highlighted in the dialogue with the pupils.
Frustration control 'There should be some such maxim as "Problem solving should be less dangerous or stressful with a tutor than without."'	This scaffolding function occurs both before and during the interaction. The text will have been chosen taking into account its decoding difficulty but also considering its conceptual difficulty. It would be inappropriate to present a text too far removed from the reader's experiences and interests. During the lesson, the teacher should make links with the reader's background knowledge through questioning, making it worth the effort needed to understand it.
Demonstration 'Demonstrating or "modelling" solutions to a task … The tutor is "imitating" in idealized form an attempted solution tried (or assumed to be tried) by the tutee in the expectation that the learner will then "imitate" it back in a more appropriate form.'	This scaffolding function occurs during the interaction. Teachers can model the strategies they intend the pupil to use. This modelling will involve the teachers verbalizing their thought processes for the pupils.

The second important feature when guiding readers relates specifically to what happens during the interaction between teacher and pupils and embodies Bruner's (1983) concept of 'handover'. The concept of 'handover' makes the metaphor of scaffolding explicit: the adult is seen in the role of someone who provides a temporary supporting structure. The support provided by the teacher is gradually reduced as the responsibility for the learning is handed over to the learner. Eventually the support is no longer needed and the learner can complete the task, solve the problem, or achieve the goal independently. This gradual reduction in support is important because it allows the teacher to intervene and provide further temporary support if necessary.

For example, when guiding readers the teacher may want to develop the strategy of clarification. This might involve the teacher modelling how to find out the meaning of the word by returning to the beginning of the sentence or phrase or reading on to the end.

The teacher would verbalize her/his thinking on doing so. When the next word needs to be clarified, the teacher might then refer the pupils to the previously demonstrated strategy and encourage them to verbalize their thinking. If the learner is struggling with the task, the teacher can then offer more support – increasing the scaffolding. Eventually the strategy will become embedded and the learner can undertake the task independently. Once this occurs, further intervention by the teacher is unnecessary and indeed is likely to disrupt the learner's ability to clarify the word in question.

The principle of handover can be observed through a key feature of guiding readers: dialogue. We cannot know how a text has been understood or whether understanding has been deepened without talking with the learner. In this way, effective text comprehension requires the teacher and the learner to co-construct meaning between them. Productive dialogue can take place only when teachers know the pupils well and know what strategies they can already handle competently, and which strategies need further support. Examples of productive dialogue that can promote thinking are illustrated in a number of the case studies.

Conclusion

When readers engage with texts, they bring to bear their unique life experiences, including their own reading histories. Thus, the sense readers make of a text is also likely to be unique. This is equally true for young developing readers. For this reason, telling readers *what* to comprehend is of limited value. It is more helpful to give them access to tools that will show them *how* to comprehend. The strategies that teachers can use to help pupils develop these tools were described in this chapter. Young readers who are becoming proficient in these strategies will be able to engage with text and uncover different layers of meaning. However, if these strategies are to become embedded reading habits, to become skills used subconsciously and automatically, they need to be introduced and developed through scaffolded learning. The case studies that follow provide examples of how these strategies can be used in the context of scaffolded learning to guide readers through the process of text comprehension.

References

Bruner, J. (1983) *Child's Talk: Learning to use Language.* New York: Norton.

Duke N.K. and Pearson, P.D. (2002) 'Effective practices for developing reading comprehension'. In A.E. Farstrup and S.J. Samuels (eds) *What Research Has to Say About Reading Instruction* (3rd edition). Newark, DE: International Reading Association.

Palincsar, A.S. and Brown, A.L. (1984) 'Reciprocal teaching of comprehension-fostering and comprehension-monitoring activities'. *Cognition and Instruction,* 1, 117–75.

Raphael, T. E. and McKinney, J. (1983) 'An examination of 5th and 8th grade children's question answering behavior: An instructional study in metacognition'. *Journal of Reading Behaviour,* 15, 67–86.

Raphael, T.E. and Pearson, P.D. (1985) 'Increasing students' awareness of sources of information for answering questions'. *American Educational Research Journal,* 22, 217–36.

Raphael, T.E. and Wonnacott, C.A. (1985) 'Heightening 4th grade students' sensitivity to sources of information for answering comprehension questions'. *Reading Research Quarterly*, 20 (3), 282–96.

Tennent, W. (2015) *Understanding Reading Comprehension: Processes and Practices*. London: Sage.

Vygotsky, L.S. (1978) *Mind in Society: The development of higher psychological processes.* Cambridge, MA: Harvard University Press.

Wood, D., Bruner, J.S., and Ross, G. (1976) 'The role of tutoring in problem solving'. *Journal of Child Psychology and Psychiatry,* 17, 89–100.

4 Scaffolding learning through dialogue

Talk has a central role in scaffolding understanding. But not any old talk. When teachers initiate conversations in guided reading lessons, they need to be aware of the kind of talk that is likely to be most effective in developing understanding.

In a study of the quality of pupil–teacher talk in guided reading lessons in some Year 6 classrooms, Skidmore *et al.* (2003: 47) reported that 'talk in this context is teacher dominated. The teacher usually asks questions to which s/he already knows the answer, normally selects which pupil is going to speak next; keeps a tight grip on the topic of conversation; and does most of the talking.' Such talk is unlikely to stimulate deep understanding.

It was pointed out in Chapter 3 that the most important thing in guided reading is for the teacher to uncover what the pupils are thinking, not for the pupils to try to guess what answer the teacher wants. Asking the pupils to predict what will happen next and to justify their answers gives the teacher insight into the sense the pupils have made of the text. Deliberately using the 'clue' and 'thinking' questions described on p. 38 also allows the teacher to probe the pupils' ideas.

Teachers too often dominate discussions with pupils, whether with a whole class or a small group. How can they ensure that they facilitate, rather than monopolize, these learning conversations? Here are a few hints. They should:

- **wait** before offering statements, prompts, or even tentative thoughts, to give pupils an opportunity to voice their ideas first
- **support** and encourage pupils to ask their own questions and lead the discussion
- **use paired talk** as a strategy to give pupils time to think and to formulate better answers before contributing to the group discussion
- **encourage** children to respond directly to what others in the group say.

If teachers can do this, it is likely that the discussions that take place in their guided reading lessons will give all pupils the chance to:

- make tentative statements to see what they think about something
- change their minds
- listen to each other's views and responses
- formulate considered responses through verbalizing, refining, and asking their own questions.

Dialogue: a key part of teaching talk

Alexander (2008) states that there are five kinds of talk for teaching, all of which can be used effectively, depending on their purpose:

- **Rote** – the drilling of facts, ideas, and routines through repetition.
- **Recitation** – the accumulation of knowledge and understanding through questions designed to test or stimulate recall of what has been previously encountered or to help pupils to work out the answer from clues provided in the question.
- **Exposition** – telling pupils what to do, and/or imparting information, and/or explaining facts, principles, or procedures.
- **Discussion** – the exchange of ideas with a view to sharing information, solving problems, or making collective decisions.
- **Dialogue** – achieving common understanding through structured and cumulative questioning and discussion, which guide and prompt, reduce choices, minimize risk and error, and expedite 'handover' of concepts and principles.

(Alexander, 2008: 38)

While the first three are the 'traditional bedrock' of teaching, the last two – which are much more likely to develop children's thinking – are less prevalent. Almost all of these types of talk for teaching could be utilized during a reading lesson focused upon comprehension. Rote is the only kind of talk unlikely to be useful when encouraging deeper understanding. At the start of a lesson, recitation may be a way to remind pupils about what has been covered before and the previous knowledge on which they may need to draw; exposition can be used when it is necessary to explain new things or give further information, but the most fertile conversations will involve discussion and dialogue.

Alexander states that discussions, and particularly dialogue, present the greatest cognitive challenge to pupils: they are the kinds of interaction most likely to develop children's thinking. When dialogic teaching occurs, there is evidence of a positive change in pupils' thinking. The challenge for the thoughtful teacher, therefore, is to ensure that discussion and dialogue become an integral part of the talk repertoire of every guided reading session.

Principles and characteristics of dialogic talk

Alexander defines dialogue succinctly as 'conversation with cognitive challenge' and summarizes its three key aspects as follows:

- It achieves shared understanding through structured and cumulative questioning and discussion. There may or may not be a right answer, but justification and explanation are sought.
- Pupils' thinking is challenged and so their understanding is enhanced. The teacher is likely to share several exchanges with a particular child several times in order to move her/his thinking on.
- The pupil's response is the fulcrum of the exchange.

An example: so what does dialogue in a reading session look like? The following example is taken from Year 3.

Before this session, pupils had been asked to prepare by reading two short stories from the anthology *The Upside-Down Mice and Other Animal Stories,* edited by Jane Merer. The stories were: 'The Upside-Down Mice' by Roald Dahl and 'At the Zoo' by Brian Patten.

The children had been asked to think about which of the two stories they preferred and to think of one or two reasons to justify their choice. The objective of the session was for pupils to: 'Use criteria to evaluate two stories that they have read and justify preferences with evidence from the text.'

The beginning of the session was devoted to a discussion about what makes one story 'better' than another, and a number of agreed criteria were written down. One of these criteria was 'easy to read'.

The dialogue below is from the end of the session, following the paired discussion within the group, where the pupils had the opportunity to state and justify their preference with a partner.

Teacher: Jack, please tell us which story you preferred, and why.

Jack: I preferred 'At the Zoo' because it was very mysterious and you didn't find out what was looking at what until the very end because when I first heard the story I thought there were some new arriving animals and the children were looking at them for a school project but at the end I found that these aliens were actually looking at humans at the zoo and the humans were the new arrivals.

Teacher: The story sounds very confusing. When did you understand that the children were in the cages?

Jack: Oh, not until the very end. In fact, the first time I read it I didn't get it at all. It took two readings and then I thought, '*Now* I know what's going on!'

Teacher: But on our list of 'what makes a book worth reading' that we wrote earlier, we put 'Easy to read'. 'At the Zoo' doesn't sound like it was an easy story if you had to read it twice to understand it.

Jack: Yes, but the words were easy. The story wasn't. The story was a mystery, and I like mysteries, so that is why I like 'At the Zoo' better.

Teacher: So Jack prefers 'At the Zoo'. What about you, Karen?

The teacher begins the dialogue by posing an authentic question that asks the pupils to evaluate, and reminds Jack to justify his answer. Jack's initial response is expressed in an extended utterance. He has had a chance to prepare his thoughts through the paired discussion. He states that 'At the Zoo' is preferable because it is 'mysterious' and offers some evidence of this from the text.

The teacher's response is crucial in building a dialogic sequence. First she responds directly to the content of what Jack says, rather than commenting on the qualities of his answer (for example, she *doesn't* say 'Well done! What a good answer' or 'You have justified your preference very well'). At this point in the conversation it is much more important to extend, clarify, or challenge his thinking. Excessive praise at this moment would have the effect of closing down the conversation. The teacher does not ask another question immediately but makes a comment, indicating to Jack that this is not just a simple matter of recall that is now finished. The teacher then asks a 'when' question. This is not as straightforward as it sounds. It requires Jack not only to develop his point, but to explain further, demanding that he be more explicit and clarify what he means.

Jack's second response then reveals that he had to work hard to make sense of the story, particularly at the end. He had to read it twice before the twist at the end was understood. The teacher in her next response again builds on the content of what Jack says. However, in this utterance there is an explicit challenge to move his thinking on. The teacher refers back to the agreed criteria and reveals a contradiction between what Jack is saying and the previous discussion. How can it be a better story when it does not seem to meet the criteria for 'easy to read'? This statement implicitly demands a response, and Jack, after a short period of silence, reveals a much more subtle and sophisticated understanding about what it is to be a reader – it is clearly more than just being able to say the words on the page, and simple words can combine to make complex meanings.

The teacher then decides that this response shows that she has moved his understanding forward in a conversation that has encompassed three exchanges. It is now time to move on to another in the group. Again, it is interesting that at this point she doesn't pause to praise but carries on to get Karen's response. Praise and specific feedback are saved for the conclusion of the lesson, when the group will review what they have learnt.

This short transcript shows that the key test of dialogic classroom talk has been fulfilled. The conversation has led to a development of Jack's thinking.

Alexander (2008) says that there are five principles of dialogic talk. Teaching through dialogue is:

- **Collective** – teachers and learners address learning tasks together, whether as a group or as a class, rather than in isolation.
- **Reciprocal** – teachers and children listen to each other, share ideas, and consider alternative viewpoints.
- **Cumulative** – teachers and children build on their own and each other's ideas, and chain them into coherent lines of thinking and enquiry.
- **Supportive** – children articulate their ideas freely, without fear of embarrassment over 'wrong' answers; and they help each other to reach common understandings.
- **Purposeful** – teachers plan and facilitate dialogic teaching with particular educational goals in mind.

(Alexander, 2008: 28)

In the example of dialogue above, all five principles are evident. The session is *collective*, because all of the pupils have a shared knowledge of the texts under discussion and are involved in listening to and learning from the dialogue with the others in the group. It is *reciprocal*, because the teacher listens to the responses given and builds upon them, pressing for further information and clarification, rather than immediately moving on to another pupil. It is *cumulative*, because the ideas are built on by the teacher and the pupil, allowing a chain of thought to be created. It is *supportive*, as Jack expresses himself freely even when the teacher challenges his thinking. He knows that the teacher is listening to him and will respond to what he says rather than criticizing how he says it or making judgements about his ability. It is *purposeful*, because the session has a clear focus, aimed at exploring preferences and developing shared understandings. There is considerable cognitive challenge as pupils are asked to explain and justify their answers, extend their contributions, and respond to the views of the teacher herself.

Alexander goes on to say that 'dialogic teaching harnesses the power of talk to engage children, stimulate and extend their thinking, and advance their learning and understanding. Not all classroom talk secures these outcomes, and some may even discourage them' (ibid: 31).

In the exchange between Jack and his teacher, there is clear evidence of the power of the talk to develop Jack's understanding of the nature of reading. Crucially, the teacher knows that Jack's response is the fulcrum. What she says has to show that she has understood what he has said, and has to challenge his thinking. It is assessment for learning at its most fundamental level.

Building blocks for effective talk: questioning

If, as Alexander states above, the pupil's response is the fulcrum of the exchange, then an exchange has three elements: the opening question from the teacher, the response from the pupil, and the response from the teacher (or another pupil) that builds on the previous response. The opening question is important, but even more important is what is done with the pupil's response.

The usual three-part classroom exchange has been described as having the form: initiate, respond, evaluate; the teacher asks a question, the pupil responds, and the teacher evaluates that response. This is NOT what happens in a dialogic conversation. Teachers have to learn not to fall into their habitual teaching conversational style – but breaking the habits of a lifetime isn't easy.

Martyn Nystrand's research (Nystrand *et al*., 2003; Nystrand, 2006) helps us to unpick this area. Nystrand, like Alexander, also emphasizes the importance of moving away from questions and answers that focus solely on factual recall and towards more cognitively challenging classroom interaction. In a review of research into this area, Nystrand (2006) identified four *discourse moves* that shifted the classroom conversations into a more cognitively challenging mode. These are:

- the teacher asks more authentic questions
- the teacher responds to the content of the pupil's answer (which Nystrand calls 'uptake')
- there is time devoted to discussion
- pupils have opportunities to ask questions.

Nystrand defines authentic questions as questions that allow various answers, *including those not anticipated by the teacher* [emphasis added]. This is a very useful definition and is more helpful than the more common use of the terms 'open' and 'closed' questions. Open and closed questions can have a monologic perspective on the part of the teacher: *there is one answer in my head that I want the children to reach and I will continue to prompt them until they get there!*

In the transcript above, the opening evaluative question is authentic because the teacher does not know which story may be the preferred one. Other examples of questions that are authentic include prediction (What do you think this character will do next and why?), inferential questions (How do you know that Mole is happy to be free?), and life to text (Do you think the king was right to do that? Why?).

Authentic questions are much more likely to give rise to extended answers on the part of children, because they have to include their reasoning. This means that the teacher has an opportunity to listen to and make a judgement about the current state of the children's understanding and thus can respond appropriately to the content of the response, building further understanding or dealing with any apparent misconceptions. The power of this 'uptake' is seen in the way the teacher responds to Jack's utterances in the transcript above.

Summary: what can a teacher do to help dialogic talk happen?

The teacher:

- poses genuine questions that do not merely ask the children to guess what the teacher is thinking, or to recall simple and predictable facts
- expects the children to provide extended answers
- gives the children time and opportunities to formulate ideas and views
- shows the children what she/he expects, by providing models of the patterns of language in her/his contribution to the conversations
- expects the children to speak clearly and audibly and doesn't repeat or evaluate the children's answers
- responds to what the children say, building chains of exchanges that move thinking on, by debating and telling the children things, rather than just asking questions.

Conclusion

When readers engage with texts, they bring to bear their unique life experiences including their own reading histories. Thus, the sense readers make of a text is also likely to be unique. This is equally true for young developing readers. For this reason, telling readers *what* to comprehend is of limited value. It is more helpful to give them access to tools that will show them *how* to comprehend. The strategies that teachers can use to help pupils develop these tools were described in Chapter 3. Young readers who are becoming proficient in these strategies will be able to engage with text and uncover different layers of meaning. However, if these strategies are to become embedded reading habits, to become skills used subconsciously and automatically, they need to be introduced and developed through scaffolded learning, and the vehicle for this is dialogue. Dialogic talk is talk that skilfully probes and deepens pupils' understanding.

References

Alexander, R. (2008) *Towards Dialogic Teaching: Rethinking classroom talk* (4th edition). Cambridge: Dialogos.

Nystrand, M. (2006) 'Research on the role of classroom discourse as it affects reading comprehension'. *Research into the Teaching of Reading*, 40. Online. www.english.wisc.edu/nystrand/RTE%20 Classroom%20Discourse%20&%20Reading.pdf (accessed 4 April 2016).

Nystrand, M., Wu, L., Gamaron, A., Zeiser, S., and Long, D. (2003) 'Questions in time: Investigating the structure and dynamics of unfolding classroom discourse'. *Discourse Processes,* 35, 135–96.

Skidmore D., Perez-Parent, M., and Arnfield S. (2003) 'Teacher–pupil dialogue in the guided reading session'. *Reading Literacy and Language*, July, 47–53.

Part 3

Case studies:
Lessons from the classroom

Chapter 5: Introduction to the case studies

Chapter 6: Examples of guiding reading for 7–9 year olds (Years 3 and 4)

Chapter 7: Examples of guiding reading for 9–11 year olds (Years 5 and 6)

Chapter 8: Examples of more challenging reading lessons for 10–12 year olds

5 Introduction to the case studies

The case studies that follow are divided into three groups, according to age: we present examples of lessons for 7–9 year olds and 9–11 year olds, and also more challenging texts that may also be suitable for the early years of secondary school. In each of the groups, we have included case studies using a fiction text and a poem; there are also two case studies using non-fiction texts, and one using a digital text (a film clip).

Starting points

These case studies are examples of real lessons that have been taught as described here. They are not blueprints to be followed, but starting points for teachers to use flexibly. They are not intended as a straitjacket. Some of the case studies last no more than a single lesson, while others describe sequences of lessons or parts of a sequence. Some describe a guided reading lesson with a small group, others with a whole class. Schools organize reading in different ways, as these case studies demonstrate.

They illustrate some of the key principles we have described elsewhere in the book – the importance of text selection, preparation, planning, thinking about how to encourage the pupils' discussion (NOT how to lead it) and when and how to intervene, guiding where necessary, deciding what comes next on the basis of formative assessment, and evaluating children's developing understanding.

The school context

The brief description of the school and class contextualizes the guided reading lesson that is described. It should help the reader to appreciate the authentic situation in which it took place. In many of these classrooms, a substantial proportion of the pupils have English as an additional language; we have found that the same strategies apply as when working with a class where all the pupils have English as their L1, but more use of the clarification strategy (see Chapter 3) may be needed to support their literal understanding. They may also be bringing to the text a different range of life experiences, and the teacher needs to recognize and utilize this diversity.

Planning

The case studies exemplify different approaches to planning. In some case studies, teachers have planned the lessons tightly beforehand, preparing questions in advance, while in others teachers have planned more flexibly. Some teachers prefer to start with an exploratory lesson and then to plan the subsequent lesson(s) in more detail depending on the pupils' initial responses to the text. This approach ensures that the focus is determined by the pupils' reactions rather than by the teacher's preconceptions about what should be covered. Some teachers feel that over-detailed planning can close down rather than open up opportunities for discussion of ideas, and preparing a sequence of questions in advance may limit rather than liberate the exploration of deeper levels of meaning. Both approaches can be successful; which one is chosen will depend on the particular class, teacher, and text. The exploratory approach does not negate the need for planning; it simply postpones this stage until the pupils' initial ideas have been evaluated, and it is at that point that the teacher needs to be able to respond to whatever openings are offered.

The text chosen

Since text selection is a vital part of the process of teaching guided reading, the text is described briefly in these case studies and in some cases is included in its entirety. Some of these texts will be familiar to many teachers. Others, like the particular advertisements used in Case Study 1, are not valuable in themselves, but the reason for choosing them is important. The text that the teacher decides to use must provide sufficient challenge and have enough depth to justify the time spent on it. In order to help you, the teacher, to make this crucial decision, the text potential diagram is a useful tool. Becoming familiar with the text you hope to use is essential, and the text potential diagram provides a way to analyse the features of the text in order to see what potential it offers to the group or class with whom you intend to use it. After filling in as many boxes on this diagram as are relevant, you may decide at the end of the process that the text is not suitable – for example, it may present too many challenges for the group you have in mind, or be too superficial and not challenging enough; either way, that's an important decision to make!

In each case study, the text potential diagram indicates which features of the text the teacher has considered and which may therefore become a focus for instruction. When using a sequence of lessons, the text potential diagram can also be used to map which aspects have been covered in each lesson, and which remain to be examined. The teacher continues to make judgements about the most productive next steps, using the diagram as a guide. It isn't necessary to aim for complete coverage, and the level of the pupils' interest in the text is an important factor when deciding how much time should be spent on it.

Organizing the class for guided reading

In most of the case studies described here, the lesson has been conducted with a particular group of pupils. Guided reading is often organized in this way, with the teacher working with one group in the class, while the other groups have different tasks, some working with a teaching assistant while others work independently. In two of the case studies, the organization for the other groups is described, but teachers will have their own ways of doing this. In four case studies, the teacher works with the whole class for part of the time, for example, presenting the material, and then introducing individual and small group work.

Groups – large or small?

Why is guided reading usually done in small groups? For an effective guided reading lesson, the text must be accessible and relevant to all of the pupils, and this is usually achieved by grouping them according to their reading attainment. In one of the case studies, the teacher prefers to use single-sex groups because she finds it easier to source material that matches the pupils' interests. Teachers often use groups of six, but this may be because a class of 30 pupils can be organized into five groups of equal size; such a managerial solution may not be the most appropriate for guided reading. As the teacher in one of the case studies notes, a group of four pupils works better than six. In groups larger than four, some pupils will 'hide' while others will dominate; in pairs, threes, and fours, everyone contributes.

More importantly, the teacher's role in guided reading is critical. Scaffolding the pupils' learning requires the teacher to be aware of each student's comprehension and possible misunderstanding. That is harder to achieve when the number of pupils is large and the range is correspondingly wide.

In order to help pupils to manage group work effectively, parameters such as time limits and outcomes should be clearly specified at the start so that the pupils can take responsibility for them.

We have included examples of guided reading carried out with the whole class, and this may come as a surprise to some readers of this book as it seems to be breaking our own rules. In our view, whole-class lessons can be successful when there are plenty of opportunities for the pupils to discuss issues together in small groups (that is, there is more talking than sitting listening), and where the teacher develops their ideas by giving appropriate challenges to deepen their thinking.

Dialogue and discussion

In Chapters 3 and 4 we emphasized the importance of the teacher's talk in a number of ways: asking questions to deepen pupils' comprehension through inference-making; utilizing the strategies that form the basis of reciprocal teaching (Chapter 3, Table 3.1, p. 36) to ensure that pupils have understood all aspects of a text; and encouraging the kind of dialogic talk that challenges pupils' thinking. In a number of the case studies, the teacher deliberately says very little, establishing an expectation that the pupils will listen to and learn from each other. Often the teacher's opening comment sets the tone by indicating that everyone's ideas are valid (for instance, 'Why do you think ...?' rather than 'Why does the author ...?'). In this way, the teacher is permitting the pupils to give *their* views, not to guess the 'right' answer that is in the teacher's head.

Because these are *real* extracts from classroom discussions, there are plenty of hesitations and false starts, lots of *erms* ... and incomplete sentences. We have not tidied them up more than necessary; they are illustrative examples, not model lessons.

The guided reading lesson

The account of the lesson generally falls into three parts:

1. Before the lesson – the teacher's planning and any preparation of materials.
2. During the lesson – what happened during the lesson, together with some commentary on the activities and discussion that took place.
3. After the lesson – the teacher's reflections on the lesson or sequence of lessons, some evaluation of the learning that has taken place, and an assessment of what the next steps might be.

And finally ...

These are not recipes to be followed; each lesson included here has some ingredients that we hope the reader will be encouraged to try out – activities, texts, ways of recording ideas – in a mix-and-match way. The important principles for guiding reading successfully were described in the earlier chapters. Here, we show how they have been put into practice. We hope that when you've read these case studies, you will appreciate how it can be done.

Examples of guided reading for 7–9 year olds (Years 3 and 4)

Advertisements from children's magazines

Context

Elder Junior School is a large school for 7–11 year olds in outer London. The school has a very high proportion of pupils from different ethnic backgrounds, for whom English is an additional language; furthermore, it supports an above-average proportion of children with special educational needs. However, pupils make good progress by the time they leave the school at the age of 11.

Gerald has a class of 30 (Year 3) 7 and 8 year olds. They are divided into five ability groups for guided reading. Guided reading takes place every afternoon, immediately after lunch.

Planning

The following case study shows how persuasive texts, in the form of two advertisements, can be used with a guided reading group. It is a stand-alone guided lesson. There was no preparation for the lesson by the children and only limited follow-up was planned. It was taught by the author of this case study.

Text selection

Children's magazines are a good source of persuasive texts in that they carry advertisements aimed at the 7–11 age range. Any comic or magazine will provide at least one advert that can be worked on by groups of children throughout the upper primary school.

Reproduced by permission of Whale and Dolphin Conservation. This advertisement has now been amended.

The two advertisements chosen for this lesson come from two children's magazines: *LEGO Chima* and *LEGO Friends*; they are both readily available from newsagents and are very popular with 7–9-year-old children.

Text potential
Exploring what the text offers

Vocabulary

Use of superlatives: 'ultimate', 'awesome', 'cool', 'amazing'.

Narrative features

Historical, social and cultural context

Adverts are ubiquitous in the contemporary world. They pervade every aspect of our cultural lives. Therefore to develop a critical literacy we have to explore with children how advertising works to persuade the reader to consume at whatever age.

Making links to background knowledge

Bringing their experience of adverts both on screen and in print to the focus adverts. Who are these products aimed at? What strategies are being used to persuade, such as free gifts, and do they know of other examples of these strategies? Do you have to buy the product?

Language features

Use of imperative verbs clear in one advert *(Doctor Who)* and the use of questions to persuade in the other (Will you keep me safe and free?).

Grammar; Syntax

Comparison between short, sharp text in *Doctor Who* advert and more extended sentences in dolphin advert.

Coherence

When making sense of the adverts, how do we read them? Do we read the *Doctor Who* advert in the same way we would read a story? How then do we put the parts of these texts together to make them coherent?

Literary features

Mapping text potential
Advertisements

Theme

Buy, buy, buy!

Subject

Two adverts: one advertising a *Doctor Who* comic, the other to persuade the reader to send money to 'adopt' a dolphin.

The adverts are contained in two LEGO magazines aimed at children from approx. 6–9 years old: *LEGO Friends* and *LEGO Chima*.

Visual features

The relationship between image and text. What information do they each give us? How are the words framed to draw our attention to them? Why are the colours important? Why are different fonts and font sizes used?

Text type, purpose and intended readership

Adverts from comics, each aimed at a specific readership. Their purpose is clear – to persuade their young readers to buy the *Doctor Who* comic or send funds to 'save' dolphins from harm.

The gendered nature of the comic context and the adverts themselves are worth exploring. *Doctor Who* (and the *LEGO Chima* comic) aimed at boys? Dolphins (and *LEGO Friends*) aimed at girls?

Advertisements usually have a limited amount of written text and can therefore be read quickly. However, they are also truly 'multi-modal': the meanings they convey are communicated through visual images and design as well as through words. It is this relationship between all the modes used that produces the effect upon the reader. When reading advertisements, pupils should be considering the effect of the images, as well as paying attention to the words and the way in which they are positioned within the overall text.

As Bearne *et al*. (2004: 5) state:

> Many books and other media now available in schools cannot be read by attention to writing alone. Much learning in the curriculum is presented through images, often in double page spread of books, which are designed to use layout, font size, and shape and colour to add to the information contained in the words … We read them differently from the way we read continuous print, making different choices about where to start reading; often the eye falls on the strong central image, or a coloured text box presented as a 'fascinating fact'. Or the arrows of a diagram might direct our gaze.

Advertisements are always aimed at particular groups of people and have a clear purpose: they seek to persuade a given group of people to act in a particular way – usually to buy or do something. In these children's magazines, if the ages of the children contributing letters and drawings are anything to go by, the target audiences are boys and girls of around the age of this class (7 year olds) up to 10 or 11 year olds.

It follows that these texts have the potential to develop comprehension and response in a way that looks explicitly not only at the persuasive techniques used by the (anonymous) authors, such as the interplay of language and image and the use of hyperbole, but also at how the texts are designed to appeal to a particular audience, in this case boys and girls of the same age as this class. They are an excellent resource to develop critical literacy and understanding of bias, particularly the explicitly gendered and stereotypical elements present in these advertisements.

Lesson planning and organization

These advertisements were part of a longer sequence of work on comprehension and the development of inference aimed at deepening the children's understanding of, and response to, a range of texts. The planned questions were formulated to take account of the particular purpose and intended readership of these advertisements and to ensure basic comprehension of what the texts were about: they focus on literal comprehension, persuasive features, and purpose and readership, and fit into the three types of question described in Chapter 3: 'looking', 'clue', and 'thinking'. (See Chapter 3, p. 38, Questioning.)

THE THREE TYPES OF QUESTION
Comprehension – making meaning from texts:

- literal
- inference/deduction
- evaluative/responsive

Therefore three areas for formulating questions:

- literal ('looking', e.g. When? What? Who?)
  What are these texts? What is their purpose? What are they advertising?
- inference/deduction ('clue', e.g. How do you know that …?)
  How do we know they are adverts? Who are these adverts trying to persuade? How do we know?
- evaluative/responsive ('thinking', e.g. Do you think that …?)
  Did these adverts make you want to spend your money/find out more? Why? Why not?

The learning objectives selected for this lesson were drawn from the Reading Programmes of Study in the 2014 National Curriculum (England):

- Checking that what they read makes sense to them, discussing their understanding, and exploring the meanings of words in context.
- Drawing inferences and justifying inferences with evidence.
- Identifying and discussing themes.

The adverts were duplicated on A4 sheets of paper – enough for one copy for each pair of children in the group. The three questions were also copied onto paper for each pair.

The lesson

Introduction

The teacher worked with a group of six pupils; he outlined the learning objectives, gave out the adverts and questions, then told them what they were to do. The rest of the class were engaged in other reading activities, some supported by the teaching assistant. One group prepared for their guided lesson the next day; another followed up their session from the previous day. A third group worked with the teaching assistant to reread and discuss a familiar short story, while the fourth group read quietly individually.

The teacher started by making sure that the group had read and understood the questions. The pupils worked in pairs; they were told they could annotate the adverts if they wanted to. The children were encouraged to reread the adverts carefully and to discuss the questions in order, while at the same time identifying vocabulary that was unknown or puzzling or which needed clarification if the meaning was not to be compromised.

During the lesson

Exploration and discussion in pairs

The children worked in pairs in the guided group; this lasted no more than five minutes. The three pairs then reconvened for a discussion with the teacher. Each pair had made some brief annotations on the adverts. Two examples follow:

It wants you to adopt and save a dolphin. SO ADOPT ONE NOW! The dolphin need a better life.

MerWil and Shelden

ADVERTISEM

YOU MUST IT NOW buy

About monsters

Freaky, ugly, pure powerful, monsters

Group discussion

The initial questions were dispensed with quickly. All of the children were aware that the texts were advertisements and designed to persuade the reader to spend their money:

Extract from the conversation: purpose and features of the texts:

Teacher (T): OK, now you have looked at them – those two pages – what do you think they are? What have you written underneath?

Boy (B) 2: Freaky, ugly, powerful monsters.

T: And what have you written under yours?

B3: Newspaper. Comic. Advert. Fake.

T: OK.

B3: Something fake.

Girl (G) 1: It wants you to adopt and save a dolphin. They want you to adopt a dolphin so they can have a better life.

T: And you looked at the *Doctor Who* one. What did you write under yours?

G2: It is advertising and it is a *Doctor Who* comic. It is forcing you to buy it, and it is making you want to buy it. It is making you interested in the *Doctor Who* comic.

T: So you think they are adverts, and they are advertising a *Doctor Who* comic – and what else are they advertising?

G1: They are forcing you to buy it.

T: What do you mean, they are forcing you to buy it?

G1: All around it, it is saying you must buy one now and 'Pick up a copy today!' 'Packed with awesome scares.' It says every issue has free gifts and it's scary.

B2: It's persuading you to get the comic – to read more or to see more.

B3: It's trying to get you to do more or see more.

T: Yes, the gifts are there to try and persuade you to buy it, aren't they?

G2: [Unclear]

T: And you mentioned all these words – 'You must buy it NOW!' Are you going to?

B2: Maybe, because it's running out …

T:	... could be. So now that you have read it ...
G1:	... it wants to raise money.
T:	So you wouldn't buy a *Doctor Who* or you wouldn't adopt a dolphin?
B2:	No. I would buy a TV.
B4:	I would buy something I want.
	(General agreement)
T:	But it says you must buy it.
G1:	You don't have to. You can choose to buy it. It is saying that you must buy it.
G2:	But then if you don't buy it, what happens? Nothing happens.

Commentary

As this extract continues, the children develop their understanding of some of the persuasive techniques used by the advertisers: imperative verbs in the text, as well as incentives such as free gifts and a promise that the content will be scary. The children are also aware that, although the modal verb 'must' may suggest that it is necessary to buy the comic, they do not have to follow the injunction: *'but then if you don't buy it ... Nothing happens'* – there are no sanctions if you don't.

In this way, a sophisticated, critical understanding of these texts – both their purpose and their linguistic features – is developed and shared quickly by the group.

By far the liveliest part of the lesson came when the group discussed who the adverts were aimed at, particularly in the context of the magazines in which they appeared. This started when one of the boys pointed to the dolphin advert and said, 'That's for girls.' The teacher took up this line of enquiry.

Extract from the conversation: gender and magazines:

T:	Why are you saying this one's for girls?
B2:	(flicking through the pages of *LEGO Friends*) 'Cos inside it's for girls. If you turn over the pages you can see it's for girls.
B1:	(pointing to *LEGO Chima*) This is for boys cos it's got lots of scary stuff in it and it's for boys.
T:	If this advert's in a girls' magazine [*LEGO Friends*] and this advert's in this one [*LEGO Chima*], are you saying this [magazine] is for girls and this one's for boys?
B3:	Yes.

G1:	No!
	(General hubbub)
G1:	No – I have LEGO and I have loads of boys' stuff in my house.
T:	OK, I am interested in what you are saying about this. How do you know this one is for girls?
G2:	It doesn't matter if they are for boys or girls. Boys can buy that one and girls can buy that one. It doesn't matter.
T:	They could. So do you think that some boys would buy that one [*LEGO Friends*]?
B1:	No.
G1:	Yes! My brother would buy it!
T:	But would he be buying it for himself or would he be buying it for you?
G1:	For *himself*.
G2:	Boys would look in it and see what's interesting, and then they would buy it for their little sisters.
T:	Do you think then that some boys would buy that [*LEGO Friends*]?
Boys:	No.
Girls:	Yes. Yes.
G2:	A boy might buy it for himself and see what's good in it.
B1:	I think he would be buying it for his little sister.
	(The girls then look more closely at *LEGO Chima*.)
G1:	I like looking at that.
B2:	No you don't.
G1:	Yes, I watch Lego. I watch everything.

Commentary

What is very clear at this point is that the girls will happily read, and be interested in, a comic that has been aimed at boys, but the boys do not believe that the girls would (or should!) be interested in one that has been aimed at boys; furthermore, the boys would not contemplate buying *LEGO Friends* under any circumstances. The distinction between the girls' and the boys' attitudes to the texts, and particularly their highly gendered reactions, were based on markers that they took for granted: the stylized drawings of the girls in *LEGO Friends*, the almost complete absence of male characters in *Friends* and of female characters in *Chima*, and the focus on collaborative activities in *Friends* (e.g. cake making and knitting) compared with battles and action in *Chima*. This strong reaction overtook the discussion about making explicit the differences between the two adverts and the features that seemed to indicate their intended audiences.

The conversation moved on to a re-examination of the advert about saving dolphins. One of the boys expressed interest and the teacher picked up on this.

> **T:** I think that this advert is in this magazine because someone who makes the magazine and gets the adverts thinks that it is likely to appeal more to girls than boys. And I think that I quite like dolphins and I might be interested in sending money to help dolphins and I am just interested in 'Why is it in a girls' magazine?'

There was little response to this comment, so the teacher finished the lesson with a suggestion designed to try to reach an agreed conclusion that would encapsulate the understandings that the group had reached through their discussion:

> **T:** OK. If you wanted to write a letter or an email to the people who write and make these magazines, what would be your message to them?
>
> **Boy 1:** Why … why have you put it [the advert] in the girls' magazine?
>
> **T:** Why have you put it in the girls' magazine …
>
> **G2:** … we could have a magazine for both boys and girls, and then it would have the dolphins in it and both boys and girls could see it.
>
> **T:** So would the question be: why don't you have magazines for both boys and girls?
>
> (General agreement.)

This seemed a good place to stop. Time had run out and a general agreement had been reached with the whole group. Their thinking had developed and it was clear that they had taken a critical look at the adverts and the magazines in a way that had brought the gendered elements to the surface.

A possible follow-up activity for this group would be to discuss and formulate the content of a comic or magazine that would appeal to both boys and girls of their age.

Teacher's reflections

The teacher had this to say after the lesson was completed:

> This lesson was really lively! The children were not used to looking at these kinds of text in guided reading, and they were very excited by it. They were keen to express their views and there was quite a lot of talking over one another. I spent time calming them down a bit, and insisting they listened to the person speaking before jumping in with their own contributions. Despite that, the pupils did build on each other's views, even if they disagreed amongst themselves, and they did not always address their contributions to me, the teacher. I would definitely plan to continue this focus on audience and purpose in adverts and persuasive techniques both with this particular group and with the whole class, and I would include discussion on which adverts are specifically aimed at boys and girls.

What the pupils learned and showed they could do:

> I think the pupils showed a really good understanding of the purpose of adverts and of the audience they are aimed at. During the lesson they developed their understanding of some of the persuasive techniques used by the advertisers: imperative verbs in the text, incentives such as free gifts, and a promise that the content will be scary. They knew that you do not have to buy the product even if the advert tells you that you 'must'.

> The pupils developed a more sophisticated, critical understanding of these texts as a result of the conversations around them, and drew both on the texts we considered as well as their prior experience, thereby moving their thinking on. All the children were able to justify their opinions using evidence from the text. It was a really good discussion.

What next?

More talking about adverts with a focus on audience, and on how particular words, images and design features carry messages about who the adverts are aimed at. We will look at adverts in newspapers and magazines aimed at adults, and compare them by drawing out similarities and differences as well as discussing possible stereotypes.

Conclusion

This lesson was the starting point for an exploration of the purpose of and specific audiences for advertisements. The way that the children responded to the adverts and magazines as being for a gendered audience deserves further exploration and, in particular, a focus is required on how the images and colour within the adverts and the contexts of the magazine themselves all led the children to make assumptions about the intended audience. A subsequent lesson could therefore look explicitly at the clues in the design and content that lead the children to their implicit judgements and help them consider the issues of stereotyping further.

Reference

Bearne, E., Ellis. S., Graham, L., Hulme, P., Merchant, G., and Mills, C. (2004) *More Than Words: Multi-modal texts in the classroom*. London: Qualifications and Curriculum Authority.

The Lost Thing by Shaun Tan

Context

Birch Primary School is a very large school for children aged 4–11, in outer London. It has a high proportion of pupils for whom English is an additional language and children with special educational needs. In addition, the pupil population is highly mobile. Despite this, pupils make rapid progress and achieve very highly by the time they leave the school at the age of 11.

Kate has a class of 30 (Year 4) 8–9 year olds. These are divided into five ability groups for guided reading; this takes place every day for half an hour, first thing in the morning, as part of a dedicated reading lesson. Each group has a clear focus for each day of the week.

Planning

Kate organizes her groups for guided reading in this way:

DAY 1	Preparation for guided reading. This could include predicting, reading part of the text, and considering the key questions to be discussed in the guided reading lesson with the teacher on the following day.
DAY 2	Guided reading lesson with the teacher.
DAY 3	Follow-up to the guided reading lesson: mainly activities to extend their understanding of, and response to, the text.
DAY 4	Reading on screen (including e-books) – free choice.
DAY 5	Quiet reading. Books chosen from current selection of topic books (at the time of this case study, around 30 books about Ancient Greece and retellings of Greek myths).

Texts are selected for each group. Most are used with more than one group but not necessarily all groups.

Text selection

The Lost Thing (2000) is written and illustrated by Shaun Tan, a highly acclaimed picture-book maker from Australia. It is typical of his work: a picture book in which the narrative is conveyed through both the words and the pictures, and through the interplay between them.

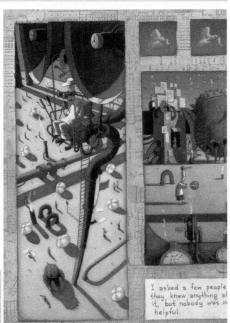

Like Shaun Tan's other well-known books, such as *The Arrival* and *The Red Tree*, *The Lost Thing* tells a straightforward story (boy finds a lost thing, tries to find out where it belongs, and reflects on his choices) illustrated by surreal and dream-like pictures. It could be considered science fiction or fantasy as it seems to be set in an alternative world where alien creatures coexist with human beings. However, the strange yet detailed images help the reader to explore themes such as difference and belonging, character relationships, and society and the individual.

The story is told simply in the first person. The vast majority of the sentences are straightforward and the vocabulary is not particularly challenging for young readers.

The narrative itself, the intricacies of the illustrations, and the intriguing way in which the book is designed make this a challenging, yet engaging and accessible, text that can be explored by children throughout upper primary school.

Text potential
Exploring what the text offers

Vocabulary
These words will probably need to be clarified: 'demanded', 'shrieked', 'dramatic', 'filthy', 'dunno', 'smoothing over', 'anonymous'.

Language features
The story is simply told in the first person.

Literary features
The words relate a simply told story. Much of the literariness comes from the illustrations. The details act as similes and metaphors to be interpreted. What do the features of the lost thing itself (and the other strange creatures and surreal setting) tell us about what it is like?

Narrative features
Plot is simple but the character and setting are worth exploring. The story appears to take place in an alternative world where alien creatures coexist with human beings. Is this a science-fiction setting? The characters are very clearly drawn. Do their relationships change as the story plays out?

Historical, social and cultural context
Focus on the individual and her/his place in the wider society. If you are different, how does that affect what you can and cannot do?

Coherence

Mapping text potential
The Lost Thing by Shaun Tan

Grammar; Syntax
Written sentences are straightforward with no great complexity. This should not create any problems for young readers to make meaning.

Theme
Potential themes:
- difference and belonging
- family relationships
- society and the individual.

Visual features
Illustrations are very important – they carry much of the detail of the story. Children can explore the interplay between the words and the surreal and dream-like pictures.

The backgrounds on each page, behind the pictures, are also intriguing. Could explore how they add to meaning.

Making links to background knowledge
Could make links to other Shaun Tan books such as *The Red Tree* and *The Arrival*. What they have in common: powerful illustrations that enhance as well as carry much of the narrative.

Making links to life. Did the main character do the right thing?

Text type, purpose, and intended readership
A multi-modal, richly illustrated picture book. It invites the young reader to reflect on the nature of relationships, family, friends, and the wider society.

Subject
This is a straightforward story about a boy who finds a very strange lost thing, tries to find out where it belongs, and reflects on his choices.

This text has the potential to develop comprehension and response in a wide variety of ways. Both the words and the illustrations have to be considered together if the text is to make full sense, and the development of comprehension monitoring in this multi-modal text is important. As ever, clarifying word meanings together with a concern to show how making life-to-text links can enhance comprehension are both integral to the session. In this case study, the teacher's intentions are to develop the children's ability to infer reasons for actions and events based on evidence from the text, and in particular to show how the words and illustrations work together to make meaning and inspire response. Vocabulary development, too, is a focus for teaching through the strategy of *clarifying* (see Chapter 3, p. 39).

Lesson planning and organization

The teacher decided to spend five sessions during the autumn term with a group of five children whom she describes as 'above average but not my top group', to thoroughly explore the potential of *The Lost Thing*. She divided the book into five sections and planned three questions to support group discussion for each section.

Teacher and school: Kate (Birch Primary)	Year group and decoding level: Year 4
Title and author: *The Lost Thing* by Shaun Tan (ISBN: 9780734411389)	
Section 1: Pages 1–6 Introducing the new book – Predicting – Questioning – Clarifying – Summarizing	Key questions: Where did he see the thing? Why do you think no one else noticed the thing? How do you think the thing felt? Why?
Section 2: Pages 7–12	Key questions: Who did he take the lost thing to? Why were his parents worried about it? Should people always be helpful?
Section 3: Pages 13–18	Key questions: Why couldn't he keep it in the shed? What was the building like? Why did the thing make a small, sad noise?

Section 4: Pages 19–24	Key questions:
	What was the man given?
	Would it have been a good idea to leave the 'thing' at the tall, grey building?
	Why do you think there are 'lost things' in the world? Whose job is it to put them back?
Section 5: Pages 25–30 (end)	Key questions:
	What was the boy's hobby?
	Why do you think the author is being vague with the details?
	Why do you think the boy is seeing 'that sort of thing' less and less these days?

The questions were focused on literal comprehension ('looking'), inference ('clue'), and making text-to-life connections ('thinking').

THE THREE TYPES OF QUESTION
Comprehension – making meaning from texts:
• literal • inference/deduction • evaluative/responsive
Therefore three areas for formulating questions:
• literal ('looking') *Who did he take the lost thing to?* [answer is in the text] • inference/deduction ('clue') *Why were his parents worried about it? How do you know they were worried?* [infer from text] • evaluative/responsive ('thinking') *Do you think people should always be helpful?* [give your opinion]

Each section of the text then became the basis for a guided group lesson. These lessons were structured using a variant of the Reciprocal Teaching process: predicting, question-making, clarifying, and summarizing. The following lesson plan shows the teacher's plans for the class.

Thursday:	Learning objective:	Guided group: **Bananas**	Next steps:
<u>Teaching resources:</u> Reading books Topic books Laptops Journals Writing frame	I can answer and discuss questions based on a text, giving evidence for my answers. <u>Steps to success:</u> Read questions Clarify for understanding Answer questions through discussion	*Prediction*: Children discuss what has happened previously in the book to recap, and then predict what they think will happen next. Encourage them to give reasons for their predictions. *Question-making*: Share the questions with the children, ensuring they have a clear understanding of them. Encourage them to be considering the questions as they read. *Looking*: **Who did he take the lost thing to?** *Clue*: **Why were his parents worried about the lost thing?** *Thinking*: **Do you think people should always be helpful? Why/why not?** Children to *read* the text section given. Encourage them to look at the pictures in this book for extra information. *Clarifying*: Ask children to think about what they have read. If there are any words of which they are not sure, or they have any questions, ask them to record them on a whiteboard for discussion. (Ensure that 'demanded' and 'shrieked' are discussed and clarified.) Do not spend longer than five minutes on this section. Children then discuss the questions. Allow the children time to develop their viewpoints. Ensure the conversation stays on task. Facilitate the discussion, encouraging all children to participate. *Summarizing*: Children summarize what they have read in this session, focusing on the key points. Pairs or individuals, depending on length of previous discussion.	Guided group to write story summary for this section of the text.

Links to assessment	Vocabulary to clarify:	Other activities (carousel):
Focus group:	'demanded' – asked someone to do something forcefully	**Peaches**: Complete next section of story to summarize text from previous lesson.
AF3: Infer reasons for actions and events based on evidence from the text.	'shrieked' – very loud high-pitched voice/noise	**Oranges**: Bug club – children to read books allocated to them for their specific level. (If computers are being temperamental, children to read home/ school reading book.)
AF5: Comment on the choice of language the author has used.		**Apples**: Task related to reading book – write a letter from Daddy complaining to the police about the break-in and the mess that has been left. Address needs to be filled in, using text as clues. **Supported by TA**: ensure they recap on what Daddy discovered and consider why he is cross/ angry.
		Encourage synonyms to vary their vocabulary.
		Grapes: Reading topic books (Ancient Greeks).

The lesson described below is the second guided lesson on *The Lost Thing*. In it, the teacher employed two broad assessment foci:

1. Infer reasons for actions and events based on evidence in the text.
2. Comment on the author's choice of language.

During the session

Predicting

Children discussed what had happened so far in the story, and then predicted what might happen next; when doing so, they had to refer to evidence in the story so far to support their views.

The following extracts from the second session deal with reading and discussing the book, and provide good examples of how the teacher is able to build learning conversations through a variety of discourse moves, enabling the children to develop their thinking around vocabulary, and to draw on evidence in the text and their own life experience to support insights into the characters through collaborative talk.

Extract from the conversation: recalling the previous session:

Teacher (T): Before we go to the predicting, let's remind ourselves of what we read last week. What can you remember?

Boy (B) 1: Basically what happened was Sean was playing on the table to carry on with his bottle top collection. Then he went to the seaside to get …

B2: … seaweed …

B1: … more bottle tops and then he saw a big lost red thing on its own on the beach and nobody else noticed it.

T: OK. Does anyone else have something to add to that?

B2: It was lost. It was this big red robot, I think … and it was so big that no one else noticed it on the beach. Cos it was standing there like a statue and it was baffled …

Girl (G) 1: … and it was … it was … very lonely and scared because he was only he … and a mum and dad said no don't go near it because it might be dangerous and …

G2: … so basically it's lonely because … because they think it's dangerous and anybody else wouldn't see it because they was too busy doing other beachy stuff.

T: OK.

B3: I remember I kind of said last time – it looks like tubes cos there's tubes on the sides as well and on the round. Because it's got tubes it can do whatever it wants and it's just a tube and, well, why would they all like want to play with a tube?

G1: It could be part of the wire under the ground.

T: It could be …

B2: … and I think it just stands there and might be able to move to different places when people weren't looking and I reckon it's floating on webs.

Commentary

This is the very beginning of the session. The teacher's opening question, '*What can you remember?*', is an authentic one. It indicates that the individuals in the group might remember different parts, but that together they can reconstruct a literal understanding of what has happened so far. This turns out to be correct as the members of the group build directly on each other's contributions without going through the teacher every time. There is time for thinking as each member is given time by the others to get their thoughts in order as they speak; pauses are allowed and other children do not jump in as the individual reaches for the next word or phrase.

The children quote directly from the text: both *beachy stuff* and *baffled* are important words from the first part of the text that had been discussed in the previous session; these words have stuck in their minds. The children not only recall the facts of the story; they also rehearse or recall the judgements or inferences they made about the characters they have met so far and what the characters might be.

Note how the children say much more than the teacher at this point. The teacher asks an authentic question to open up the talk, nudges children to say more or join in, and affirms some interesting speculation (*It could be …*). In this way, the teacher has set up a context in which the children themselves are enabled to collaborate and remember how they have made sense of the text so far; this is powerfully demonstrated by the fact that all five children contribute.

Extract from the conversation: predicting:

T: Anybody else have any thoughts about what they think might happen?

B3: I reckon that what will happen next is that, like, they go and play hide and seek, play It …

G2: … that's already happened.

T: So OK. You think they will carry on playing. Do you think he is going to keep him forever then?

B2: I reckon they would be best friends.

G2: I think there is like agents would come and they would start coming to the Thing and they told everybody to get out of the way and then people would put up signs saying about warning: people do not enter the beach.

T: Oh, OK – why would they do that then?

G2: Because it might be dangerous, because they would have spikes on top of it.

T: OK, be like bombs they had a long time ago which had spikes on them.

B3: And I reckon it might be a big ball and they carry on playing with it … after like he takes it home and the bomb, the red ball just goes BOOF!

T: Explodes. It explodes. Yes.

B2: It could be an alien ship …

G1: They could be holes. They could be bullet holes.

T:	What could be bullet holes?
G1:	Where bullets have gone in the top here.
T:	So let's think of our questions now.

Commentary

This part of the lesson starts with an authentic question from the teacher. It has a variety of possible answers and is designed to get children to think for themselves, and not just report someone else's thinking. Once again, the children build directly on each other's contributions. The teacher manages this section more tightly than earlier on, when the children were asked to recall the previous section. To do so, she very effectively deploys a wide range of talk in a short space of time. Her utterances were as follows:

- Manage: *So OK. You think they will carry on playing.*
- Probe: *Do you think he is going to keep him forever then?*
- Ask for justification: *Oh, OK – why would they do that then?*
- Contribute own thoughts while summarizing and affirming what has just been said: *Explodes. It explodes. Yes.*
- And finally, probe again to get a child to develop her thinking: *What could be bullet holes?*, before moving the session on to the next part.

This is a clear example of a teacher using a repertoire of types of questions and responses to encourage children's thinking to move forward in a short space of time.

The teacher then read aloud the next section of the book (pp. 7–12) to the children, who followed the text in their own copies.

Clarifying

The children were then asked to read the same section of text, and to note on their whiteboards any unfamiliar vocabulary or any aspect of the story that puzzled them. The children identified the following words to be clarified: 'demanded', 'shrieked', 'dramatic', 'filthy', and 'dunno'.

The group and the teacher then quickly discussed each word in turn.

Extract from the conversation: clarifying:

B3:	Dramatic.
T:	Dramatic. What does dramatic mean?
B2:	Like when you are doing drama like you're being dramatic, when you are doing drama.
T:	So OK, when we are doing our acting, when we have been up on stage practising, how do we want to express ourselves?
B3:	By being dramatic.

T:	So what does that mean you are doing on top of what you normally do?
B3:	You're like expressive.
T:	Being expressive, being over the top, making yourself more than what you normally would. OK? What else do we have?
B3:	Demanded.
T:	Demanded. What does demanded mean? Don't all talk at once!
B2:	Like when you are asked to do something.
T:	Are you asked in a nice way?
B3:	No – rude.
T:	Maybe not rude, maybe very forceful. You are demanding someone to do it so you are quite forceful.
B3:	Like shouting to do something.
T:	Is that what your mum's doing, demanding that you clean your room?
Boy 2:	I don't clean it though …

Commentary

This exchange is typical of the way unknown vocabulary can be clarified during this part of the reciprocal teaching process. The children identify words that they do not know, and which are getting in the way of understanding the piece. The child offers the word and the teacher then offers it to the group.

As we see here, the two boys and the teacher together develop an understanding of two words while the others listen. The boys are skilfully moved towards understanding by a conversation that is carefully structured by the teacher. In each case, Boy 3 introduces the word and Boy 2 adds helpful comments; these are summarized and then amplified by the teacher (*Being expressive, being over the top, making yourself more than what you normally would*). The teacher adds explicitly to the explanation, but not by asking a lot of questions that compel the children to guess what is in her head. She has made a decision that it is better to tell, rather than elicit from the group.

Boy 3's final comments in both cases show how he has a better understanding of the word meanings; his thinking has moved on (*You're like expressive. Like shouting to do something*).

Questioning

The following questions were given to the children before they independently read the relevant section of the text. The purpose was to ensure that they understood the questions clearly, and that they kept them in mind when reading. They were:

1. Who did he take the lost thing to? ('looking')
2. Why were his parents worried about the lost thing? ('clue')
3. Do you think people should always be helpful? Why/why not? ('thinking')

The group then considered these questions, and they were guided, not dominated, by the teacher. The teacher encouraged all of the children to participate (see Teacher's reflections below).

Extract from the conversation: evaluative question (developing an opinion):

T: OK. We are going to move on now to our thinking question. Should people always be helpful? Sean is being quite helpful here, isn't he?

G2: I don't think Pete was helpful because when Sean took the lost thing to him he said it was cool but he didn't know much about that.

T: OK, so did he end up being helpful in the end?

G2: No.

T: What do you think, Girl 1? Should people always be helpful?

G1: Not every time. Maybe because if like you be rude to them, then why should they be helpful? If they bully you why should you help them? Then they carry on bullying you, then you shouldn't be nice to them. You should just walk away.

T: How is Sean being helpful so far? What has he done?

G2: He saw the robot on the beach and he saw no one doing nothing with it and he realized it could stay with him for a little while to play some games and show people.

T: And then he was a bit lost to know what to do with the lost thing, wasn't he? So he has ended up having to take him to Pete and he didn't know what to do with him. He ended up having to take it home. Mum and Dad aren't too happy with him. So has it been good for Sean to be helpful? What position has it put him in then?

G2: It's put him in a bad and very lonely position.

B2: Angry. It's put him in an angry position as well.

Commentary

This short extract from the conversation, arising from the questions that the teacher had prepared, reveals how effectively the teacher uses talk to support the children to develop a more sophisticated understanding of the consequences of the main character's actions. She does this by asking a planned question that is designed to get the children to make links **beyond** the text to develop their comprehension **of** the text. For example, she follows the original question (*Should people always be helpful?*) with a new one (*Sean is being quite helpful here, isn't he?*) to ensure that this connection is encouraged.

The teacher's talk during this part of the session is different again from that in the previous extracts. In this part of the session, she takes on a much more challenging stance in order to move the children's thinking on. After Girl 1's extensive contribution, where she draws from her own experience to suggest that in real life there are circumstances where one might be better advised not to be helpful, the teacher challenges the group to apply that insight to the main character in the text (*How is Sean being helpful so far? What has he done?*). There follows a contribution from Girl 2 where she illustrates how Sean has been helpful. However, the teacher intervenes with a question about the consequences of that episode of helpfulness, and challenges the group to think more deeply (*So has it been good for Sean to be helpful? What position has it put him in then?*). The subsequent contributions from Girl 2 and Boy 2 show how they have a much more subtle, precise, and complex understanding of the character's predicament.

G2: It's put him in a bad and very lonely position.

B2: Angry. It's put him in an angry position as well.

This is a clear episode of dialogue developing thinking and leading to a significant insight.

Summarizing

Finally, working in pairs, the children summarized what they had read and understood in this session and whether their thinking about the characters had changed in any way.

After the session

The children were asked to reread this section (pp. 7–12) of the text again, and summarize it by adding a few more sentences to their ongoing summary in their reading journal books.

Teacher's reflections

The teacher had this to say after the session was completed:

What the pupils learnt

> I enjoyed the lesson. The children were enthused by this book and have enjoyed discussing it in both lessons so far. They showed a good understanding of the book throughout the lesson and engaged with each other well. There was some unusual vocabulary (e.g. 'demanded') that they were able to explain to each other, and they were able to make sense of the text, and to infer some of the deeper meanings, drawing both on the words and on the illustrations.

> All the children were able to justify their opinions by using evidence in the text to back up their answers. They built on each other's contributions and did not always look to me. There were examples of this during the clarifying part and when they were discussing the thinking question.

> By the end of the session, they had a very good understanding of the problem that Sean was now facing and of the predicament he was in by trying to be helpful.

What next?

> I will carry on with this book and we will continue to work on the same learning objectives, particularly comprehension monitoring, drawing on both illustrations and words.

Kate also reflected on how helpful she finds Reciprocal Teaching strategies in supporting her effective teaching in guided reading:

> This structure really helps me focus much more clearly on key elements of comprehension and inference. It gives me a good feel for where everyone in the group is, and whether they understand the story. It helps me to understand the text too as I am thinking about and planning each type of question to ask. I also get children to come up with clue questions after they are used to the process and this has also really helped them to develop inference and understanding, although they find it quite challenging at first.

Conclusion

The lesson was successful and, in the teacher's evaluation, resulted in positive learning experiences. The tight planning of the three types of questions and the use of the Reciprocal Teaching structure was very helpful for a group of pupils who were new to this kind of approach, as it was a new class near the beginning of the academic year. In this lesson, the teacher modelled the types of questions they will be considering over the coming months and provided effective ways of discussing these and other questions as a group. By using such a clear approach, the children are introduced to the overall framework that they will be expected to begin to take over more independently in future lessons.

Reference

Tan, S. (2000) *The Lost Thing.* Sydney: Lothian Books (ISBN 978-0-73-441138-9).

'Maggie Dooley' by Charles Causley

Context

This lesson was taught to a small group of 8–9-year-old girls in a two-form primary school in west London. Levels of achievement are well above the national average, especially in writing.

The class teacher organizes her guided reading lesson in single-sex groups as, in her judgement, the pupils express their points of view more confidently when working in this way. She also considers it easier to match texts to the reading interests of the group.

Planning

The teacher was finding the demands of working with long novels quite taxing, especially when attempting to use a different novel with each group, as had been the school practice. In the teacher's assessment, the pupils needed a greater variety of texts to enable them to develop their ability to make inferences, particularly about character and character motivations. Prior to this lesson, the class had been reading a range of fiction texts, but poetry had rarely been used in guided reading. Poetry was poorly resourced in the classroom and the school library, and was not represented in the guided reading resources.

Text selection

The selected text, 'Maggie Dooley', is a short poem in five stanzas by the children's poet Charles Causley. A former teacher, Causley was a Cornishman whose work was inspired by local legend, folklore, and eccentric characters and is infused with a timeless quality. There is an apparent simplicity in the language that makes it accessible even to very young children, but this belies the more sophisticated nuances that may be revealed through close, reflective reading and discussion.

A theme running through Causley's poetry is the movement from innocence to experience. Most adults reading the poem will bring to bear knowledge of the social circumstances behind Maggie's situation. These circumstances are hinted at, but never explicitly stated: she is an 'old' woman with little to occupy her days; she looks forward to the regular routine of feeding the stray cats in the park; she is steadfastly loyal to her 'family'. The use of the word 'family' and the fact that the place that she visits regularly is the 'children's roundabout' suggest that she has no other family. They may have grown up and gone away, or perhaps she never married and had children. We may infer that she is Irish from her name and because stout is a popular Irish drink, but the use of the delicate word 'sip' in 'takes a sip/From a bottle of stout' indicates that she is not an alcoholic but rather a lady who allows herself this small luxury. It was thought unlikely that all of the pupils in this Year 4 class would have experience of, or would be able to understand, Maggie's circumstances: they did not share the same social or cultural context as Maggie, and their responses could therefore have been limited or stereotypical, although those who had seen or read *Mary Poppins* might, when prompted, be able to make connections with the Birdwoman who sells seed to 'feed the birds'.

A subtle transition between first and final stanzas reveals a shift in viewpoint. Initially, the reader is invited to watch and listen to Maggie as she feeds the cats, and is then invited to learn more about her thoughts and feelings as she explains them to an unidentified listener.

The only thing the reader can be certain of is what Maggie does at eight in the morning and eight in the evening. What she does in between those times is left to the reader's imagination.

The text

'Maggie Dooley'

Old Maggie Dooley
Twice a day
Comes to the park,
To search for the stray,
Milk in a bowl,
Scraps on a tray,
'Breakfast time!'
'Supper time!'
Hear her say.

Alone on a bench
She'll sit and wait
Till out of the bushes
They hesitate;
Tommy No-Tail
And Sammy No-Fur
Half-Eye Sally
And Emmy No-Purr.

She sits by the children's
Roundabout
And takes a sip
From a bottle of stout.
She smiles a smile
And nods her head
Until her little
Family's fed.

Whatever the weather,
Shine or rain,
She comes at eight
And eight again.
'It's a saint you are,'
To Maggie I said.
But she smiled a smile
And shook her head.

'Tom and Sammy,
Sally and Em,
They need me
And I need them
I need them
And they need me.
That's all there is,'
She said, said she.

Charles Causley

'Maggie Dooley' from *I Had a Little Cat: Collected poems for children* by Charles Causley, originally published by Macmillan Children's Books. Printed by kind permission of David Higham Associates.

Text potential
Exploring what the text offers

Vocabulary

'Stout' – needs simple explanation.

'Family' – central concept for the poem. Nuances of meaning need exploring and application to the poem.

'Saint' – non-religious meaning. Needs to be applied to the poem.

'Stray' – used as a noun with a definite article 'the stray'.

Language features

Repeated references to routine

'Twice a day', 'Breakfast time!', 'Supper time!', 'She comes at eight, and eight again'.

Narrative features

Grammar; Syntax

Some stanzas are just one sentence. Children may need support in recognizing that this is the expression of a complete thought.

Visual features

Mapping text potential
'Maggie Dooley' by Charles Causley

Literary features

Poem in five stanzas with two voices.

The voice of the poet intrudes into the poem through direct speech. How does this affect the poem?

Movement through the poem from external viewpoint to more intimate (conversation) and then internal.

Historical, social, and cultural context

Images of poverty. Possibly (but not explicit) Irish immigration to the post-war UK.

Coherence

Use of pronoun 'they' before the cats are introduced could be confusing.

Theme

Potential themes:
- alone and lonely
- family
- outsiders and belonging
- routine and safety.

Making links to background knowledge

Homeless people, the elderly, social deprivation, mental illness. There is a high probability that the children's experiences will be limited, informed by stereotype of received opinions.

Text type, purpose, and intended readership

Poem from a collection of poetry for children. Uses traditional form, which lends a timeless quality to the text. Invites the reader to reflect on the circumstances of people who live outside the norms of society.

Subject

An old woman who fills her days with a regular routine looking after stray cats.

Lesson planning and organization

Each child in the group had a copy of the poem.

A large sheet of paper, marker pens, and small whiteboards were also available to the group for recording ideas.

The lesson

First encounters

The children listened while the poem was read aloud by the teacher. As the children had little experience of reading poetry, it was important to help tune their ears to the cadences and rhythm. After the first reading, the children were invited to offer their initial responses to the poem. After a short exchange of ideas during which the pupils shared their emotional responses ('I think the poem is quite sad') and sought clarification of vocabulary ('What is stout?'), the teacher began to check what they had understood. She posed the question:

How does Maggie Dooley spend her day?

The responses were confident, and all of the children agreed that it was a poem about a solitary old woman whose daily routine involved feeding four stray cats. When asked why they thought Maggie had established this regular routine, they all suggested that she liked cats; typical responses included 'Perhaps she had a kitten when she was younger' and 'I think she loves cats. I think she has lots and lots of cats at home and she takes the cats the leftovers from their bowls.'

To try to explore the emotional landscape of the poem, particularly the potential back-story, the teacher used hot-seating: getting volunteers to be in the hot-seat as Maggie Dooley and asking her questions in an attempt to try to delve beyond the obvious. Questions that might have provoked thoughtful answers would have been 'Why do you feed the cats?' or 'Where do you go when you've fed them?', but these did not occur to the group. It quickly became apparent that the children found it difficult to think beyond the lines of the poem, or made fanciful suggestions (e.g. 'What did you have for your dinner?') that were not rooted in evidence in the poem.

Identifying explicitly stated information

To help the pupils better understand how to access the potential stories behind the words on the page, the teacher used a graphic organizer, a simple two-column table that she explained as follows:

Teacher (T): I have divided this large sheet of paper into two columns. In the heading for this column on the left, I am writing things that we know because the poem tells us. And in this column on the right, I'm writing things that we think because we can work them out from clues in the poem.

WHAT WE KNOW BECAUSE THE POEM TELLS US	WHAT WE THINK (OR CAN WORK OUT) BASED ON **CLUES** IN THE POEM

She then returned to the left-hand column and invited the pupils to make suggestions:

T: So, I wonder if we can start by finding five things that we know to be true about Maggie Dooley because the poem tells us.

Girl (G) 1: She goes to the park every day.

T: Do we definitely know that?

(Chorus of voices): Yes.

G2: She goes <u>twice</u> [stresses the word] a day because it says, 'Twice a day/Comes to the park'.

T: Yes, so you have taken us back to the words in the poem to support what you know. Sometimes we call that 'evidence'.

G2: She's old.

G1: Yeah, the first line is 'Old Maggie Dooley' so we know that she is old.

T: OK, while you're thinking of more things that we know about Maggie, I'm just going to write down what you've told me. So far we have two things that we definitely know about Maggie. If you don't agree with anything that I'm writing down, just let me know.

G3: She has four cats.

G2: They're not hers.

G4: She just feeds them. She feeds four cats.

G5: 'Tommy No-Tail/And Sammy No-Fur,/Half-Eye Sally/And Emmy No-Purr.' Four cats.

T: So what would you like me to write?

G4: She feeds four cats.

G2: All the cats she feeds are stray cats.

T: Do you want me to add that?

G2: Yes, she feeds four stray cats.

T: Do we definitely know that they are stray? Perhaps they all have homes but they come to the park for an extra meal, like Six-Dinner Sid.

G2: No, because it says 'search for the stray'.

T: OK good, so you are really good at using the words of the poem to check what we know about this character, Maggie Dooley.

G2: All the cats are injured.

T: All of them?

G2: No tail …

G3: … no fur, half-eye …

G2: … and Emmy No-Purr. Their names tell us that they are injured.

T: So they all have disabilities.

G6: She always sits by the children's roundabout.

T: I'm going to write that down. So you have come up with five things we definitely know about Maggie Dooley. Does anyone disagree with anything that I have written down so far?

G2: She sits on a bench. You can add that, 'she sits on a bench by the children's roundabout'.

T: There are lots of other things that we definitely know about Maggie Dooley. But I'm going to stop there for a moment.

The pupils talk confidently, identifying explicitly stated information with ease. They demonstrate a clear literal understanding of the poem, picking up salient details to build on and supporting each other's suggestions; they demonstrate an understanding of the difference between 'stray' and 'belonging'; prompted by the teacher, they quote from the text to support their ideas (e.g. *It says "search for the stray"'*). From the cats' names they infer that the felines have all been injured or are disabled.

After satisfying herself that that the children are secure with this, the teacher moves them on to think about making inferences from clues in the text.

Using clues in the text to make inferences

T: OK, so now we're going to have a look at this second column: 'What we think or can work out, based on clues in the poem'. At the moment this column is completely blank. We are going to look for ideas that we can work out based on clues in the poem. Sometimes we call it 'reading beyond the lines'. A text can be like a jigsaw; some of the pieces are there and some seem to be missing. When we read, we use these clues to help us find the missing pieces.

Usually you do this naturally – instinctively – when you are reading, but we are going to have a closer look to see exactly how some of those clues can help us work out other things about the character. I'm going to start by showing you what I mean.

The teacher reads the lines 'And takes a sip/From a bottle of stout'; 'sip' has already been defined earlier in the lesson, and now she explains what she might infer about Maggie from this line. She talks about Maggie's surname and says that she thinks she might be Irish from those two clues, but this is just a guess. She writes this inference in the form of a question. *I wonder if Maggie is Irish? Her surname and the bottle of stout suggest that she might be.*

T: OK, so now I wonder if we can work out some other ideas using clues in the poem. Let's take this line: 'I need them'. What does that clue suggest to you?

G3: It makes me think that she's really lonely and the cats are the only things that come to her. They're like her friends. She needs them; otherwise, she would be <u>really</u> lonely.

G2: I think she's lonely.

G1: Yes, she goes to the park twice a day. I only go once every two weeks.

G2: She goes in the morning and in the evening, so I don't think she has much to do. I don't think she has any friends.

G4: Let's write 'I think she's lonely'.

G6: I think she used to have friends and they broke up, but now there are just the cats and she tells them how she feels.

T: Do you think that's why she needs them then?

G2: She confides in them.

T: That's a good word for describing how she might tell them her troubles …

G5: … cos you know it says … no … here … 'Tommy No-Tail/And Sally No-Fur' … it says they hesitate. Tommy's tail might have fallen off because he's been hurt. So they are scared to come out of the bushes.

T: It doesn't actually say that, does it? But you have thought about that word 'hesitate', and used that as a clue to think about why they might behave in that way. They are being cautious and careful. How do you want me to write that?

G5: The cats might be might be scared of people because they hesitate to come out because of their injuries.

T: Here's another line. I wonder if we can do any clue-spotting with this one: 'She sits by the children's/Roundabout'. We've written that down as one of the things that we definitely know. I wonder if we can use it as a clue to work out anything else?

G6: Maybe it's because she likes children but she never got any of her own.

T: I like your thinking. Charles Causley could have written: she sat by the duck pond, or she sat by the flower-bed but he didn't: he chose the children's roundabout, and that's created another picture in your head. Are there any other lines in this poem that would make us think that perhaps she doesn't have children?

(Pause while the children look at the poem.)

G1: 'they need me' because children do need their mum like I need my mum.

G2: And it says 'family'.

T: Can you read that for us?

G2: 'Until her little/Family's fed.'

T: So there are a few clues that could support that idea. I'm going to write it in this column.

G3: 'She smiles a smile', so I think she's happy seeing the children playing.

G2: Maybe she smiles because it reminds her of happy times.

G6: Can we talk about my idea now? It could be that's where the cats usually go, so that's why she goes there.

G5: I've got another fact: she comes at eight and eight again. Perhaps eight is her lucky number.

T: Could it be anything else?

G2: It could be that she wakes up early and goes straight to the park and then just watches TV in the afternoon and goes back in the evening.

T: Which of those makes most sense to you?

G2: That she wakes up early. Or the cats are only hungry then.

T: So she plans her day around when they are hungry, perhaps?

In this extract, the pupils are demonstrating their ability to make inferences based on the information provided in the poem. This contrasts with their earlier responses during the hot-seating, which either reiterated what was stated in the poem or moved away from the poem. When Girl 5 makes an inappropriate inference (*'Perhaps eight is her lucky number'*), the teacher asks her to consider other possibilities. In this exchange of ideas they are deepening their responses, in particular the idea that Maggie may never have had children and the cats are her surrogate family.

The pupils then work in pairs to find more things that are stated in the poem, and they use those pieces of information as clues to make inferences about Maggie's character. The discussion is lively and they comfortably express tentative thinking. At one point a child says she is not sure whether Maggie was homeless or poor because she had money to buy stout and had possessions like the bowl of milk. They then talk about homeless people they have seen drinking in shop doorways, and about buskers and homeless people sometimes having animals, especially dogs, to keep them company. One of the girls suggests that animals don't judge you like other human beings. This is supported by another girl who adds, *'Just like Maggie Dooley's cats'*.

At this point the teacher pulls the lesson together, and makes an explicit reference to the way the children have been discussing the poem.

T: I like the way you were talking then, really listening to each other's ideas. I was quiet because I was enjoying listening to your ideas. It's really good learning when you learn from each other like that. Do you feel that you all need to agree when you are talking like this?

G1:   No.

T: Why do you think you don't have to agree?

G1:   We all have different opinions about things that are not actually said in the poem.

G2:   No one really knows the answer except Charles Causley.

G6:   And Maggie Dooley [laughs], if she's true.

T: So there are right and wrong answers to the things you have put in this column [indicates left-hand column]. But for these things [right-hand column], there are lots of possible answers. It's not that any old answer will do, but there are more possibilities. They could be true because there are clues in the poem to support them.

Teacher's reflections

The teacher was pleased at how readily the children responded to the distinction between explicitly stated information and inference-making using clues in the text. It was evident that some of the pupils understood that the cats were a likely substitute for children, family, or friends, and this created in their minds a back-story for Maggie's current circumstances. This was more subtle than their initial responses, which suggested the poem was simply about an old lady who liked cats. Using the chart as a graphic organizer helped the pupils to understand the difference between explicitly stated information and inferences drawn from clues in the text, and the teacher felt they would be able to apply this to future learning. On reflection, the teacher felt that hot-seating had been the least successful element of the lesson as the children did not have the experience of this technique to be able to develop a deeper level of discussion. The hot-seating might have been more successful if it had followed the discussion about inference-making as the pupils would have had a greater resource on which to draw in order to ask and answer questions. Throughout the session the teacher utilized terms that are commonly used such as 'evidence' and 'support', making sure these were understood in context.

Conclusion

From observations of many guided reading sessions, it would appear that poetry is an underused resource. The compressed and allusive qualities of poetry afford many opportunities to explore subtle, underlying ideas and themes that might be more difficult to access in longer texts. It also allows complete texts to be read during one session: this can be satisfying, especially if reading longer texts is spread over a long period with gaps between lessons with the teacher. Graphic organizers can support children's thinking by making the process visible. The children in this case study had, with prompting from the teacher, already developed skills in working as a group and were attentive to each other's ideas; this in turn enabled them to reflect not only on the content of the lesson but also on the process.

Reference

Causley, Charles (1996) 'Maggie Dooley'. In Causley, Charles, *I Had a Little Cat: Collected poems for children.* London: Macmillan Children's Books (ISBN 978-0-330-46411-6).

Case study 4: poetry, 9–10 year olds

Case study 4: poetry, 9–10 year olds

'The Malfeasance' by Alan Bold

Context

Elder School is a large school for children aged 7–11 in outer London. It serves an ethnically diverse neighbourhood. The proportion of pupils who speak English as an additional language is much higher than average, and the school also has a very high proportion of pupils with special educational needs. Despite this, pupils make good progress by the time they leave the school at the age of 11.

The teacher, Catherine, has a class of 30 (Year 5) 9–10 year-olds.

Planning

The following case study shows how a challenging poem can be approached with mixed-ability groups across a whole class, either working with groups sequentially or through whole-class teaching, with a view to developing comprehension and response. The lesson was taught jointly by the writer and the class teacher. It is possible to use this poem following a similar teaching sequence, with a small guided reading group.

Text selection

'The Malfeasance' (in *The Oxford Book of Story Poems*, 1999) is a powerful and humorous modern poem with a serious theme that becomes apparent as we read through it. Children are likely to identify a number of different messages and themes and may not agree on a single meaning.

The text

'The Malfeasance'

It was a dark, dank, dreadful night
And while millions were abed
The Malfeasance bestirred itself
And raised its ugly head.

The leaves dropped quietly in the night
In the sky Orion shone;
The Malfeasance bestirred itself
Then crawled around till dawn.

Taller than a chimney stack,
More massive than a church,
It slithered to the city
With a purpose and a lurch.

Squelch, squelch, the scaly feet
Flapped along the roads;
Nothing like it had been seen
Since a recent fall of toads.

Bullets bounced off the beast,
Aircraft made it grin,
Its open mouth made an eerie sound
Uglier than sin.

Still it floundered forwards,
Still the city reeled;
There was panic on the pavements,
Even policemen squealed.

Then suddenly someone suggested
(As the beast had done no harm)
It would be kinder to show it kindness
Better to stop the alarm.

When they offered it refreshment
The creature stopped in its track;
When they waved a greeting to it
Steam rose from its back.

As the friendliness grew firmer
The problem was quietly solved:
Terror turned to triumph and
The Malfeasance dissolved.

And where it stood there hung a mist,
And in its wake a shining trail,
And the people found each other
And thereby hangs a tail.

Alan Bold

Text potential
Exploring what the text offers

Vocabulary

Some unusual words that are crucial to meaning: 'bestirred', 'dank', 'Orion', 'lurch', 'eerie', 'dissolved'.

Language features

Use of verbs is strong and could be examined; how do the verbs ('lurch', 'slithered', 'floundered') help us to build a clear picture of the creature's movement?

Theme

Theme: a range of possibilities:

- nothing to fear but fear itself
- kindness brings its own reward
- overcoming problems.

Narrative features

This is a narrative poem so has a plot sequence that can be identified.

Mapping text potential
'The Malfeasance' by Alan Bold

Grammar; Syntax

The poem has a straightforward structure of four-line stanzas with an abcb rhyme pattern.

Other aspects of repetition also can be explored.

Visual features

Pupils could perform this poem, visualizing and creating tableaux as it is recited.

Historical, social, and cultural context

Literary features

Both simile and metaphor feature heavily. Similes include 'taller than a chimney stack' and 'more massive than a church'.

The Malfeasance creature itself can be seen as a metaphor, which is explored through the theme and by asking 'what is the lesson the poet is teaching us in this poem?'

Coherence

Use of the pronoun 'it' ensures coherence between stanzas.

Making links to background knowledge

Children can explore the themes by relating it to their own experience of fear and kindness and solving problems collectively.

Text type, purpose, and intended readership

A humorous poem probably written to appeal to children, but adults will also appreciate the humour and theme.

Subject

A narrative poem about a dangerous monster threatening a city and the solution the population found through being kind.

In the above diagram, the boxes show the areas where the teachers felt the text lent itself most powerfully to teaching.

The text has the potential to develop comprehension through inference and response in a wide variety of ways, and the lesson focuses on powerful themes as they emerge from the narrative of the poem.

The linguistic features used to describe the Malfeasance quickly build up a vivid picture in the mind of the reader. These features include simile and metaphor, the syntax of the poem, and the effect this has on meaning. The vocabulary has been carefully chosen and placed in such a way that multiple meanings can be explored. The children can be asked to examine the effect of the verbs used to describe the creature's movements ('lurch', 'slithered', 'floundered') and other structural features such as repetition ('still', 'still'; 'squelch', 'squelch'; the repetition of 'and' at the beginning of the last four lines) and patterns of rhyme, rhythm, and stanzas. The lesson therefore focuses on the particular language and vocabulary that the poet has carefully chosen to help readers make sense of the text.

The poem also lends itself to performance. Pupils could prepare a reading of the poem, using purely voice or props or their own pictures to enhance their response to, and interpretation of, the poem as they perform for their peers or other members of the school community.

Lesson planning and organization

This poem was part of a longer sequence of work on comprehension and the development of inference to deepen understanding and response.

Overall plan

Year 5 English

'The Malfeasance' by Alan Bold

Focus and teaching objectives	Developing effective exploratory talk in group work.
	Setting up structures to ensure argumentation/discussion is effective in deepening learning in the context of working with a narrative poem.
Link to 2014 National Curriculum POS for Spoken Language	<ul><li>Listen and respond appropriately to adults and their peers.</li><li>Ask relevant questions to extend their understanding and knowledge.</li><li>Articulate and justify answers, arguments, and opinions.</li><li>Maintain attention and participate actively in collaborative conversations, staying on topic and initiating and responding to comments.</li><li>Use spoken language to develop understanding through speculating, hypothesizing, imagining, and exploring ideas.</li><li>Speak audibly and fluently with an increasing command of Standard English.</li><li>Participate in discussions, presentations, performances, role play, improvisations, and debates.</li><li>Gain, maintain, and monitor the interest of the listener(s).</li><li>Consider and evaluate different viewpoints, attending to and building on the contributions of others.</li></ul>

Lesson Plan

Introduction	Introduce children to key teaching objectives:

Spoken language:

* To work effectively in small and large groups, giving reasons for what is said and responding to other people's comments.

English:

* To develop an understanding of a poem, both literal and beyond, using inference, and justifying inferences and opinions with evidence from the text.
* To ask questions to clarify meaning and discuss how the use of figurative language contributes to understanding.

Paired work: remind each other of the ground rules for working well in pairs/groups.

Main teaching segment	What are good ways of saying things that help us to work together in groups? Some examples:

* I think that … because …
* What do you think?
* What is your idea?
* Why do you think that?
* I don't understand what you mean. Could you say a bit more?
* I agree because …
* I think I disagree because …
* Those are good reasons, but I'm not sure about that idea because …
* Has everybody said what they wanted to?
* So do we all agree that …?

Can you come up with any more? Collect them and explain why they are useful when talking directly to each other both in small groups, and the whole class.

English input:

We will read the poem and then discuss in our groups:

Literal comprehension (looking question):

What is happening in this poem? (It is a narrative poem, so it tells a story.)

	Clarification (asking questions to clarify meaning): **Is there anything about the poem that puzzles you or you don't understand**? (This could be particular words or it could be a question about the meaning of the poem you would want to ask the poet if he was here now.) Inference (clue question): **What is the Malfeasance?** (And why do you think that?) Thinking question (if time): **What lesson is the poet trying to teach us in this poem?** Please note down your thoughts if that is helpful. Reminder that as they work in groups they should try to use the examples of good group talk above.
Group work 1	Groups work through the first two questions. Adults hover but do not intervene unless they have to!
Whole class plenary	Discussion of question 1. What do you think? Do we all agree? Further reminder that as they talk in the whole class directly to each other they should still try to use the examples of good group talk above.
Group work 2	Inference (clue question): **What is the Malfeasance?** (And why do you think that?) Thinking question (if time): **What lesson is the poet trying to teach us in this poem?** Please note down your thoughts if that is helpful. Reminder that as they work in groups they should try to use the examples of good group talk above.
Whole class plenary	What did you think? Do we all agree? Reflecting on the talk. What words and phrases did you use that helped the group work well together? What will you remember to do next time as a result of what you have done today?

Three core questions were formulated to shape activities and discussion of the poem. They focused on literal comprehension ('looking'), inference ('clue'), and making 'text to life' connections ('thinking'). See Chapter 3, p. 38, for a more detailed explanation of these kinds of questions.

THE THREE TYPES OF QUESTION
Comprehension – making meaning from texts:
• literal   • inference/deduction   • evaluative/responsive
Therefore three areas for formulating questions:
• literal ('looking')   *What is happening in this poem?*   • inference/deduction ('clue')   *What is the Malfeasance? How do you know?*   • evaluative/responsive ('thinking')   *What lesson, do you think, is the poet trying to teach us in this poem?*

The poem was duplicated on A3 sheets of paper – enough for one copy for each pair of children.

There was also a hard copy of the three questions for each pair.

The lesson

Introduction

The teacher outlined the learning objectives, gave out the poem and questions, and then read the poem aloud to the class while the children followed in their pairs.

The questions were read aloud and discussed to ensure that all of the children understood what they were expected to do.

Children worked in mixed-ability groups of four or in pairs. They were told they could annotate both the poem and the questions on the paper, but had to agree as a group how they would do so and what they would write. The children were also encouraged to reread the poem carefully and to address the 'looking' question first, while at the same time identifying vocabulary that was unknown or puzzling, or which needed clarification if the meaning was not to be compromised.

During the lesson

Exploration and discussion in groups

Each group reread the poem and then worked on the questions and annotated their copies.

Below are two typical annotated outcomes.

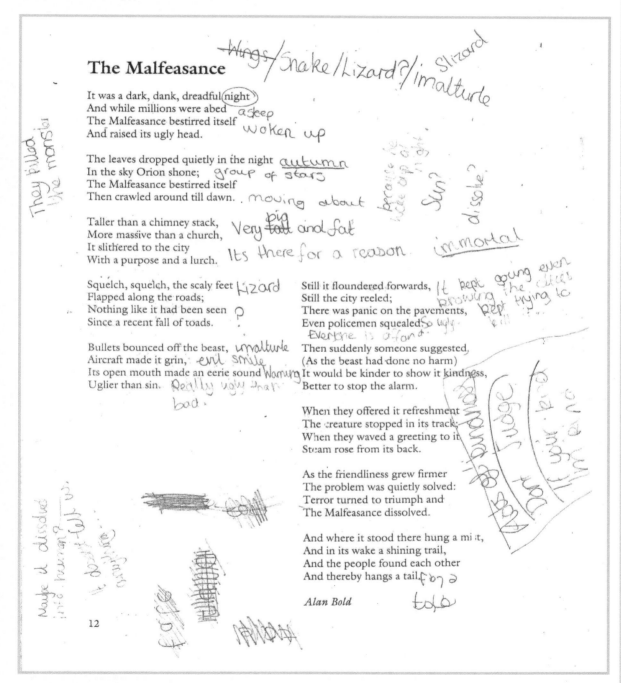

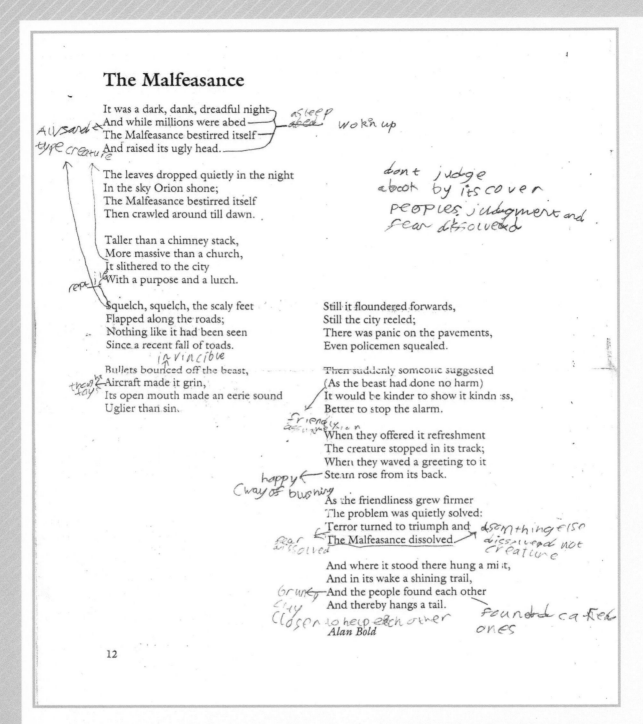

The Malfeasance

It was a dark, dank, dreadful night
And while millions were abed
The Malfeasance bestirred itself
And raised its ugly head.

The leaves dropped quietly in the night
In the sky Orion shone;
The Malfeasance bestirred itself
Then crawled around till dawn.

Taller than a chimney stack,
More massive than a church,
It slithered to the city
With a purpose and a lurch.

Squelch, squelch, the scaly feet
Flapped along the roads;
Nothing like it had been seen
Since a recent fall of toads.

Bullets bounced off the beast,
Aircraft made it grin,
Its open mouth made an eerie sound
Uglier than sin.

Still it floundered forwards,
Still the city reeled;
There was panic on the pavements,
Even policemen squealed.

Then suddenly someone suggested
(As the beast had done no harm)
It would be kinder to show it kindness,
Better to stop the alarm.

When they offered it refreshment
The creature stopped in its track;
When they waved a greeting to it
Steam rose from its back.

As the friendliness grew firmer
The problem was quietly solved:
Terror turned to triumph and
The Malfeasance dissolved.

And where it stood there hung a mist,
And in its wake a shining trail,
And the people found each other
And thereby hangs a tail.

Alan Bold

12

These annotated examples show considerable evidence of a high engagement with the poem, and of a deep understanding of both the narrative told and the possible themes that it addresses.

Both examples also show how the groups carefully and methodically worked through the poem to co-construct the literal meaning, addressing both individual vocabulary items and the action in each verse, as well as going well beyond the literal to infer what kind of creature the Malfeasance could be.

Clarification of vocabulary and making meaning

The groups paid attention to the unusual vocabulary and made notes to remind themselves of their meaning: in the first verse in both examples above, they identified 'abed' and 'bestirred', and noted that they mean 'asleep' and 'woken up' respectively. Group 1 carried on with their careful annotation of each verse, looking for unusual words but also looking for clues with which to infer meaning. In the second verse, they agreed that the line 'The leaves dropped quietly in the night' indicated an aspect of the setting; it is autumn.

Both groups kept the 'clue' question in mind as they read the poem, and noted the clues that might suggest what the Malfeasance could be. Group 1 ascertained that, as the poem says it is 'more massive than a church', the Malfeasance must be 'very big and fat'.

Group 2 decided to draw arrows from the fourth verse to the first to show how the new information was building a fuller picture of the creature. They noted that it must be a lizard-like creature, as the clues in the fourth verse suggest reptilian qualities: 'the scaly feet/Flapped along the roads'.

As the groups read on into the second half of the poem, they showed evidence of being able to grapple with what was happening to the creature and why; and while doing so, they simultaneously addressed all three question types: 'looking', 'clue', and 'thinking'. The line 'Aircraft made it grin' provoked two different, but very interesting, responses: Group 1 interpreted it as meaning that the creature had an evil smile, while Group 2's view was that it meant the creature thought the planes were 'toys'.

As the groups discussed the final three verses – that is to say, when the people in the poem start to show the creature kindness – the pupils had to think carefully about what was happening and the reasons why.

Group 1 decided that, because the steam rose from the creature's back after the people waved to it, it must be that the creature was now blushing with happiness. However, it was the significance of the creature dissolving that was more intriguing. Group 2 were clear that this did not mean the creature was dissolving ('something else dissolved not creature'); it therefore had to be a metaphor. Furthermore, 'fear dissolved' was a significant insight into one of the possible underlying themes of the poem. They also noted that 'people's judgement dissolved'.

Group 1 were a little puzzled and frustrated by this development in the action ('maybe it dissolved into human? It doesn't tell us anything …').

The strategy of working in groups, discussing the poem verse by verse, and agreeing what to note down as they went along were very powerful strategies in helping the children to make sense of the story the poem was telling, but also helped them to co-construct a deeper response to the themes that seemed to be implied by the way the narrative developed.

The teacher did not tell the pupils what to think about the poem; instead, the structure of the lesson made it possible for the groups to explore the poem in a way that enabled them to have insights into both narrative content and theme. An awareness of all three questions as they explored the poem was also crucial in focusing their discussions and helping effective meaning-making to take place.

Themes and messages

The groups also noted what they thought about the theme or message in the poem in response to the third question.

One group noted down:

> Don't judge creatures by their looks. Get to know them better.

Group 2 came to a similar conclusion: 'don't judge a book by its cover'. This was the conclusion reached by virtually every group and was picked up by the teacher for a whole-class discussion after the group work.

Plenary: exploring responses to the poem

The following extract from the whole-class conversation took place after the class had discussed the questions about what had happened in the poem and what they thought the Malfeasance was.

Teacher (T): Now we've got a view about the Malfeasance as this beast which people are really scared of to begin with and then … something happens to it in the second half of the poem, doesn't it, which we're puzzling over. There are a number of things that people said it might be due to: it might be the lifting of a curse, might be about sunlight, might be about being allergic to food, you know, all sorts of things which we're not quite sure about. So let's now consider what you think the poet is trying to say, you know, the big thing he's trying to tell us, the lesson he's trying to teach us when we read through this poem; the theme of the poem. And themes are, you know, the kind of big idea that we get out of the poem rather than the detail.

So what I want you to do is to turn back to your groups and have a read of those last two or three verses again, and then just think about what actually is this poem about, what's it trying to tell us. I'll give you about five minutes.

Five minutes then passed and the groups were invited to share their thoughts one by one about what they thought the theme might be.

T: OK. This time I'm going to ask each group in turn to say what they think without interruption, and then you can all join in when we've heard everybody's ideas, OK?

Child (C) 1: I think the poem is trying to say like don't judge a book by its cover because it's like the people, like, judge it and I feel that happens through the story. And I think it taught people of the city and the reader that you should help everyone because … something like that … not like real but it's sort of something like that could happen, like a war or something.

T: OK. Thank you. Next group, tell us your idea.

C2:   I think Child 1 is right, and if you show kindness to someone then they'll show kindness back to you.

C3:   We thought that there were two lessons that the poet showed. One was about judgement because the creature was ugly, but in that other paragraph it says that he had done no harm, and the next one is kindness because the other person who said that the beast, like they should give him a refreshment so he wouldn't harm them and then … and that … and when he showed kindness the beast didn't harm them anymore.

T: OK. Thank you.

C4:   We thought that the lesson was kindness isn't always for the best because in the end it ended up with someone killing somebody; the creature dissolved.

T: Thank you.

C5:   The poet taught me that we should get to know people better before we judge them.

T: OK. And why do you say that?

C5:   You can't judge people by their looks because you don't know how they are inside and you have to like them for who they are instead of their looks.

T: Hmm hmm. Is that fair? Is that what you decided in your group? Yes? OK. Last group.

C6:   You also shouldn't … you should think about people, what they're feeling, not … like you should think about their inside, not the outside.

T: OK.

C3:   And people, in the olden days they used to judge them by their colour. So it's like racism. So if like a black person is sat on the bus and the white man wanted to sit there they'd have to move.

C5:   I agree with what Child 6 said before, well, even though he might be ugly outside, he might really … their feelings …

C7:   … they could be thoughtful.

C8:   Yeah, they could be thoughtful on the inside, so you don't really need to judge them from their looks.

C9: You should show kindness because, just because the creature dissolved it doesn't mean that like … just because they showed him kindness. Because sometimes … let's say a child was like sitting in a corner crying because someone's been nasty or something and then a teacher went up to the child and showed them kindness …

T: … so let me get this right. Virtually everyone around the room is saying that the message of this poem is something to do with showing kindness and that that would be a good thing; but we've got one group that's saying that actually showing kindness meant that this creature dissolved, disappeared, and that it says in the last verse, *'and the people found each other'*. I presume that means the people in the city, so … And I think that's perhaps a good thing that the people found themselves. So the creature dissolving might be a good thing. So if the kindness they showed made the creature dissolve, is that a good thing or is that a bad thing? I'm not sure.

C3: I think it's a good thing because, like you said, they found each other so that means they might have showed them kindness and they might do it again.

Commentary

The above extract from a longer exploration of the theme of the poem is worth considering because, in a short space of time (less than seven minutes), nine different children get to contribute to the class's thinking and all have an opportunity to speak in extended ways, justifying their views with evidence drawn from the text. There is general agreement on the theme of kindness, though there is one different view that is not developed, even though the teacher refers to it in one of the challenge interventions when she says, 'So the creature dissolving might be a good thing.'

After the children have had an opportunity to discuss the theme in groups, the teacher asks one person in each group to report back in turn before opening out to a whole-class discussion. This enables all of the groups' thinking to be shared equally. Note that the teacher doesn't praise or give feedback or interrupt at any point in this sharing of ideas. She thanks each group in turn, occasionally prompts for justification, and checks that what is stated is what the group has agreed. This strategy reinforces the classroom ethos that all views can be shared and considered as part of the co-construction of knowledge and understanding; the children's voices have equal worth. It also ensures that more voices are heard even though, during the more open discussion, particular children are able to contribute more than once.

Teacher's reflections

The teacher had this to say after the lesson was completed:

> This lesson went really well! The strategy of getting the children to annotate their own copy of the poem resulted in them slowing down and discussing what was happening in each verse in turn, and considering the unusual words carefully to work out what they meant and how they helped to construct a mental picture of the Malfeasance creature. They were grabbed by this poem and loved discussing it in their groups. The size of the groups helped too. We decided to try groups of four rather than six to see if we got better participation in the group work, and we did. There wasn't really anybody on the periphery or not joining in, which you usually get if they are working in my usual groups of six. I am going to do much more group work in fours now.

What the pupils learned and how they showed what they could do:

> The pupils showed a really good understanding of the narrative plot through their careful reading throughout the lesson, and engaged well with each other. In particular, they developed their word-meaning strategies, using context. There was a lot of unusual vocabulary, and they were able to read around the word and make really good decisions about the word's meaning in that context. All of the annotated poems [two of which have been included here] showed that they could interpret the text and the poet's message by drawing on the text and making connections with their own experience. All the children were able to justify their opinions using evidence in the poem. They built really well on each other's contributions, whether they agreed or not, and did not always address their contributions to me, the teacher; it was a proper class discussion!

> In the end, I wasn't sure I agreed that kindness was the only theme, and perhaps I should have challenged them more about what the beast represented – whether it was metaphorical, representing the emotion of fear, rather than the mythical creature that they suggested and stuck to throughout.

What next?

> We will carry on with narrative poetry and we will continue to work on similar areas, particularly identifying themes and how the poet's precise choice of words not only underpins the way we interpret the literal meaning but also affects our personal responses.

Conclusion

This case study transcript contains evidence of dialogic teaching taking place.

Robin Alexander states that dialogue requires:

- interactions which encourage students to think in different ways
- questions which invite more than simple recall
- answers which are justified, followed up and built upon rather than merely received
- feedback which informs and leads thinking forwards
- contributions that are extended
- exchanges that chain together into coherent lines of enquiry
- discussion and argumentation which probe and challenge
- professional engagement with subject matter which liberates classroom discourse from the safe and conventional
- classroom organization, climate and relationships which make this possible.

Alexander (www.robinalexander.org.uk/dialogic-teaching/)

In this extract, it is clear the children have been asked to think in a range of ways about the poem, the questions having been designed to do much more than simply get them to regurgitate what they already know. Their answers are justified and followed up both by the teacher and by other members of the class. The teacher's contributions in the second part of the transcript are designed to probe, challenge, and move their thinking on. There is definitely a coherent line of enquiry about the theme of the poem, and the respectful ethos of this classroom makes possible the sharing of ideas. What is more, the children listen carefully, their answers are built on, and they feel that their contributions are of significant value.

Poetry is an excellent context for this kind of talk and, if presented in engaging ways, ensures that the discussions and contributions lead to a deepening of both the teacher's and the children's understanding.

Reference

Bold, A. (1999) 'The Malfeasance'. In *The Oxford Book of Story Poems*. Oxford: Oxford University Press (ISBN 978-0-19-276212-5).

Chocolate

Context

Bernice teaches a class of 10–11 year olds (Year 6) at Chestnut Primary School, a larger than average-sized primary school in outer London where the proportion of pupils who speak English as an additional language is well above average, as is the proportion from minority ethnic backgrounds. Despite low levels of achievement when they start, pupils achieve exceptionally well and standards by the end of Year 6 are usually above average.

For a number of years Bernice has been using the Reciprocal Teaching approach to guided reading, supported by the three levels of questions that aim to access different layers of meaning: looking questions, clue questions, and thinking questions. She has used this approach successfully with fiction texts and was interested to see how it could be applied effectively to non-fiction texts.

Planning

Bernice had previously worked with a group of 'reading champions' consisting of other teachers from the local School Improvement Learning Community (SILC) – a consortium of five schools who work closely to share practice in all areas of the curriculum – where a number of issues had arisen when teachers had attempted to use non-fiction texts. For example, the lack of appropriate texts became apparent. A look in one of the school's libraries revealed that, while suitable material on the topic was available for younger children, it was not appropriate for children at the upper end of the primary school. Another issue was that of background knowledge. By their nature, non-fiction texts relate to the development of domain knowledge (knowledge in specific areas) and often assume some sort of knowledge of the domain already, on which the new information can be built. However, if children do not have this domain knowledge in place, it becomes very difficult to build new knowledge onto this.

Text selection

Bernice attempted to address these problems before she planned her non-fiction guided reading lessons. First, she ensured that she obtained what might be considered age-appropriate texts through contact with the local authority's schools' library service. This is a very useful service for resourcing literacy in schools as it provides access to a range of high-quality texts that might not be available in individual schools.

Second, to address the issue of the knowledge children were bringing to the text, Bernice ensured that the guiding reading lessons she planned were developed from a context with which the children were familiar. In this instance, her guided reading sessions were developed from a topic the children were studying at the time, entitled 'From Bean to Bar'.

This topic, examined by the classes of 9–11 year olds in the school, was about chocolate, with an explicit focus on geography and PSHCE (Personal, Social, Health, and Citizenship Education). It also covered such matters as life on a cocoa plantation (which raised issues around child labour), the issue of fair trade (particularly in relation to chocolate production), and the impact of deforestation and the devastating effects of flooding on farmers. The learning from this topic was made explicit in the learning environment through the use of classroom displays.

As part of the topic, the children also spent some time reading fiction texts related to the theme of chocolate. Before beginning non-fiction work in guided reading, the children in Bernice's class completed a series of guided reading lessons on *The Whizz Pop Chocolate Shop* by Kate Saunders (2012). Bernice planned to follow this with two guided reading lessons using non-fiction texts.

Text potential

Exploring what the text offers

Vocabulary

Technical vocabulary – e.g. 'caffeine', 'carbohydrate', 'stimulant', 'chemical', 'nutrient'.

Language features

- Use of passive tense
- Glossary
- Fact box
- Headings and sub-headings

Theme

Potential themes:
- healthy eating/living
- child labour.

Subject

The material used here is from specific pages of a factual information book about chocolate. There is no attempt to use the whole text. The focus is on where chocolate comes from and potential health issues.

Narrative features

Grammar; Syntax

Apart from some passive tenses, the text presents little difficulty.

Sentences tend to be short.

Mapping text potential

Chocolate Non-fiction study

Visual features

- An illustration of molecules will need explaining.
- Readers will need to consider contrasting images of cartoon-like drawings and photographs.
- Being able to locate non-fiction layout features will be important.

Historical, social, and cultural context

Plantations in rural Africa are described as a place where modern-day slavery still exists.

Scientific diagram of molecular structure – how clear to children?

Literary features

Voice – differences in authorial voice between the two similar texts.

Metaphor – 'the dark side of chocolate'.

Coherence

Making links to background knowledge

Most children are likely to have little background knowledge of cocoa production.

They may have some knowledge about 'harmful' effects of caffeine.

They may have some concept of slavery.

Text type, purpose, and intended readership

This non-fiction text aims to provide information about chocolate production. There is bias in the text as the writer aims to deal with the moral issue of child labour.

The text also aims to present a 'scientific' tone to the content.

Lesson planning and organization

When Bernice came to plan the guided reading lessons on the theme of chocolate she selected the book *The Story Behind Chocolate* by Sean Price (2009). She also used *Ideas Box! Chocolate* by Jillian Powell (2011) for comparison.

Rather than working sequentially or systematically through the books, she focused on points that were linked closely to the work the children had completed as part of the topic. Once again she took the reciprocal teaching approach and focused on three levels of questions to access different layers of meaning. She selected specific double-page spreads and developed two lessons that she felt would be appropriate.

Lesson 1

The first double-page spread, on pages 16–17 of the book, is entitled 'Cacao farms and plantations'. This section of the book is closely related to the work previously completed as part of the geography/PSHCE work. By choosing this particular section of text, Bernice was able to guide the children more deeply through this theme, and had planned the following key questions to engage with the three different layers of meaning:

1. What have cocoa plantations often been linked to? ('looking')
2. Does the author agree with child slavery? How do you know? ('clue')
3. Do you think the author has used structure well to support the text type? ('thinking')

These questions allowed Bernice to focus on the theme of child slavery, to discuss this in the context of the life of children on the cocoa plantation and to explore the authorial intent in non-fiction. This double-page spread text has very little written text – approximately 250 words.

As a follow-up activity, the children were asked to undertake some comparative work between the sections of text studied in *The Story Behind Chocolate* and similar material presented in *Ideas Box! Chocolate*. The children were given envelopes containing labels for the features of non-fiction text: they included 'Caption', 'Sub-heading', 'Fact box', 'Introduction', 'Diagram', and 'Photograph'. Once they had finished reading pages 16–17 of *The Story Behind Chocolate*, and had thought of possible answers to the key questions, they were asked to work in pairs to identify the relevant feature on this second text, *Ideas Box! Chocolate*; they did not have to read the text in detail. The rationale for this is that there is often a question in the Reading SAT that asks for these features to be located. This second text would also feature in the planned follow-up activity.

They were asked to complete the following activity:

> Compare pages 16–17, which we read together, with pages 4–5 in the *Ideas Box!* book. Which features are similar? Which features are different? Do the authors have different viewpoints? How do you know?

Cacao farms and plantations

Cacao trees are often grown on **plantations** (large farms). Workers collect the pods off the trees.

Working with cacao trees can be dangerous. Workers use big knives called machetes. These are used to cut down cacao pods. Workers also get sprayed with pesticides. These are chemicals used to kill bugs. Pesticides can harm people's eyes, skin, and **nerves**.

The dark side of chocolate

Chocolate farms and plantations have long been tied to slavery. Starting in the 1600s, **slaves** were used on cacao plantations. Over time, most types of slavery ended. But in 1999, reporters found that some types still exist. Children in Africa are often bought and sold. Many become workers on cacao farms. Some children are sold to African cacao farms by their parents. Other parents make their children work for them. In both cases, the parents are very poor. They need the money to survive.

Child labour

The problem of child labour is hard to solve. Companies cannot just stop buying cacao beans. Many children need to work at least some of the time. If they do not, their families will starve. The problem of child labour cannot end overnight. Countries in Africa must make it illegal. They must also build schools for child workers. These changes will give children a better life.

▶ Many poor children have to work on cacao plantations to help feed their family. They must cut down pods and collect the beans.

True Stories: The Story Behind Chocolate, page 16, by permission of Capstone Global Library Ltd.

True Stories: The Story Behind Chocolate, page 17, by permission of Capstone Global Library Ltd. Photo © Tyler Hicks/Getty.

Where does chocolate come from?

Kim has just baked a chocolate cake. Mmm, everyone likes chocolate. Polly likes chocolate ice cream. Eddy likes chocolate biscuits. Ash's favourite book is *Charlie and the Chocolate Factory*. "If only chocolate grew on trees!" he says. "But it does!" Sal tells him.

Karina goes to school in Peru.

Sal's class has been writing letters to pupils at a school in Peru. In Peru they grow cacao beans, from which chocolate is made. Her pen pal, Karina, has told her how farmers grow cacao trees and harvest the beans. The cacao trees sound amazing. They grow up to 18 metres tall and can go on producing beans for over 100 years.

From *Espresso Ideas Box: Chocolate* by Jillian Powell, first published in the UK by Franklin Watts, an imprint of Hachette Children's Books, Carmelite House, 50 Victoria Embankment, London EC4Y 0DZ. Photo © Danita Delimont/Alamy.

These men are harvesting cacao seed pods.

Kim wants to know what everyone's favourite kind of chocolate is, so he has organised a chocolate tasting. Everyone has to put on a blindfold, taste little pieces of different kinds of chocolate then say which they like best. The bar chart shows which was most popular.

5
4
3
2
1

Dark | Milk | White | Fruit and nut

Quiz:
What does the Aztec word chocolate mean?

A) Sweet water

B) Bitter water

C) Sugar water

Quiz answers are on page 32.

5

From *Espresso Ideas Box: Chocolate* by Jillian Powell, first published in the UK by Franklin Watts, an imprint of Hachette Children's Books, Carmelite House, 50 Victoria Embankment, London EC4Y 0DZ. Photo © BrazilPhotos/Alamy.

Lesson 2

The second double-page spread, on pages 20–21 of *The Story Behind Chocolate*, is entitled 'What's in chocolate?'. This focuses on the chemistry of chocolate and its possible positive and harmful effects. Again this text was short – approximately 300 words. The key questions generated for this lesson were as follows:

1. What are theobromine and caffeine? ('looking')
2. Is chocolate healthy? ('clue')
3. Why do you think the author chose to use a scientific diagram? ('thinking')

These questions allowed Bernice to take a focus on health issues related to chocolate, and to revisit the idea of author intent in non-fiction.

A similar follow-up activity was prepared, using the same pair of books for comparison:

> Look at the four pages beginning overleaf to compare pages 20–21 in *The Story Behind Chocolate*, which we read together, with pages 20–21 in the *Ideas Box! Chocolate* book. Which features are similar? Which features are different? Which is the better text for giving the same information? Why do you think this?

Extracts from lesson 2

What follows are extracts from the second of the two lessons, with a group of six higher-attaining readers, together with a commentary. This lesson took place about six weeks before the children took their Standard Assessment Test (SAT) in Reading. This is a test taken by all children in England towards the end of their primary school education, and prior to entry to secondary education.

Revising the layers of meaning in context

Bernice started by revising the layers of meaning through the question types. The children were asked to explain the meaning of the looking, clue, and thinking questions, which she referred to as reading questions, inference questions, and opinion questions, making an explicit link to the terminology they would encounter in the SAT for Reading. So prior to engaging with the text itself, the teacher ensured that the children had a metacognitive understanding of the layers of meaning they were likely to encounter.

This did not result in the children simply repeating definitions that they had previously learned because Bernice ensured she made a link back to session 1, where the children had difficulty answering the 'looking' question: 'What have cocoa plantations often been linked to?' This appears to be the simplest type of question to answer because it taps literal understanding; however, in the previous session the children could not find the answer to this when they referred to the text. This surprised Bernice because the answer was written in bold. Bernice identified the source of difficulty in the fact that the text stated, 'Chocolate farms and plantations have long been *tied* [our italics] to slavery', whereas the question asked what plantations had been *linked* to.

Teacher (T):	Now last week, some of you got caught out. Why? Why did you get caught out on that particular question? Charlie I'm going to ask you because you were one who got caught out with it.
Child (C) 1:	Linked …
T:	Yeah, yeah, it said linked in my question and what word did it use in the text? Do you remember?
C1:	Ummm, we said farmers …
T:	Yeah, you said farmers, didn't you? But was that the answer? What are they often linked to? Think about our story.
C2:	Oh, slavery.
T:	Slavery. OK, we have to be quite careful with that reading question because although we know the answer is there, it may not use *exactly* those words.

In this interaction, Bernice has asked the children to recall the area of difficulty from the previous session. Using both questions and prompts from the teacher, the children are able to do this. At the end of this interaction, Bernice simply makes the point that literal questions can be misinterpreted because of the use of different vocabulary. Bernice has guided them to engage carefully with the literal layer of meaning.

Bernice then presented the three key questions to the children and asked them to read the text themselves.

1. What are theobromine and caffeine? ('looking')
2. Is chocolate healthy? ('clue')
3. Why do you think the author chose to use a scientific diagram? ('thinking')

What's in chocolate?

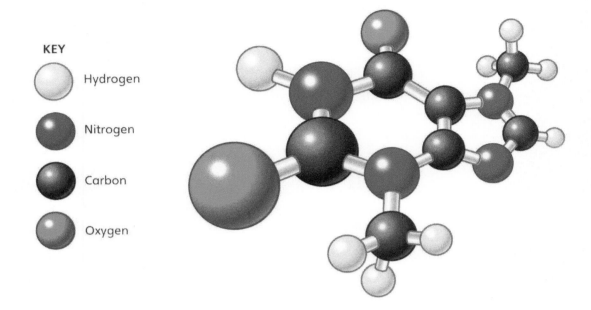

KEY

Hydrogen

Nitrogen

Carbon

Oxygen

▲ The chemical theobromine is the active ingredient in chocolate. It is made up of oxygen, nitrogen, carbon, and hydrogen **atoms**.

The chemistry of chocolate

People love chocolate. Eating chocolate seems to lift people's spirits.

The reason for this lift is a chemical called theobromine (see diagram). Theobromine is the active ingredient in chocolate. The active ingredient is the most important chemical within something.

Theobromine is a mild **stimulant**. But it is not the only stimulant. Chocolate also contains caffeine. Caffeine is the same stimulant found in coffee and soft drinks. However, chocolate has much less caffeine than coffee or soft drinks.

Some chemicals in chocolate are healthy. Scientists believe that chemicals called antioxidants in dark chocolate can lower a person's blood pressure. That is an important health benefit. High blood pressure can cause strokes and other serious illnesses.

20

True Stories: The Story Behind Chocolate, page 20, by permission of Capstone Global Library Ltd.

Chocolate's drawbacks

Many chocolate products can also harm a person's health. Most chocolate products contain a lot of **fat**. Most of them also have sugar added. Fat and sugar cause people to gain weight. Eating too much chocolate can cause people to be severely overweight.

Chocolate is fine to eat in small amounts, but too much of it will harm your health.

Chocolate allergies ✓

Many people think that they are **allergic** to chocolate. However, very few people are allergic to chocolate itself. Usually they are allergic to something that has been added to chocolate. That can include milk or nuts.

▼ Theobromine poisons dogs and other animals, including horses. Even a small taste of chocolate can kill them. Keep chocolate away from pets.

True Stories: The Story Behind Chocolate, page 21, by permission of Capstone Global Library Ltd. Photo © Tim Platt/Getty.

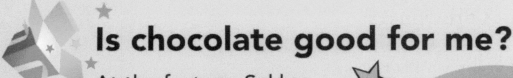

Is chocolate good for me?

At the factory, Sal has learned some interesting facts about chocolate as food. She has written a report about it for her school newspaper.

 ## Chocolate report

Espresso Extra

Chocolate: a feel good food!

Did you know that chocolate contains over 300 chemicals and some may make you feel more alert or cheer you up? Chemicals like theobromine can increase the activity of your brain cells.

Is chocolate healthy?

Chocolate also contains flavenoids and antioxidants which may protect the body against damage and ageing. Dark chocolate contains over twice as many antioxidants as milk chocolate – and fewer calories!

Chocolate also contains sugar, a kind of carbohydrate that is high in calories. It gives you energy but can also make you put on weight. Sugar also attacks the enamel on your teeth if you don't brush them regularly. Finally, the cocoa butter in chocolate contains saturated fats, and you should only eat these in small amounts. However, it also contains healthy fats like oleic acid. So, as long as you don't eat too much of it, chocolate really can be good for you!

20

From *Espresso Ideas Box: Chocolate* by Jillian Powell, first published in the UK by Franklin Watts, an imprint of Hachette Children's Books, Carmelite House, 50 Victoria Embankment, London EC4Y 0DZ. Photo © Richard Semik/Shutterstock.

Warning!

Theobromine is poisonous to dogs and cats so eating chocolate can harm and even kill them. Never give your pet chocolate, except for the special pet brands.

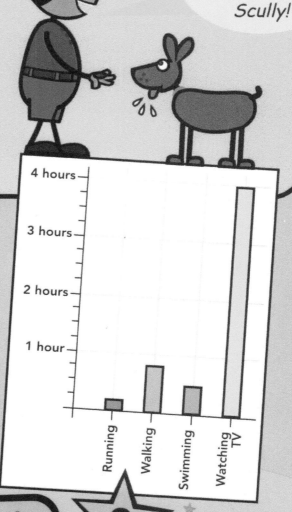

Here's a special doggy chocolate, Scully!

Kim has made a bar chart showing how long it takes to burn off the calories in a small chocolate bar.

Science spot: nutrients

Carbohydrates and fats are nutrients in food. Investigate other nutrients found in chocolate including vitamins and minerals, using the information on the packaging.

Feedback...

How much chocolate do you eat in a typical week?

21

Clarification

After the children had read the text and completed the task, Bernice spent some time on clarification. Again, she provided a rationale for this:

T: So, is there anything you want to clarify? Anything which you've read in this text and thought 'I don't want to answer those questions until I've had a chance to talk this over'?

One word that required some clarification was 'stimulant'.

C4: Stimulant.

T: Stimulant? What do you think a stimulant is? Because, actually, look, it's in bold. So where would we find that?

C3: Er, in the glossary.

T: In the glossary, so …

C3: But I know what a stimulant is.

T: Go on then.

C3: A stimulant is basically like caffeine and, erm [checks in the text] theobromine. Basically, erm, things that make you more aware of … that make you wake up.

C1: And makes you happy.

T: That makes you happy.

C1: Yeah.

T: OK, so it can make you happy as well. How do we know that caffeine is a stimulant? Think about the environment that we are in.

C3: You have coffee in the morning.

C1: Yeah, coffee in the morning.

T: When do I say it's going to be a good day?

(Numerous children together): When you've had a coffee.

This interaction shows the importance of clarification as a strategy to support comprehension. Here, we see Bernice supporting an understanding of how non-fiction texts work by eliciting from Child 3 that a glossary is likely to exist when words are presented in bold. She then allowed Child 3 the room to clarify the word for his peers. Child 3's clarification was supported by Child 1. Bernice also encouraged the children to make the link to their wider understanding of the world – in terms of both their home and school lives. This is important because non-fiction texts are likely to present new information, and linking this new information to what children already know, about the domain itself or the wider world, is essential.

Ensuring literal comprehension

The discussion around clarifying the word 'stimulant' led neatly onto addressing the first key question. It is designed to develop literal comprehension.

Question 1:   What are theobromine and caffeine?

T: What then are theobromine and caffeine, Child 4?

C4:   Theobromine and caffeine is like a stimulant and the chemical inside the, erm, theobromine is hydrogen, nitrogen, carbon, and oxygen.

T: I like how you've used the diagram there to help explain what's inside it.

C4:   And caffeine is put inside erm, coffee and soft drinks, and it allows you to wake up.

T: Absolutely, so they are stimulants – they allow you to get your body going and wake your brain up.

C1:   That's why you drink coffee.

T: That's why I drink <u>lots</u> of coffee. [Children laugh.] Anything else to add on this one?

   (Pause.)

C5:   Theobromine and caffeine are both active ingredients.

T: Yeah, they are both active ingredients in chocolate.

By asking if there is anything else to add, the teacher moved from the key literal question to an assessment of the children's broader literal understanding. The discussion turned to understanding what an active ingredient might be, and then to the atoms shown in the diagram on the double-page spread. After discussing these aspects of the text, Bernice could be sure that the children had developed enough of a literal understanding of this text to move on to deepening their understanding.

Using evidence in the text

The next question was a clue question, or what Bernice calls an inference question. Here, the aim was to support the children in developing a deeper understanding of the text by using available evidence.

Question 2:   Is chocolate healthy?

The text itself presented information that gave positive and negative answers to this question – though these weren't presented explicitly. Bernice gave the six children time to talk in pairs to consider how they might answer the question. As the children discussed the question, Bernice listened carefully to them.

T: Child 6, can you give me a comment that says that chocolate <u>is</u> healthy – that says that chocolate <u>is</u> healthy – without over-quoting the text too much?

C6: OK, it says in, erm, that scientists believe that in chocolate, there, erm, is a chemical, called antioxidant – in dark chocolate – can help lower a person's blood pressure.

T: Ok, so you picked out that one. Is there anything else that supports Child 6's comment that 'yes, chocolate can be healthy'?

C1: Erm, it says that it can help with blood pressure.

T: Yes, did we not just have that?

C2: Yes, but that's an important health benefit.

C3: It also says it is fine to eat in small amounts but if you have too much then you might be poorly or overweight or …

In this interaction we see Bernice trying to get Child 6 to reformulate her ideas in her own words. In this way, Bernice can see that not only has the child been able to locate the important piece of evidence, but also has some deeper understanding about what has been stated: it's not simply a matter of searching the text. Bernice also asked the other children in the group. Initially, it seemed that Child 1 was simply repeating the point raised by Child 6 about blood pressure but her talk partner emphasized the point that there was more to say about the issue by providing the information about the health benefits.

Bernice opened up the discussion by bringing to the fore the knowledge that children are likely to have about the health benefits of chocolate, which is often presented as an unhealthy option.

T: What is it that's in chocolate that makes us think that it is unhealthy, Child 1?

C1: Sugar.

T: OK, sugar. What else is inside it?

C6: Erm, erm, not natural fat, so, erm, I forgot, erm, saturated fat.

T: OK, is that a word that was featured in there?

C6: No.

T: So that's something you are bringing to it, that you know that saturated fat is not as good. OK, can you explain saturated fat?

C6: Saturated fat is when you have fat in things like, erm, fruit for example, that's healthy fat. That's good for your body. But saturated fat is artificial so your body doesn't necessarily like it.

T: I don't know if that's completely the best definition to give but I think it fits fairly well when you give the example of fruit versus erm …

C2: Chocolate.

In this interaction we see how Child 6 was encouraged to bring knowledge from outside the text to the text being read, when he talked about saturated fat. While Child 6 has some understanding of saturated fat, a misconception emerged in relation to fats and fruit. Bernice acknowledged that the definition needs some further development. At this stage she was happy to have the health differences between fruit and chocolate made clear.

This dialogue developed further when Child 3 made a link back to the earlier discussion on caffeine by attempting to explain why caffeine might be considered a positive reason to eat chocolate.

C3: Because it also says that … that they add caffeine to it, so it could also help you get up in the morning.

T: Right, so is your advice to me to eat a bar of chocolate and drink a cup of coffee for my breakfast?

C3: [Laughs] No. My advice is to just eat chocolate but not too much.

T: For breakfast or just generally?

C3: Generally.

T: Something I heard Child 1 and Child 3 talking about was about dark chocolate. You know, dark chocolate versus milk chocolate, or white chocolate. So is one type of chocolate more healthy than another?

C2: Yeah, dark chocolate.

This interaction shows that Child 3 was able to refine his thinking based on his previous knowledge and what he has learnt in the session, and he showed that he was aware that chocolate is acceptable in moderation regardless of the caffeine issue. Eventually the discussion moved on to the benefits of dark chocolate over milk or white chocolate. At this point, Bernice built on points she had heard the children discuss in their pairs.

Bernice then moved the dialogue on to a discussion about the negative aspects of chocolate. The issue of fat and sugar once again emerged.

T: Anything other than the fat and sugar to say that chocolate is unhealthy?

C1: It's … people gain weight.

C2: Some people have allergies to things that are in it, like nuts and milk. People who are allergic to nuts and milk might have a bad reaction and they might have to go to hospital.

T: I think they probably would if they have an allergy to it, wouldn't they?

Bernice did not spend much time on this part of the dialogue as it was obvious that the children were aware of the negative aspects of eating chocolate and could explain these.

Expressing an opinion

Given this, Bernice moved on to the third key question. It required the children to make a judgement, give an opinion or offer an evaluation. The third key question was as follows:

Question 3: Why do you think the author chose to use a scientific diagram?

The diagram shows the molecular construction of theobromine in terms of how it breaks down into hydrogen, nitrogen, oxygen, and carbon particles. Bearing in mind that this is a book designed for primary school children, Child 2 offered a reasonable and reasoned response to the question.

C2: Erm, it fits in, with the, erm, with some of the paragraph – the chemistry of chocolate – so they use these scientific diagrams to represent all the different, erm, all the atoms, and related things.

As a group, the children agreed with this reasoning; Bernice then proceeded to ask the children to consider how effective such a diagram might be, to encourage them to evaluate it critically.

T: Does it help you to understand anything?

C3: Yes.

C1: A little bit.

C3: It helps you to begin to understand atoms if you don't know anything about it, and it sort of tells you how much carbon, tells you how much of each other thing there is …

T: Do you think it is a good use of a diagram, Child 1?

C1: Erm, a bit.

T: Why only a little bit?

C1: Because it's good in one thing – it shows you what's inside the theobromine but if you don't know what that is and what it can do, it isn't going to help.

T: Yes, if you don't know what it's showing you then it is pretty useless, and it almost becomes a picture rather than a diagram, doesn't it?

In this interaction, Bernice explored the limitations of using such a diagram in the context in which it is presented. Note how she took Child 3's comment and then asked Child 1 to build upon this.

Following this, Bernice returned to the labelling activity completed when the text was read initially. The rationale for this was that this task led onto the follow-up activity. The children showed how they had labelled the features of the second piece and then transferred the labels to the main text that they were reading. Here, Bernice was reinforcing the generic features of non-fiction texts. She had included among the labels a 'red herring'; not all of the labels applied to the first text, and this led to some interesting discussion as the children were completing the task.

Follow-up activity

In both planned guided reading sessions the children were asked to undertake some comparative work between the sections of text studied in *The Story Behind Chocolate* and the *Ideas Box! Chocolate*. The sections in the *Ideas Box!* text covered virtually the same content but were presented very differently.

The children were asked to complete the following activities:

Guided reading: session 1

Compare pages 16 and 17 that we read together, to pages 4 and 5 from the *Ideas Box!* book. Which features are similar? Which features are different? Do the authors have different viewpoints? How do you know?

Guided reading: session 2

Compare pages 20 and 21 that we read together, to pages 20 and 21 from the *Ideas Box!* book. What features are similar? Which features are different? Which is the better text for giving the same information? Why do you think this?

Essentially, the children were asked to compare and contrast the two texts and to decide which one they preferred. This was completed as a discussion task. The children were able to locate the similarities and differences between the two but they all preferred the *Ideas Box! Chocolate* text. Their reasoning for this was that *The Story Behind Chocolate* book seemed dated, although it was published in 2009 – not that long ago.

Teacher's reflections

From this work, Bernice felt that she had been successful in developing the children's understanding of how non-fiction texts should be read. She was surprised at times about the extent of guiding that was required. She noted points in the session where she felt she was having to probe the children quite deeply to ensure they had achieved a literal understanding. She felt that the children were able to make links to their background knowledge that supported their comprehension, but she had to develop some facets of this knowledge so that the children were not coming 'cold' to the text. She felt that her careful question planning and deliberate text selection had been rewarded.

Conclusion

Using a non-fiction text in guided reading requires a different approach in terms of planning. To begin with, great care must be taken when choosing the text. In addition, the kind of guiding needed in the lesson may be different. In the lesson described here, there was more teacher talk than would have been expected in a lesson on a fiction text. The greater amount of teacher talk may be entirely appropriate; since the purpose of reading non-fiction texts is largely to gain new knowledge, young readers may not be bringing much to the text. To use this kind of text successfully, these key factors need to be considered if readers are to be guided effectively through the process:

- Any text used for non-fiction work in guided reading has to be embedded in a clear and accessible context if it is to be used effectively.
- Sufficient time is needed for clarification. If it takes a long time to clarify the text, it is either too difficult or there is too much text.
- Small amounts of text are perfectly acceptable.
- The questioning strategies used with fiction texts are also appropriate for non-fiction texts.

References

Powell, J. (2011) *Ideas Box! Chocolate*. Franklin Watts (ISBN 978-1-44-510392-1).

Price, S. (2009) *The Story Behind Chocolate*. Heinemann (ISBN 978-1-43-292347-1).

Saunders, K. (2012) *The Whizz Pop Chocolate Sho*p. Scholastic (ISBN: 978-1-40-712986-0).

Black Hole by Literacy Shed

Context

Pinewood Primary School is a large, three-form entry primary school in outer London. A very high proportion of pupils come from a range of minority ethnic groups, and the number of pupils who speak English as an additional language is significantly above the national average. The largest group of pupils are those with Pakistani heritage. Pupils' attainment and progress is good.

Neave is a teacher of a class of 10–11 year olds who has been using the Reciprocal Teaching approach (see Chapter 3, p. 36) in his guided reading sessions. He has been able to use dialogic practices as part of his work, and was curious to know how the approach could be applied to moving images.

To begin with, this needed a change in perspective in that the moving image had to be considered as a text in itself. Neave was interested in using moving images as he was aware of the extent to which children are exposed to these kinds of texts.

Planning

Text selection

Neave watched a number of short film clips on The Literacy Shed website (www.literacyshed.com/the-thinking-shed.html). Eventually he chose a clip called *Black Hole* as he thought it would engage the group of pupils he had in mind. He then watched the clip several times so that he was familiar with its content. This wasn't an onerous task as the clip itself lasts only two minutes five seconds. It also allowed him to assess its text potential and he was particularly interested in the bleak setting, the moral issue of what constitutes theft, and the fact that there was a twist at the end of the narrative. So the text was selected on the principles outlined in Chapter 2: it offered enjoyment to the reader; it was carefully chosen and allowed for different layers of meaning to be explored; and the teacher was familiar with it. **Of particular interest is the fact that the text had no dialogue whatsoever. The text potential diagram relates to its visual features.**

In this clip, a man is seen working in an office late at night on his own. He seems tired and somewhat stressed as he completes some photocopying. While completing this task, one of the copies comes through as a very large black circle. Much like an enlarged full stop, it covers most of the page. There is nothing else on the sheet apart from this. The man places the large black dot to one side, on top of a nearby scanner, and continues with his photocopying. He finishes the coffee he is drinking from a plastic cup and places the empty cup on the paper with the large black circle. As he does so, the cup disappears into the black dot – which has now become a 'black hole'. The man is amazed and gingerly places his hand over the black dot, and this too 'disappears' into the black hole when he tries to touch it. He reaches in further and retrieves the plastic cup.

He then goes to a vending machine in the office. He places the piece of paper with the black hole on the glass front of the vending machine. He puts his hand into the black hole and finds he can take a chocolate bar from inside. After eating the chocolate bar, he goes into a small inner office where there is a safe. He then sticks the black hole onto the front of the safe, reaches in, and finds he is able to take out wads of bank notes. He tried to reach further into the safe but finds this difficult, so instead he crawls into the back hole and disappears into the safe. Obviously, the man did not attach the black hole very securely to the front of the safe as it drops to the floor, leaving the man trapped inside.

Text potential

Exploring what the text offers

Vocabulary

Unknown words (relating to oral vocabulary):

- 'vending machine'
- 'photocopier'
- 'safe'.

Language features

Subject

The film clip is about a man working late in an office. As he is doing some photocopying, a black dot emerges from the machine on a piece of white paper. This is the black hole of the title. He is able to place this black hole on objects, such as a vending machine and a safe. This allows him to reach in through the hole and take out the contents inside.

Grammar; Syntax

Visual features

The film clip uses colour to create a rather depressing office space.

Historical, social, and cultural context

The film clip is set in a modern office.

Coherence

Mapping text potential
Black Hole Film clip

Narrative features

Plot

- Character – Downtrodden worker turned potential criminal.
- Setting – The action moves from a large office to a small room containing a safe. The rooms are dark, and drab.

Theme

Potential themes:

- greed
- fear
- stealing
- the world of work.

Literary features

The ending has an interesting ironic 'twist'.

Making links to background knowledge

Life to text – fantasy/sci-fi.

Text to life – devices that make life easier in the home/office.

Text to text – other sci-fi fantasy texts (Harry Potter).

Text type, purpose, and intended readership

The mood of the film clip is humorous. It deals with a moral issue relating to theft. The viewer may feel some sympathy for the downtrodden office worker.

Lesson planning and organization

Neave knew that frequent stopping and starting disturbs the flow, in much the same way as interrupting the reading of a written text. So he decided to adopt the process he used when planning for Reciprocal Teaching sessions. He split the film into two sections – the clip lent itself to being divided in this way – and themes raised in the first part were revisited and extended in the second part. The first part of the film went as far as the point at which the man was eating the chocolate bar he had taken from the vending machine; the second part went from this point to the end, when he became trapped in the safe. So he planned two guided reading sessions.

He developed three questions for each part: a 'looking' question, a 'clue' question, and a 'thinking' question. These questions tap the three layers of meaning outlined in Chapter 3, p. 38. The questions were as follows:

Lesson 1

1. Where is the man? ('looking')
2. What does the black hole do? ('clue')
3. Is the black hole a good thing or a bad thing? ('thinking')

Lesson 2

1. What was in the small room? ('looking')
2. Is the man likely to get out easily? ('clue')
3. Did he get what he deserved? ('thinking')

Neave completed these two lessons with a group of four 10–11 year olds (two boys and two girls) of average attainment. He chose to work with only four pupils both because he was experimenting with text-type and because he was interested in testing out group size. He wanted to see whether the dialogue might be different if he reduced the size of the group from the usual six pupils to four.

The lesson

This section provides a description of how children were guided through their reading of the first part of the *Black Hole* clip. It lasted 1 minute 25 seconds, and generated 18 minutes of dialogue.

Before watching the first half of the film, the children were presented with the three key questions related to the different layers of meaning. The film was then played and paused at the appropriate point, halfway through, and the children began to discuss the clip *immediately without being invited to and without reference to the key questions.* Neave let the discussion develop and, as we shall see, was able to elicit responses at all the different layers of meaning. Given the dialogic nature of the entire interaction, the focus of the discussion moved between these layers. This was handled effectively because of the way Neave steered the discussion – allowing new lines of enquiry to develop and linking them with ones that had been discussed previously.

Using dialogue to explore literal understanding

To begin with, Neave did not move straight into asking the first question, 'Where is the man?'. This was answered during the course of the discussion without being asked explicitly. Instead, Neave followed up the children's initial engagement with the film.

Child (C) 1: That is awesome!

C2: That is epic!

(The children laugh.)

Teacher (T): So why is that – why is that awesome?

C1: Because he doesn't have to pay for the … er … er … chocolate, and he's actually getting it out.

In this short exchange, Neave asks Child 1 to explain why he felt the first section of the film was awesome. Child 1's response that the character in the film was able to get some free chocolate immediately opens up a line of discussion that explores a potential moral issue. However, Neave chose not to take this line at the time as he was interested in establishing the nature of the children's literal understanding – their 'reading in the moment' (see Chapter 1). Given the focus question relating to whether the black hole is a good thing or a bad thing, he decided that the moral issue was a point that he could pick up later. Child 1 points out that the character in the film used the black hole to get some chocolate from the machine. Neave then elicits further responses from the children that reveal their emotional responses to the text in order to examine their literal understanding. Child 3 made the following comment:

C3: That's creepy as well. That's creepy. Like, if that happened normally, then you wouldn't think that was awesome because you can do that anyway, but you can't do that normally – you can't just go and get a black hole and go somewhere and put your hand through it.

C1: It's like a dream.

T: Go on.

C1: It's like a dream because you wouldn't like, normally, you wouldn't find this stuff [the black hole] in this world unless there was … you know …

T: … unless what?

C1: Unless there was an alien invasion.

T: Right, OK.

C2: Unless there was like, actually a machine that could do that but then with a normal piece of paper [holds up a piece of A4 paper] that had nothing except a big black hole [meaning a dot, presumably] it would be normal.

What we can see here is that Neave has drawn from the children their shared literal understanding of the text by eliciting any relevant background knowledge (see Chapter 1). This background knowledge encompasses both the text-to-life comments made by Child 2 and Child 3 about the nature of what you would expect a piece of paper to be used for, and Child 1's text-to-text comment on aliens (presumably derived from books or films). This shows Neave that the pupils have realized the fantasy element of the story but are able to explain it in the context of what they already know. It is also notable that the children feel able to contribute to the discussion and build on each other's ideas – a feature of effective dialogic talk (see Chapter 4). Here we see Child 1 building on Child 3's ideas and Child 2 building on Child 1's. Neave's prompting here is minimal and he gives the children room to explore their thoughts. He is able to do this because the children's comments are not random: they stem directly from their reading of the text.

Using questioning to develop understanding from textual evidence

To deepen the children's understanding, Neave chose to focus on the black hole itself. On one level, this seems more of a surface issue – the black hole allows things to pass through it somehow – but it is this 'somehow' that Neave wanted to explore. At this point, his intervention directly moves the dialogue away from the surface understanding that it is essentially a piece of paper that objects can pass through. Three ideas emerge, each of which is explored. Neave begins directly where Child 2's previous comment finishes:

> **T:** So, this black hole, what are you saying that it actually does?
>
> **C2:** It's like a teleporter, like … er … if it was bigger, yeah, and you just put it on the wall, you could, just like, teleport through or if it was like this size [uses arms to create a person-sized arched shape] you could just go through the wall, like put it there, so it's like a teleporter.

C4 follows this comment in what appears to be a slightly random way.

> **C4:** It's like when you are washing up and you can't be bothered to open it, or unlock something. You stick it [the black hole] on the wall with Blu-Tack and just chuck it into the cupboard … [starts laughing]

Then, Neave neatly brings the two ideas together by intervening and bringing the conversation back to Child 2's comment.

> **T:** Say that again? [looks at Child 2] What is the word 'teleporter' that you used? Because I'm … What does that mean?
>
> **C2:** [Pauses for thought] It takes something somewhere.

We have two very different responses in this interaction so far. Child 4 makes a text-to-life link to explain what the black hole actually does by relating it to the process of washing up and putting the plates away. By contrast, Child 2 provides a reasoned speculation about the nature of the black hole linked to his background knowledge. This possibly relates to some sort of experience of science-fiction films, so there may be some level of text-to-text linking taking place. Neave has elicited a clear definition of a 'teleporter', and straight away we can see that the black hole doesn't fit the definition given of a teleporter.

To demonstrate this, Neave takes the discussion back to the real-life example of washing up, and this encourages Child 1 to develop a third idea as he says:

C1: It [the black hole] is actually like … it's actually like … an invisible seal opener.

Child 1 speculates that it might be some kind of 'invisible seal opener'. After further prompting, Child 1 clarifies this statement by saying that the black hole breaks the 'seal' on any solid object with which it comes into contact.

Neave then steered the discussion to the vending machine, and asked the children to consider how the character was able to reach into it without breaking the glass – again choosing at this point not to follow a line of enquiry that investigates the moral issue of theft. He wanted to explore the idea of the 'invisible seal opener' and address the misconception over the word 'teleporter'. The group asked for that section of the film to be shown again, and Child 3 then picked up on the idea of the idea of an invisible seal and noted the following:

C3: See, the whole glass didn't break. He's probably just broken the seal of the actual black hole, and then he closed it again.

C1: I don't think it's a teleporter because you know there's things like time-machines and things, where you go through and it takes you into a different time? It doesn't just drop you through like a hole. I think this is not like that.

C3: Yeah. Teleporting is more taking you to another place.

T: What do you think [Child 2]?

C2: Yeah, I think that's kind of true because you're not actually going there, you're not actually popping up somewhere else. You're just going through a hole.

At this point, Child 1 claims that the 'invisible seal opener' idea is more likely to be correct than the idea of the teleporter. They re-examine what the definition of a teleporter might be, and Child 2, who had initially come up with this idea, agrees that the concept of teleportation is not correct in this context. By so doing, he has reformulated his initial thinking, another feature of effective dialogic talk (see Chapter 4).

By showing the requested section of the film to the children again, Neave allowed them to revisit the text – to read it again. This led to a further discussion relating to what the black hole might actually be. In the film, the man places a plastic coffee cup onto the black hole, and the cup disappears into the scanner on which it is lying. Child 2 asked how, if the black hole could be used to create holes in walls, the man had been able to retrieve his plastic coffee cup when he dropped it inside the scanner? Why didn't the coffee cup just drop through the floor? This led to further discussion during which Child 3 made the following point:

C3: It probably floats. Because if you put your hand in there and you didn't have to go so much in … It's probably like … In here [pointing to where he is sitting] there is so much gravity. So we're at the bottom, we're right at the bottom. We're staying down here. But if there's no gravity in there [pointing to the black hole] it's probably just floating.

Child 3 speculates that the coffee cup was floating – that in some way gravity did not have an effect on it. So in this dialogue we see how the children have been able to reason why something happened, and to justify it by applying text-to-life knowledge. Child 3 is making an inference supported both by evidence in the text and through links made to background knowledge (see Chapter 1).

Encouraging dialogue to justify a moral position

In the course of the first half of the clip, we see the man place the black hole over the vending machine and retrieve a chocolate bar. Neave wanted to consider the morality of this as highlighted by his initial key thinking question, 'Is the black hole a good thing or a bad thing?'. However, he didn't have to ask the question as Child 4 took the dialogue in this direction by noting a potential negative consequence of the black hole.

C4: If the black hole is actually true, and you put your hand in there like he [the man in the film] did – he just put it on the machine and took the chocolate out – he could easily be like … Ooh, OK! What if he wants to go to the jewellery shop! And he could just be randomly getting things out, and then you could be like some thief.

At this point, Child 4 is bringing text-to-life knowledge to the action.

What Neave does next is to build on this line of enquiry by asking the children whether the character had done a good or bad thing in the action so far. He steers the dialogue to the point at which the character uses the black hole to take the chocolate from the vending machine.

C1: He just done it as a test to see if it still works. Like, say, with the printer. He gets the glass [the paper cup in the scanner] back out, but he wanted to test – does it only work with the printer or does it work anywhere?

Child 1 then makes a prediction, without being directed to do so:

C1: I think because we stopped it half way … I think … the more video that's coming … I think he, he's gonna try it in, like, different places: a wall – maybe on the door or something.

Neave was particularly keen to probe this line of argument further as the children seemed to engage with the idea that the man was just testing out the black hole without seriously considering any real moral issue. He asked the children to consider the character's actions more carefully:

T: One of you said it was like a test. He was doing it for a test at the moment … um … with that vending machine, because you've mentioned before about … er … if you go to take jewellery out, you'll be a thief, yeah? So in this one there [pointing at the still image of the man eating the chocolate that is visible on the screen] are we saying he's using it in bad way or not? Because it's a test.

C4: A bad thing is that it has an impact on everyone else because that vending machine could be someone else's. Like, they own it.

Child 4 points out that the man not only tested the black hole, but ate the chocolate as well. At this point the issue of stealing was raised again in connection to the character in the film. This led to an interesting dialogue on the man's motivation, which lasted until the end of the lesson.

Teacher's reflections

At the end of the lesson, Neave was quick to note how the strategies he used regularly to support the development of written text comprehension were equally applicable to film. He felt that, by making the children aware of the layers of meaning within the text, they were able to deepen their understanding of it. This lesson took place with four children in a small room, and Neave felt there would be practical difficulties in attempting to run a lesson like this in the classroom, although these might be addressed through the use of tablets, iPads, and headphones. However, given that he frequently used film clips in whole-class interactions to exemplify teaching points, Neave was confident that the skills the children were applying here would have benefits within a whole-class context. Neave also suggested that having a group of four rather than six appeared to have benefits in terms of pupils contributing to the dialogue and having more space to express their ideas.

Conclusion

In our digital age, children are likely to be interacting with film and moving images on a daily basis, so it makes sense to use clips such as *Black Hole* to support the teaching of comprehension of such media. In this instance, the teacher took the bold step of first acknowledging film as a legitimate text, and then using it in the context of a guided group lesson. It became clear that the children approached this text in the same way as they discuss a written text. The same processes are involved in understanding both text-types, on the whole. With teacher guidance, these children were actively seeking deeper levels of meaning. This was achieved by allowing the dialogue to develop, but steering it when necessary. This involves very careful listening on the part of the teacher and encouraging dialogue that requires the pupils to develop their responses in a thoughtful, considered manner. Of course, the choice of film clip supported this – it is an engaging clip that can be explored at these different levels. The teacher recognized the text potential.

This case study shows once again that we must consider the interaction between the reader and the text, and also the value of developing dialogic interactions that allow developing readers to explore their thinking.

Reference

Sansom, Philip, and Williams, Olly (2008) *The Black Hole* (short film). London: HSI. Online. www.literacyshed.com/the-thinking-shed.html

The Wildman by Kevin Crossley-Holland

Context

This reading session took place with a Year 6 class in a high-performing primary school where the philosophy is to teach children of all abilities together. Challenging texts are chosen for all year groups and whole-class interactive teaching is interspersed with group work. The principle of providing challenge for all readers through the use of whole-class texts is well established. Teachers have studied the work of Robin Alexander (see Chapter 4, p. 110) and are often requested to do training for other schools in the locality. Teachers frequently film their lessons and share them for professional development purposes with other teachers and the senior leadership team.

Planning

Prior to reading *The Wildman*, the class had been reading Kevin Crossley-Holland's version of *Beowulf*, illustrated by Charles Keeping, with the class teacher. The lesson reported here was one of a sequence and was taught by one of the authors of this book, with the aim of developing understanding and providing appropriate challenge for the highest-attaining readers.

Text selection

One of the foci for the guided reading in this school was to consider the place of 'bridging texts', that is, to look at ways in which a planned sequence of texts could be used together to deepen understanding, either by making a more complex text accessible (see Case Study 9, 'The Nightingale and the Rose', in Chapter 8) or to present an alternative way of reading the original text. *The Wildman* was selected for this second purpose. It is a particularly interesting story as Kevin Crossley-Holland is revisiting the territory of *Beowulf*, his award-winning version of the Anglo-Saxon epic poem, masterfully illustrated by Charles Keeping. However, in this story he is writing from the point of view of Grendel, adversary to the heroic Beowulf (although the Wildman is never identified as such). Leaving the character unnamed, the Wildman stands for all outsiders. One of the dominant themes is how we deal with the outsider whose motives are beyond our comprehension. In this respect, an interesting comparison could be made with Armin Greder's *The Island*, a contemporary picture-book fable about the way that societies respond to outsiders and also with Ted Hughes's *The Iron Man*. *The Wildman* offers the potential to explore parallels with historic and current world crises.

This short story is barely a thousand words long, but its rich language and thought-provoking themes make it an ideal choice for guided reading, whether used in connection with other texts or read as a stand-alone.

The text employs a number of poetic techniques. This novel and unusual use of language draws attention to individual words and encourages the reader to stop and think about the Wildman in new ways.

The title is ambiguous; who is the Wildman? This short, poetic story tells how a 'wild man' is captured from the sea, released, and then, believing that his captors are his friends, returns voluntarily to the shore only to be met with violence and hostility. Most readers will naturally assume that the creature from the sea is the Wildman. He is certainly viewed this way by the others (men). We sense their disgust as he refuses to eat fish but gorges on raw meat, sucking the blood from the corpses of dead animals. Yet the first-person perspective allows the reader to understand that he refuses fish because they live in his world and he regards them not as potential food but as friends. His refusal is evidence of a sensibility that evokes the reader's empathy. This use of dramatic irony may not be appreciated by all readers without some support.

The first-person narration also reveals a naivety that tugs at the reader's heartstrings. The use of questions throughout shows the creature's lack of comprehension and further irony is used when the Wildman sees the others waving at him from the shore. He mistakes this as a sign of friendship, while they interpret his return to the land as a sign of aggression. The miscommunication is tragic and the creature is recaptured and assaulted before finally escaping back to his watery home.

The text

The Wildman by Kevin Crossley-Holland

Don't ask me my name. I've heard you have names. I have no name.

They say this is how I was born. A great wave bored down a river, and at the mouth of the river it ran up against a great wave of the sea. The coupled waves kicked like legs and whirled like arms and swayed like hips; sticks in the water snapped like bones and the seaweed bulged like gristle and muscle. In this way the waves rose. When they fell, I was there.

My home is water as your home is earth. I rise to the surface to breathe air, I glide down through the darkening rainbow. The water sleeks my hair as I swim. And when I stand on the sea-bed, the currents comb my waving hair; my whole body seems to ripple.

Each day I go to the land for food. I swim to the shore, I'm careful not to be seen. Small things, mice, shrews, moles, I like them to eat. I snuffle and grub through the growth and undergrowth and grab them, and squeeze the warm blood out of them, and chew them.

Always before sunset I'm back in the tugging, laughing, sobbing water. Then the blue darkness that comes down over the sea comes inside me too. I feel heavy until morning. It I stayed too long on the land I might be found, lying there, heavy, unable even to drag myself back to the water.

My friends are seals. They dive as I do, and swim as I do. Their hair is like my hair. I sing songs with their little ones. They've shown me their secret place, a dark grotto so deep that I howled for the pain of the water pressing round me there and rose to the surface, gasping for air. My friends are the skimming plaice and the flickering eel and the ticklish trout. My friends are all the fishes.

As I swam near the river mouth, something caught my legs and tugged at them. I tried to push it away with my hands and it caught my hands and my arms too. I kicked; I flailed; I couldn't escape. I was dragged through the water, up out of the darkness into the indigo, the purple, the pale blue. I was lifted into the air, the sunlight, and down into a floating thing.

Others. There were others in it, others, others as I am. But their faces were not covered with hair. They had very little hair I could see except on their heads, but they were covered with animal skins and furs. When they saw me they were afraid and trembled and backed away and one fell into the water.

I struggled and bit but I was caught in the web they had made. They took me to land and a great shoal gathered round me there. Then they carried me in that web to a great high place of stone and tipped me out into a gloomy grotto.

One of them stayed by me and kept making noises; I couldn't understand him. I could tell he was asking me things. I would have liked to ask him things. How were you born? Why do you have so little hair? Why do you live on land? I looked at him, I kept looking at him, and when the others came back, I looked at them; their hairless hands, their legs, their shining eyes. There were so many of them almost like me, and I've never once seen anyone in the sea like me.

They brought me two crossed sticks. Why? What are they? They pushed them into my face, they howled at me. One of them smacked my face with his hand. Why was that? It hurt. Then another with long pale hair came and wept tears over me. I licked my lips; the tears tasted like the sea. Was this one like me? Did this one come from the sea? I put my arms round its waist but it shrieked and pushed me away.

They brought me fish to eat. I wouldn't eat fish. Later they brought me meat; I squeezed it until it was dry and then I ate it.

I was taken out into the sunlight, down to the river mouth. The rippling, rippling water. It was pink and lilac and grey; I shivered with longing at the sight of it. I could see three rows of webs spread across the river from bank to bank. Then they let me go, they let me dive into the water. It coursed through my long hair. I laughed and passed under the first net and the second net and the third net. I was free. But why am I only free away from those who are like me, with those who are not like me? Why is the sea my home?

They were all shouting and waving their arms, and jumping up and down at the edge of the water. They were all calling out across the grey wavelets. Why? Did they want me to go back after all? Did they want me to be their friend?

I wanted to go back, I wanted them as friends. So I stroked back under the nets again and swam to the sandy shore. They fell on me then, and twisted my arms, and hurt me. I howled. I screamed. They tied long webs round me and more tightly round me, and carried me back to the place of stone, and threw me into the gloomy grotto.

I bit through the webs. I slipped through the window bars. It was almost night and the blue heaviness was coming into me. I staggered away, back to the water, the waiting dark water.

Text potential
Exploring what the text offers

Vocabulary

Familiar vocabulary with multiple meanings – 'wild'.

Making the familiar strange:

- 'web' instead of 'net'
- 'floating thing' instead of 'boat'.

Potentially unfamiliar vocabulary: 'flailed', 'coursed'.

Plural – fishes

Language features

- Short paragraphs.
- Questions used throughout to show confusion and evoke empathy: 'Why do you have so little hair?', 'Why do you live on land?', 'Did this one come from the sea?'
- The Wildman's awareness of colour throughout is indicative of a poetic soul – an appreciation of the natural world.
- Language used to describe the Wildman is similar to the language you would use to describe the environment.
- 'I glide … currents comb my waving hair … my whole body seems to ripple.'

Grammar; Syntax

Use of adjectives as verbs: 'The water sleeks my hair as I swim.'

Unusual, poetic use of verb: 'I stroked back under the webs'.

Mapping text potential
The Wildman by Kevin Crossley-Holland

Narrative features

First person narration and naive point of view 'I was caught in the web they had made'. 'I put my arms round its waist but it shrieked and pushed me away.'

Short prose paragraphs. Poetic language of the speaker is juxtaposed against the apparent savagery of the 'Wildman'

Subject

A short poetic story about the capturing of the 'Wildman', his imprisonment, and escape into the sea. Although the story starts 'Don't ask me my name. I have heard you have names. I have no name', Kevin Crossley-Holland wrote this as an alternative perspective on the story of Beowulf.

Historical, social, and cultural context

An original contemporary tale published in a collection of folk tales. A reworking of the great Old English epic poem *Beowulf*.

Visual features

Coherence

Literary features

Poetic text with strong aural qualities, e.g. 'grub through the growth and undergrowth and grab them'.

Empathy evoked: 'my friends are seals'.

Irony: 'My friends are the skimming plaice and the flickering eel', 'I wouldn't eat fish. Later they brought me meat; I squeezed it until it was dry and then I ate it.'

Juxtaposition: 'My home is water as your home is earth.'

Making links to background knowledge

- Fenland environment.
- Beowulf legend, though this isn't made explicit and the story can be read independently

Text type, purpose, and intended readership

- Short story.
- Alternative perspective on the Beowulf story.
- Short story, published in *Folk Tales from East Anglia and the Fen Country*, but also in children's collections of stories. Therefore a publishing perspective is that folk tales are best suited to young readers. This is unlikely to be the point of view of the author.

Themes

- Civilization and wilderness
- Heroism and bravery
- Freedom and captivity

Lesson planning and organization

This single lesson followed a sequence of reading lessons, teaching Kevin Crossley-Holland's *Beowulf*. The lesson lasted for one hour, which is the time allocated for teaching literacy at the school. The objective of the lesson was to consider how word choices can prompt multiple interpretations of a text.

The lesson was planned to include a combination of individual, small-group, and whole-class activities, so that pupils would share ideas, draw on each other's thoughts, and be challenged to take their thinking deeper through scaffolded dialogue.

Pre-reading

Prior to the session, the children had read the short story and had been asked to record their initial responses on sticky notes. These responses included anything that they found strange or puzzling about the story (see also Case study 10, *Memorial* in Chapter 8, p. 173).

The lesson

The sticky notes were displayed on the wall and the pupils were given five minutes to view each other's thoughts. Pupils were invited to comment on each other's sticky notes, specifically picking out thoughts that had given them new ideas and also to respond to each other's thoughts. This short discussion lasted for about five minutes. The following are representative of the ideas written on the notes:

'It reminds me of Jungle book because he [Mowgli] is brought up by wolves. His friends are seals so he has adapted to the wildlife.'

'I don't understand how he can talk to animals.'

'I think this is about a strange alien.'

'I think this story is about a weird sea creature.'

'The Wildman is a blood-drinking savage.'

Other comments also focused on the unfamiliar use of language used to tell the story from the Wildman's point of view:

'It's really unusual the way the story has been written and it's quite hard to follow.'

'Webs are fishing nets?' [This observation was followed by the question mark as the reader expressed uncertainty about the interpretation and looked for confirmation from the rest of the group.]

The initial discussion revealed general sympathy for the Wildman. There was some uncertainty about whether the Wildman was a 'man' or an animal.

After five minutes, the teacher introduced a semantic mapping process to explore the concept of 'wild'.

To begin, the pupils were asked to think of all the words they associated with 'wild' and to make a list. This timed activity lasted just two minutes and was intended to get ideas flowing freely without any self-editing that might inhibit the inclusion of words. When the two-minute exercise was complete, the pupils were given five minutes to look at each other's lists and to 'steal' any words they would like to add to their own.

One pupil's list comprised the following words:

Savage	Lunatic
Cage	Angry
Wilderness	Tiger
Desert	Wildlife
Forest	Violent
Natural	Tame
Mad	Messy

After the words had been shared with the whole class, the teacher challenged the children to justify how their selected words were linked to the prompt word 'wild', particularly for those words where the links appeared to be more tenuous. New words were also offered where they helped to clarify a concept.

During this discussion, the pupils talked about 'wild' as the opposite of 'calm'. They suggested that wild is noisy, chaotic, and out of control. The teacher invited another child to give a different suggestion.

Teacher (T): C, can you tell us one of the words you have included on your list?

Child (C): Forest.

T: But I think of a forest as being a calm, tranquil place. And you've just told me that is the OPPOSITE of wild. So I think you are going to have to convince me that a forest can be wild.

C: Well … a forest IS wild but it's different. It's wild because it has been left to grow on its own. Things can grow any way and sometimes it's hard to walk through the forest because all the trees grow close together and you have to really bend down to get through. Sometimes the thorns catch your clothes and you can't move. I went blackberry picking with my Dad and we kept getting stuck in the brambles. And there are lots of animals in the forest as well like badgers and they're wild too.

T: Mmm, that reminds me of the book you were reading last term.

(While the pupil makes text-to-life links to their own experience, the teacher makes text-to-text links here.)

C: Yes, *Wind in the Willows*; Mole went into the wild wood and he got really scared when it got dark. Badger came and rescued him.

T:	OK, I think there are two ideas here; we'll come back to Mole being scared in a minute. You've said the forest is wild because it grows freely and naturally. So is there an opposite of that kind of 'wild'?
C:	When you grow things in the garden because you are deciding what to grow and where to put it.
T:	Any other examples?
C:	When a farmer grows wheat and stuff …
T:	Stuff?
C:	In fields, like cabbages.
T:	OK, so a farmer might grow different crops, like wheat, potatoes, and cabbages and you grow things in your garden and you think that way of growing things is the opposite of the kind of wild in the forest. Do you know a word that we can use to describe the opposite to that kind of wild?
C:	Tame?
T:	Not really, though I suppose you could talk about taming things that are growing out of control. We use the word cultivated. [Child 2], can you look cultivated up in the dictionary and find a definition for us?

In this extract from the children's discussion, the teacher helps them to make connections with their prior knowledge and experience of the word 'wild'. She also prompts them to relate their ideas to a previous text. They are encouraged to extend their vocabulary by using words that express their thoughts precisely and the use of the dictionary is embedded in the natural flow of teaching rather than being a disconnected exercise. The teacher's expectation for the children's talk is high: vague descriptions such as 'and stuff' are challenged. She also challenges their thinking by offering an alternative point of view: 'but I think of a forest as being a calm and tranquil place'. This invites the children to work a little harder to formulate their ideas and to justify their thinking.

When the class have explored a few words in depth the teacher summarizes the discussion:

| T: | I'm fascinated by the range of ideas you have come up with. What looks like a simple word seems to have many different meanings. Some of them seem to be positive, because you've told me about 'wild' meaning natural and unspoilt like the countryside, and some of them seem to have negative associations, because you talked about people behaving in wild, crazy ways. So I would like you to work in a group to have a look at words you have come up with on your lists and see |

if any of them can be grouped together. You might want to put the same word in more than one group. That is absolutely fine as long as you can give a good explanation.

For this stage, the children worked in self-selected groups of three to five.

Grouping the words using a semantic map helped the children refine and deepen their understanding of the concept of 'wild'. The following includes some of the semantic groupings the pupils identified. This wide-ranging collection of groupings contrasts with their narrower initial response to the title and character of the story.

MAD: crazy, lunatic, straight jacket, completely nuts, insane

NATURE: animals, wildlife, plants, growing (also opposites: cultivated, tamed)

SAVAGE: cruel, violent, no morals, abuse, out of control, rough

ANGRY: furious, mad, rage, shouting

UNTIDY: dirty, dishevelled, matted hair, dirty fingernails, shaggy

After ten minutes, the teacher brought the groups together to review the different meanings attached to the word 'wild', and then asked:

T: So I wonder what kind of 'wild' applies to the Wildman? [Child 2], on your post-it you said that he was a savage. Do you think that's why the writer has called him the wild man?

C2: Yes.

T: So what makes you say that?

C2: It says 'Later they brought me meat; I squeezed it until it was dry and then I ate it.' He's like a savage because he squeezes all the blood out and the people think he's disgusting.

T: Are they right? [General murmuring of agreement] But quite a few of you said that you felt sorry for the Wildman.

C3: Yeah but if I saw him squeezing blood out of an animal, I would think he was a savage, like a cannibal or something.

T: What's a cannibal?

C3: They eat people.

T: What eats people?

C3: A human eats another human.

T: Ah, so is that what the Wildman is doing? Is he a human eating another human?

C3: Sort of …

C4: No, he isn't like a cannibal because he doesn't eat the fish. He lives with the fish and he doesn't eat them because they are like his friends. So he's like the opposite of a cannibal. Can you have an opposite for that?

C1: But it says he eats mice and he squeezes the warm blood out of them and chews them. It sounds gross.

T: But humans eat meat … unless they are vegetarians. Are they gross too?

C1: I don't squeeze blood out of meat and eat it with my bare hands.

T: What would you do if you lived in the wild?

C1: Eat berries and apples and grass.

T: So you wouldn't eat meat? Lots of animals eat raw meat. What about lions and tigers – are they gross?

C1: No because they're animals and they have to eat meat. If they ate berries they would die.

In this section of pupil-teacher dialogue, we see the teacher pushing the children to consider the implications of their thoughts. The ideas are complex and the children are invited to consider why they view the Wildman as a savage and whether this automatically carries a negative connotation. The teacher then summarizes and leads the children back to the text in order to get them to apply some of this new thinking to the description of the Wildman.

T: Ok we have some interesting points of view here. These aren't things to which we can find easy answers, but I think you are suggesting that different standards apply to animals and to humans. Maybe it's OK for animals to eat raw meat but when humans do it they are behaving like animals and we don't think that's acceptable? So perhaps our response to the Wildman is determined by whether we think he is more human or more animal? And perhaps it also depends on whether we think animals and humans are different? You might already have your own views about that, but it might help if we dig a bit deeper and take another look at all the definitions of wild that you came up with. In your groups, work together to see how many of these definitions you can apply to the Wildman. You have some coloured highlighters on the table, so you can highlight different parts of the text that show where the Wildman is being 'wild'.

The pupils worked in groups for about ten minutes. Following the completion of the task, the teacher asked them to consider the different ways in which 'wild' can be applied to the Wildman. The pupils suggested:

- he is at home in nature
- he is almost like a wild animal

- he might appear to be mad or crazy because of his appearance and because he can't speak. This might be why they recoil from him when he tries to embrace them
- although he eats like an animal, he isn't savage, as in cruel or barbaric, because it is the natural thing for him to do in his environment.

Teacher's reflections

During the course of this lesson, the pupils developed an appreciation of the nuanced meanings in apparently simple words. By focusing on the word 'wild' and applying it to the characters in the story, they began to appreciate how a writer might use a word to challenge a perception. They were able to understand that the word 'wild' was open to interpretation in the context of this story and afforded a range of responses to the character. Further questions to explore might be: does the Wildman see himself in the same way that the human beings view him? Does the reader have the same perspective as the people in the story or not? To consolidate this further it would be helpful to contrast the human characters with the Wildman. At the end of the story the Wildman wonders 'why am I only free away from those who are like me, with those who are not like me?' So in the next lesson the teacher will challenge the children to think about the ways in which the Wildman and the humans are similar as well as the ways in which they are different. A double-bubble thought map will help the children visualize their thinking. It would then be interesting to challenge them to identify an authorial perspective and to consider why the story might have been given this title. There are further comparisons that can be made with the version of *Beowulf* that they have been reading and possibly with real-world scenarios and tabloid articles.

At the end of this sequence, the teacher will want the pupils to consider whether their views on the Wildman have changed in any way and, if so, to consider what made them change their mind. The teacher will also reflect with the pupils on the way in which the tools used have helped them to organize their thinking, as this is the first time they have been introduced to semantic mapping and thought maps.

Conclusion

In this lesson, several techniques were used to help pupils make their vocabulary learning more visible. The combination of structured dialogue with the use of graphic organizers made it possible for them to access complex themes.

References

Crossley-Holland, K. (1976) *The Wild Man*. London: Andre Deutsch (ISBN 978-0-2339-6801-8).

Crossley-Holland, K. (2013) *Beowulf*. Oxford, Oxford University Press (ISBN: 978-0-19-279444-4).

Greder, A. (2008) *The Island*. Crows Nest NSW, Allen & Unwin (ISBN: 978-1-74-175266-3).

Examples of more challenging reading for 10–12 year olds

'The Flowers' by Alice Walker

Context

Cherry Tree Primary School is a larger-than-average multi-ethnic school located in an outer London borough. There are four classes in each year group. The proportions of pupils from minority ethnic heritages, of those who are learning to speak English as a second language, and of those who leave or join the school at other than the usual times are higher than those found nationally.

Marie is a Year 6 (10–11 year olds) teacher. She has used the Reciprocal Teaching approach (see Chapter 3, p. 36) in her guided reading lessons for a number of years, and was interested to engage her children in more challenging texts. For this reason, she contacted a local secondary school, who recommended 'The Flowers', a short story by Alice Walker.

Planning

Text selection

In this story, set in the southern states of the USA, a girl is seen walking through some woods where she picks some flowers. The scene presented is in many ways idyllic – this is reflected in the lyrical and literary language – but when she stumbles across a dead body, the narrative takes a more sinister turn: the dead body appears to have been that of a man who has been lynched.

The text presented Marie with an opportunity to guide the group using a text to which they might not ordinarily have been exposed.

The text

'The Flowers' by Alice Walker

It seemed to Myop as she skipped lightly from hen house to pigpen to smokehouse that the days had never been as beautiful as these. The air held a keenness that made her nose twitch. The harvesting of the corn and cotton, peanuts and squash, made each day a golden surprise that caused excited little tremors to run up her jaws.

Myop carried a short, knobby stick. She struck out at random at chickens she liked, and worked out the beat of a song on the fence around the pigpen. She felt light and good in the warm sun. She was ten, and nothing existed for her but her song, the stick clutched in her dark brown hand, and the tat-de-ta-ta-ta of accompaniment.

Turning her back on the rusty boards of her family's sharecropper cabin, Myop walked along the fence till it ran into the stream made by the spring. Around the spring, where the family got drinking water, silver ferns and wildflowers grew. Along the shallow banks pigs rooted. Myop watched the tiny white bubbles disrupt the thin black scale of soil and the water that silently rose and slid away down the stream.

She had explored the woods behind the house many times. Often, in late autumn, her mother took her to gather nuts among the fallen leaves. Today she made her own path, bouncing this way and that way, vaguely keeping an eye out for snakes. She found, in addition to various common but pretty ferns and leaves, an armful of strange blue flowers with velvety ridges and a sweet suds bush full of the brown, fragrant buds.

By twelve o'clock, her arms laden with sprigs of her findings, she was a mile or more from home. She had often been as far before, but the strangeness of the land made it not as pleasant as her usual haunts. It seemed gloomy in the little cove in which she found herself. The air was damp, the silence close and deep.

Myop began to circle back to the house, back to the peacefulness of the morning. It was then she stepped smack into his eyes. Her heel became lodged in the broken ridge between brow and nose, and she reached down quickly, unafraid, to free herself. It was only when she saw his naked grin that she gave a little yelp of surprise.

He had been a tall man. From feet to neck covered a long space. His head lay beside him. When she pushed back the leaves and layers of earth and debris Myop saw that he'd had large white teeth, all of them cracked or broken, long fingers, and very big bones. All his clothes had rotted away except some threads of blue denim from his overalls. The buckles of the overall had turned green.

Myop gazed around the spot with interest. Very near where she'd stepped into the head was a wild pink rose. As she picked it to add to her bundle she noticed a raised mound, a ring, around the rose's root. It was the rotted remains of a noose, a bit of shredding plowline, now blending benignly into the soil. Around an overhanging limb of a great spreading oak clung another piece. Frayed, rotted, bleached, and frazzled – barely there – but spinning restlessly in the breeze. Myop laid down her flowers.

And the summer was over.

'The Flowers' © Alice Walker. Reproduced by permission of The Joy Harris Literary Agency and Houghton Mifflin Harcourt.

Text potential
Exploring what the text offers

Vocabulary

Unknown words – 'accompaniment', 'sharecropper', 'tremors', 'fragrant', 'brow', 'debris', 'plowline', 'benignly'. Unusual vocabulary – 'tat-de-ta-ta-ta', 'knobby stick'.

Grammar; Syntax

Many complex sentences.

Visual features

Historical, social, and cultural context

An African-American child growing up in rural southern USA at a time of oppression.

Making links to background knowledge

Unlikely to have encountered a text of this nature in other reading, or have knowledge of this world. May have seen films about the southern USA.

Mapping text potential

'The Flowers' by Alice Walker

Language features

Standard English but of a 'literary' nature.

Subject

In this story, a child, Myop, is exploring her rural locality, most of which is familiar. In a secluded spot she encounters the clothed skeleton of an African-American man who has been lynched.

Narrative features

Plot – simple but difficult to establish.

Character – happy till loss of innocence, brave, respectful.

Setting – farmyard, undergrowth/forest, darkness.

Coherence

Likely to provide challenge in terms of the number of culturally located concepts and the number of complex sentences.

Literary features

Imagery, e.g. the water that silently rose and slid away down the stream.

Metaphor – end of summer (end of childhood).

Text type, purpose, and intended readership

This narrative shows how events in childhood can change the way children perceive the world.

Themes

Potential themes:
- racism
- death
- poverty
- childhood innocence
- blindness.

Lesson planning and organization

Marie worked on this text with a group of children of average attainment. It was composed entirely of girls. She had noticed that boys tended to dominate guided reading lessons, and had decided to address this by basing her groupings on gender so that the girls could find their 'voice'.

She intended to use the text with this group for a series of three guided reading lessons as she was aware that the text had the potential to be explored in some depth; for example, the context of the story (the experience of the poor, rural African-American community), which has considerable relevance to the action; the character of ten-year-old Myop, who experiences a life-changing event (stumbling across the dead body), and Alice Walker's use of language. The teacher did not plan all three lessons in advance, but deliberately waited to see how the pupils responded to the text after each lesson before deciding in which direction she would guide them in the next one.

Lesson 1

In the first lesson, the emphasis was on ensuring that the pupils were able to gain a literal understanding of the text. Marie planned the lesson using the Reciprocal Teaching approach, although she expected to spend quite a lot of time on the strategy of clarification. To support this, she developed three questions to help the children view the different layers of meaning within the text. The questions follow the approach described in Chapter 3, p. 38, and were as follows:

1. Where is the story set? ('looking')
2. How do you know the mood is changing in the story? ('clue')
3. Why do you think the author has named this story 'The Flowers'? ('thinking')

So, even at the start of this series of lessons, Marie was aiming to make the pupils aware of the literary aspects of the text and the author's intent. In a story of this nature, this is particularly important because, unless children are able to engage with the literary aspects, they are unlikely to be able to understand it.

After the first lesson, Marie decided to focus on Myop's character, and it is this second lesson that will be described here.

Lesson 2

Summarizing

As the pupils had already read the text, there was no point in making predictions about its ending. To remind the pupils about the text, the teacher asked them to make a summary of the story. This summary was made without giving the pupils time to read the text again, but it was supported by a follow-up activity from Lesson 1 in which they had created story-maps. Girl 6 gave a summary supported by her story-map.

Girl (G) 6: There was this girl and … erm … she lived in a farm in the countryside. And we decided maybe America or Africa. And she … erm … loved picking flowers and making chains and sticking them with her mum. Er … one day she went for a walk … erm … she saw a hut but she had to go back for tea, and when she walked on she saw a dead man, and then she laid her bouquet of flowers which she had picked, and then … summer was over.

This summary is, on the whole, clear, and Girl 6's peers had very little to add. The teacher did not pick up on the metaphor of the summer being over (and the link to Myop's loss of childhood) at this point because she expected to address this at a later point in the lesson. Having established that the pupils were re-engaged with the events of the story, the teacher presented the following three questions:

1. How would you describe Myop? ('looking')
2. Does Myop change in the story? ('clue')
3. Why did you think Myop did not seem scared or frightened? ('thinking')

These questions are developed based on the 'looking', 'clue', and 'thinking' inference questions described in Chapter 3, p. 38, and focus on the character of Myop. The pupils were then given the opportunity to read the text again. When they had read the text in the previous lesson, they had not had these questions in mind; now, the dialogue initially focused on the first question:

> **'Looking' question:**   How would you describe Myop?

This is a simple but interesting question because it could be interpreted simply as describing her age and appearance. However, it also provides the opportunity to explore Myop's character, based on evidence in the text. As a result, the pupils began a dialogue that required very little teacher intervention.

> **G5:**   Myop is a girl who … she's not a scared girl, like, like for example, when she saw the man because otherwise some people might start crying maybe?
>
> **G3:**   Myop is like a girl that has her own world. And she just likes hanging around in her chicken pen, and it says that like she's ten, and it says nothing excited her like writing her own songs, you know …
>
> **G6:**   I agree with Girl 3 but I'd like to add that she's … she's really curious, so that's why she went into the forest by herself, like … and she went deeper and deeper, but she didn't get really scared. She was just curious to know what was there.
>
> **G2:**   She likes to discover things, basically.

In this exchange we see the pupils building on each other's comments without direction from the teacher. We also see them moving from making literal comments about the character (for instance, her age and the fact that she likes to write songs) to more speculative comments about her character. Girl 5 suggests that Myop can't be feeling scared because she doesn't cry when she sees the dead man. Here she is making an inference from within the text and applying it to her own background knowledge of how somebody might be expected to behave. Girl 6 adds to this by making an interesting comparison between fear and curiosity: again, this is supported by evidence in the text that Myop was happy to wander in the forest.

Resolving a metaphor

The teacher then introduces the next key question:

'Clue' question: Does Myop change in the story? .

This led to an interesting discussion as the group began to resolve the metaphor of the summer being over. Girl 2 picked up on it straight away, and was supported in this by Girl 6:

G2:	She feels a bit sad, yeah? Because you know when she like … she laid down the flowers. You know it says that summer is a happy time. You know when it says summer is over. It relates to her feelings, like saying that she's gone all sad. All of it's over.
Teacher (T):	So you think that's what that line means? You think that line proves she has changed throughout the story? [G2 nods]
G6:	I agree with Girl 2 because sometimes people love summer and that makes them happy but when it goes to like … to like … autumn or winter it goes a bit colder, then they get a bit … their mood starts changing and … and this might have happened to Myop as well.

At this point it becomes apparent that not all of the group have picked up on this; some of the group still seem to think that summer is literally over in the story.

G5:	Maybe she's not that happy when it's not summer because it seems like … she loves summer and she loves staying in the sun and stuff like that.
G1:	I agree because every day when I get home from school in the summer, I'm actually pretty happy because it's a nice warm day; but now in this season, I don't feel like going to school because it's so dark outside.
G3:	You also get more sick in the winter.

What is interesting here is that, although they have not understood the metaphor, these pupils are still trying to make sense of the text and are applying their own prior knowledge about how the seasons make them feel to the text. At this point, Girl 2 reasserts her point that the author is not referring to the literal end of the summer.

G2:	In my opinion I don't actually think she's sad about the summer – about the summer being over. I think she's sad about something else – about the old man.
T:	Ahh.

The teacher's expression of interest here opens the door for this point to be explored, but some of the group move away from the metaphorical and back to the literal. Girl 3 refers back to the question and notes when Myop was happy in the story.

G3: In the beginning of the story she's happy, when she's just singing, like Girl 6 said, like she's singing to the hens, then like when she's walking in the forest she's happy. Then at the end she's a bit sad.

G4: I think here it said in the morning she was sad.

This is a critical point in the lesson because it allows the teacher to move the dialogue back to the metaphorical meaning of the summer being over, and she does this by exposing how the evidence in the text does not support the literal interpretation offered by Girl 3 and Girl 4.

T: So how could that happen? How could the summer be over when it is still in the morning time?

G2: I don't think actually it's literally the summer is over. I think it's like … she's like … she is, she is …

G5: Maybe sometimes if you're inside the forest it gets dark.

G4: 'Cos of the trees.

Again, Girl 4 seems to be trying to make sense of the question by attempting to make a literal interpretation. However, Girl 2 follows up this time with a comment that begins to shift the thinking of her peers.

G2: I think it's because of … like when she saw the man, she <u>felt</u> as if her summer was over because in the summer she feels really happy, but when the summer is over she's really upset.

[Long pause]

G4: Yeah, maybe that's what it means: the summer is over.

G6: Yeah, that's what it means.

G1: Maybe by summer they mean happy because … it's depending on the season … erm … there are happy seasons and there are sad seasons – like summer and spring. They are happy because they are warmer, and it's more colourful outside instead of dull and gloomy.

T: I think Girl 1 has come up with quite a good point there with possibly how that might be, how the summer was over. Thinking about what the summer was. Was it actually summer? Or was it her feelings?

The teacher wraps up the discussion about the metaphor by reasserting the point made by Girl 2. The teacher wasn't confident that all of the group had grasped the point, but certainly a number of them had. In the light of this discussion, the teacher later stated that this had informed her thinking about the next lesson, when she intended to revisit the use of figurative language. For some of the pupils in this group, the application of background knowledge led to a partial understanding of the author's intended meaning; to explore this, the teacher repeatedly related their background knowledge to what was actually stated in the text.

Teacher's reflections

Marie had not used the same text over a series of guided reading lessons before, and she found this to be very productive: she was able to adjust her future planning in the light of the learning that had taken place in the previous lesson. She felt that the use of this challenging text allowed some of the pupils in the group to engage with text in a way that they would not previously have been able to: in this instance, two of the pupils were able to deal with the story's central metaphor. It was clear that some of the pupils were not quite able to resolve the metaphor, but Marie felt that exposure to this type of text would be beneficial for their longer-term reading comprehension, and that the pupils had certainly pushed themselves further than she had expected.

Conclusion

The planned lessons described here enabled the pupils to grapple with the more literary aspects of text, for example, by linking Myop's character to the metaphor of the ending of childhood. As was pointed out in Chapter 1, pp. 17–18, good writers do not make things easy for the reader; good writers make the reader work. If we want pupils to be exposed to quality texts, this exposure requires teachers to support children through the difficult process of acquiring meaning at deeper levels. This lesson showed how this can be achieved through carefully structured guidance.

Reference

Walker, Alice (1994) 'The Flowers'. In *Alice Walker: The Complete Stories*. London: The Women's Press (ISBN 978-0-7538-1907-4). Originally published 1988. Online. http://theliterarylink.com/flowers.html

'The Nightingale and the Rose' by Oscar Wilde

Context

The sequence of lessons reported here took place in an urban school in Wales. The class consisted of 10–11 year olds. A similar sequence of lessons has been used successfully in a Year 7 class in a secondary school.

The lessons were planned and presented by one of the authors.

Planning

Four lessons were planned. Three lessons were taught with the whole class, each lasting one hour, and the fourth lesson was conducted with a group of six high-attaining readers and lasted 45 minutes. The aim of this sequence of lessons was to introduce pupils to a classic short story, using a gentler introductory picture book as a bridging text – a more accessible vehicle through which to introduce the theme and some of the concepts of the classic text.

Text selection

Two texts were chosen for comparison that appear to be very different. However, as the text potential diagrams show, there are many interesting reference points to be compared and contrasted.

Tadpole's Promise by Jeanne Willis and Tony Ross (2003) is a humorous picture book depicting a Romeo and Juliet story: love across the boundaries. In this case it is the caterpillar, a creature of the air, who falls in love with a tadpole, a creature of the water. They meet at the water's edge and never the twain shall meet, or shall they? A reader with knowledge of life cycles may detect early on, as the caterpillar urges the tadpole to 'never change', that this is an impossible task for him. He cannot go against nature and eventually he turns into a frog. Ironically, this means that he can now inhabit the same space as his love, the caterpillar, who has of course turned into a butterfly. But there's no 'aaah' moment in this story. Just at the point where the reader thinks the couple may be reunited, a quick turn of the page reveals that the frog has eaten his 'beautiful rainbow' and wonders where she has gone. This is a beautifully designed and paced story, which delivers its final joke without any compassion. The

joke relies on real-world knowledge. Children who haven't yet learnt about life cycles will be disappointed by the ending, which will appear to leave them hanging. But there's another type of knowledge that some readers will bring to bear: the knowledge of relationships, promises made, and promises broken. Familiarity with stories also increases the expectation of a happy ending, if the reader has read it as a fairy tale. However, if it has been read as a fable, then the reader may conclude that the caterpillar/butterfly gets her just desserts.

'The Nightingale and the Rose' is a classic story from Oscar Wilde's *The Happy Prince and Other Tales*, his collection of fairy stories for children (1888). The version used was not illustrated and was unabridged. This is another tale of unrequited love. A student declares that he is in love with his professor's daughter, who promises to dance with him at the ball, but only on the condition that he brings her red roses. The student laments that there are no red roses in his garden. His lamentations are overheard by a nightingale who is impressed by his passion and vows to help him find a red rose. She flies around the garden seeking a red rose but learns that the only way to achieve her heart's desire is to press her breast against a thorn and turn a white rose red. She sings all night until she has no more blood to give. In the morning the student wakes to find that 'luck' has delivered him a red rose. The nightingale lies dead on the window sill. Eager to see the object of his affections, he takes her the rose only to find she rejects him, having

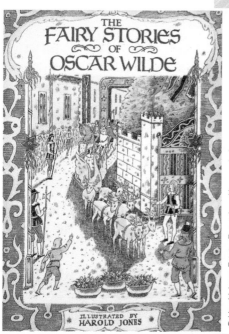

received a more precious gift of jewellery from the chancellor's son. Disillusioned, the student throws the rose into the gutter and vows that the study of metaphysics is a more worthy pursuit than love. This story can be read in many different ways. It is rich in symbolism and imagery. On one level it is a treatise on romantic love. But those coming from a Judeo-Christian background could potentially read it as a Christian allegory, with the nightingale suffering a crucifixion in order to save the unworthy student.

These two stories, separated by over a hundred years, have some similarities: they are both witty, knowing, and ironic, but the mode of telling creates a different response. Wilde's story in particular often divides readers into two camps: those who find the treatment painfully beautiful and emotive and those who find it overblown and sentimentalized. The theme of love is an obvious connection between the two stories, as is the ironic treatment and the use of a fairy-tale structure. Promises are casually made and easily broken. Animals are used to convey messages.

Tadpole's Promise will be accessible to all the children in the class and was chosen to be a good bridging text to 'The Nightingale and the Rose'. The vocabulary and the syntax of the nineteenth-century text is unfamiliar and challenging, but, having read and discussed *Tadpole's Promise*, pupils who can read at a higher level should be able to access this more complex story.

Text potential
Exploring what the text offers

Vocabulary

- Promise – central concept to the story. Ironic tone.
- Change – word with multiple meanings.
- Love – concept word.

Language features

- Direct speech.
- Repeating structure advances the story.
- Choice of 'weather', 'seasons', 'world' suggests there is something more powerful at play here than the mere feelings of a tadpole and a caterpillar (Shakespearean/epic).

Subject

Two creatures that live in different worlds fall in love. Is their love doomed or will it last?

Potential cross-curricular links to science.

Literary features

Irony – this is dependent on vocabulary and real-world knowledge.

Mapping text potential

Tadpole's Promise by Jeanne Willis and Tony Ross

Grammar; Syntax

'Where the willow meets the water, a tadpole met a caterpillar.' A complex sentence with a subordinate relative clause. What effect does this have on tone? How would it be different if Jeanne Willis had written 'A tadpole met a caterpillar where the willow meets the water'? 'Where the willow meets the water' is an alternative for 'Once upon a time'.

Coherence

Historical, social, and cultural context

Visual features

Book design – using the gutter to show above and below the water line – literally different worlds.

Design and pace of the picture book. Notice how the page turns make a difference to the anticipation and surprise that you experience as a reader.

Themes

- Love vs romantic love.
- Human relationships – adolescent and mature.
- Making and breaking promises.

Making links to background knowledge

- Metamorphosis – life cycles.
- Food chains.
- Knowledge of other stories.
- Relationships – making and breaking promises.

Text type, purpose, and intended readership

- Fictional narrative/ picture book
- Children – what age? Interesting to ask the pupils what they think?
- Also has mature humour. Likely to be read on different levels.

Narrative structure

Fairy tale: pattern of three.

Animal fable – what is the moral of this story?

Historical, social, and cultural context

Link to other texts: Romeo and Juliet; Oscar Wilde, 'The Nightingale and the Rose'.

Lesson 1

Tadpole's Promise – whole class – 1 hour

The aim of this lesson was to explore the theme of love, using semantic mapping as a technique to examine vocabulary and word associations.

The story was read aloud to the class with dramatic effect to emphasize the intensity of the joke and with a slow turn of the final pages so that the impact is increased as the frog wonders where his 'beautiful rainbow' has gone. There were gasps of shock and laughter as the final pages were turned. One small group looked disgusted.

Using questioning to encourage the application of background knowledge

Following the read-through, the teacher asked the class whether they liked the ending or not. The majority expressed delight but the teacher pursued a line of conversation with the children who hadn't enjoyed the ending.

Teacher (T): Why didn't you enjoy the ending to the story? It didn't make you laugh?

Child (C) 1: It's horrible.

C2: Yeah, he ate her. That's not nice.

T: But frogs do eat butterflies, don't they? Do you think that's horrible?

C3: It's not the same.

T: Really?

C3: No, because real frogs don't love butterflies.

T: Hasn't he turned into a real frog?

C3: No, it's a story and it's like Beauty and the Beast. You wouldn't want Beauty to kill him because she really loves him.

T: Didn't the butterfly get what she deserved?

C4: But it's sad for the frog. He LOVED her and he killed her. I think that's horrible. Like – if I killed someone I loved it would be awful …

T: You would be devastated?

Child 1 and Child 2's initial statements simply reiterate the point that they didn't like the ending because it was 'horrible' and 'not nice'. The teacher wants them to be able to explain and justify this response and to do this she encourages them to make links with their background knowledge, by making the point that in real life 'frogs do eat butterflies'.

Child 3 then responds by making a 'text-to-text' link with Beauty and the Beast. Child 3 is clearly tapping into the idea of romantic love as expressed in fairy tales. Child 4 supports this further by relating the text to her own personal experience – a 'text-to-life' comment. 'Love' is a theme the teacher wanted to use as a link to 'The Nightingale and the Rose' text, but the teacher didn't have to raise it herself. If they had used their background knowledge to raise issues other than the 'love' element of the story, the teacher could have steered the discussion towards 'love' later. This would not have negated the content of the dialogue that was developing (it's not simply about what's in the teacher's head) because the children would still have been accessing deeper layers of meaning. In this example, questioning encouraged the children to access background knowledge to justify an opinion – and we can't justify opinions *without* access to background knowledge.

Teacher talk that invites speculation

The teacher then re-oriented the dialogue to include those who *did* enjoy the ending.

> **T:** Then I wonder why some children in the class thought it was hilarious?
>
> **C5:** The frog doesn't know that the butterfly is his beautiful rainbow so he can't feel awful. That's really funny. He's waiting for her but he's eaten her.
>
> **C3:** He might be waiting forever. [laughter]
>
> **C4:** And he'll never find another beautiful rainbow because he loved her and even his thoughts are heart bubbles.

This shows the teacher using talk to create a dialogic interaction. Her opening question, which begins 'I wonder why …?' is an invitation to speculate. This type of teacher talk then facilitates Child 3 and Child 4 to build on Child 5's comment without recourse to the teacher. By steering the dialogue in this direction the teacher allows another viewpoint to be shared but at no point does she give precedence to one way of thinking over another; this allows a coherent line of argument to begin to emerge.

> **T:** I noticed that when I read the part of the story where the caterpillar says to the tadpole 'promise you'll never change' some of you gave a little giggle. I wonder why?
>
> **C6:** He can't promise …
>
> **C7:** But he did promise.
>
> **C6:** Yes but he shouldn't have promised because he can't promise not to change.
>
> **T:** But he did promise not to change. What do you mean?
>
> **C6:** He shouldn't have promised because he can't keep his promise. You shouldn't make promises that you can't keep.

In this extract, the teacher prompts the children to think about their response to the text.

Initially their response is to be horrified by the idea of the frog eating the butterfly, but their involuntary response to the tone of the text suggests that something else is going on here. The teacher prompts them to think about this apparent contradiction. Her question requires them to draw on their background knowledge about the life-cycle of a frog to make explicit the humour in the situation. They move towards talking about the dramatic irony, the fact that the frog is unaware that he has in fact eaten his beautiful rainbow.

Exploring the layers of meaning in words: semantic mapping

In Chapter 1 it was noted that vocabulary is a critical component in the comprehension process. It was also noted that the meaning of a word changes according to the context in which it is used and that people are likely to assign different meanings to the same word. Simple vocabulary can be conceptually complex. The teacher wanted to explore the theme of love in more depth as this would link to the work on 'The Nightingale and the Rose' in the next lesson. She did this by investigating the word 'love' in the context of associated vocabulary. She introduced a semantic mapping activity that had the following procedure:

- Working in twos or threes, the children were given two minutes to list as many words associated with the word 'love' as they could think of.
- Ideas were then shared and listed. The teacher added some of her own words to the list, as all of the words suggested by the pupils had positive connotations. Words she added included 'sacrifice', 'hate', 'chocolate', and 'forever'. The teacher took time to explain why she had added these particular words.
- The children developed their lists further in twos or threes. They then looked at the lists of other groups and decided whether there were any further words they wanted to add to their lists.
- The children were then asked to group these words by finding common connections between them. The teacher modelled this first using the original list to create groups of words such as 'chocolate', 'flowers', and 'Valentine's day'; and 'hate', 'angry', and 'jealousy'.
- The children shared the grouped lists with the class.

The children produced different clusters of words, showing that they did not group the words in the same way and that they had different associations for the word 'love'.

The lesson ended with a quick summary and an invitation to the children to consider whether they had started to think differently about the word 'love' during the lesson. It was explained that the semantic maps they had created would be kept in their reading journals and reviewed later.

> **T:** One of the interesting things about words is that we think we know what they mean. Sometimes we look them up in a dictionary to find out how they have been defined. But there are many words where our understanding changes over time or according to our experiences. We are going to look back at your maps when we have done some more reading.

Lesson 2

Text potential
Exploring what the text offers

Vocabulary

- Archaic/literary vocabulary: 'lit' lit upon a spray; 'want' for want of a red rose; 'heed' no heed of me.
- Vocabulary choices: 'clasped', 'wept'.
- Vocabulary choices and imagery.
- Semantic fields: love, knowledge, and nature. Identify the many references to these fields.

Language features

Elevated diction and highly romanticized language.

Contrasts: brown nightingale contrasted with opulent imagery.

Subject

On the surface, this is a romantic love story about a student and his 'true love, but this story is more a thematic exploration than a character-driven plot.

Grammar; Syntax

Noun-preposition relationships. Pronouns often precede nouns. In one case the pronoun 'she' is used five times and the noun it refers to is mentioned five paragraphs later. One of the challenges of reading nineteenth-century text is the unfamiliar construction.

Mapping text potential
'The Nightingale and the Rose' by Oscar Wilde

Literary features

Numerous instances of imagery, e.g. 'her voice was like water bubbling from a silver jar'.

Personification: Nightingale, tree, moon, and other creatures in the garden.

Symbolism: Nightingale (birds in literature), Rose (from Beauty and the Beast, Blake to Wilde), some interpretations of the imagery is very adult but others more easily understood by age group

Themes

Potential themes:

- romantic love vs true love
- love, truth, and knowledge/education
- sacrifice (could be read as religious allegory?)
- art and materialism.

Visual features

Historical, social, and cultural context

Written in 1885, inspired in part by Hans Christian Andersen's 'The Nightingale'. Also connections with Wagner's Tannhäuser (1845). Wilde's aspirations to be converted to Catholicism may also be an influence.

Coherence

Making links to background knowledge

- Nineteenth-century literary fairy story. Requires a mature understanding of the concept of love to appreciate the narrative point of view.
- Passionate story – link to Wilde's religious aspirations (connection with Dorian Gray?).
- Diction will be unfamiliar to students who haven't read nineteenth-century texts.

Text type, purpose, and intended readership

Literary fairy tale from the collection 'The Happy Prince and Other Tales'. Are these stories intended for children? Why are fairy tales often classified as 'children's books'? Could adults read and appreciate these stories?

Narrative structure

Fairy tale (assume this will be familiar to all pupils).

'The Nightingale and the Rose' – whole class, mixed ability – 1 hour

The teacher introduced 'The Nightingale and the Rose' by asking if anyone had heard or read stories by Oscar Wilde. His name was unfamiliar to the pupils. The teacher asked if they had heard or read 'The Selfish Giant' or 'The Happy Prince'. Most children in the class had come across these stories in various versions. The teacher explained that 'The Nightingale and the Rose' was originally from a collection of fairy tales written by Oscar Wilde in 1888; she then prepared to read it aloud to the whole class. The pupils each had their own copy of the text.

Before starting to read, the teacher explained to the class that when she had finished she wanted them to jot down a response to the story. She explained that it would be a quiet time to write down what they were thinking. Some prompts were suggested, but the children were told they could write what they wanted:

- Did you enjoy the story? Why or why not?
- Did you find anything difficult to understand?
- Do you have any questions that you would like to ask?

As we see in a number of the case studies, questions given prior to reading (or listening to) a text serve to tune the learners in to the content. The teacher then read 'The Nightingale and the Rose' aloud to the whole class while the children listened and followed by reading their copies of the text.

When she had finished, she asked them to write down their reactions to it, allowing ten minutes for this. When they had finished, each pupil spoke in turn about their response to the story. Some responses included an evaluation of the ending of the story. Opinions varied: one girl suggested that the ending should have been a happy one, with the professor's daughter agreeing to dance with the student. Another girl said she didn't like the rose ending up in the gutter. One boy said he didn't understand why it ended with the student going back to his 'dusty books'.

After a short discussion ascertaining that the children had understood the events in the story, the teacher asked them to return to the text and to highlight examples of language (words, sentences, or phrases) that they thought were especially powerful, that provoked thinking or evoked strong emotions. They were reminded to think carefully about why they were highlighting these as they would be required to explain why they had made those choices.

The teacher deliberately avoided starting from a list of prepared questions as she wanted the children to think more deeply about the impact of the language on them. Questions such as 'can anyone find an example of a metaphor?' or 'Why do you think Oscar Wilde chose a particular word?' or 'What do you think Oscar Wilde was trying to say to his readers?' are often asked too early in the reading process and interfere with pupils developing their own understandings. These first encounters are important and, if handled sensitively, take pupils to a deeper understanding, which will have a more lasting impact.

It's easy to get answers to questions that keep their understanding at the surface level, but in order to develop understanding, rather than test that they can name those surface features, we have to work more deeply.

Examples of the language the children highlighted:

- 'She swept through the garden like a shadow. And like a shadow ...' One girl mentioned the repetition and the effect of the nightingale sweeping across the garden, quietly, unnoticed.
- They noticed that some words were capitalized and raised a question about this. It didn't appear to match what they thought they had been taught about capital letters.
- One girl selected the following passage: *'My roses are red,' it answered, 'as red as the feet of the dove, and redder than the great fans of coral that wave and wave in the ocean-cavern.'*

This enabled the teacher to remind them of some of the literary concepts that they had already encountered; she asked: '*Do you think Oscar Wilde chose good similes to describe the red of the rose?*' This evaluative question allowed the children to reflect on the effectiveness of the author's stylistic choices and elicited different opinions, encouraging them to begin to justify their preferences.

The lesson closed when all the pupils' contributions had been heard and acknowledged.

Lesson 3

Revisiting the text – whole class – 1 hour

Identifying themes: Lesson 3 allowed the children to revisit the text with the aim of building on their understanding by identifying what they might consider to be important themes. The teacher provided this opportunity because, in her experience, children often talk about seeing things or understanding things on a second reading that they didn't notice on their initial engagement with the text. While pace in a lesson is important, the pace that matters is the one that follows the pupils' learning and interest. Sometimes this can move quickly, but at other times a slower pace is needed for deeper learning to take place. The teacher needs to make a judgement about whether the opportunity to discover something in order to find an answer to one's own questions is more powerful than being given an answer or led too quickly to an answer that is held only superficially.

Working in groups and without any specific question to answer, the children were asked to do the following:

- Revisit the text, page by page.
- Reread and discuss anything of interest on each page.
- Listen to each other and have a consensus about when to move on.

After 20 minutes, the teacher gathered the class together and asked if they had any new ideas on listening to what the other children in their group had to say. From this, the teacher moved the discussion forward and gave a brief explanation of the different ways in which the question 'What is this story about?' can be answered. This allowed the children to link their new ideas to the concept of 'themes'.

The teacher then explained the next task. The groups were asked to think about the themes in 'The Nightingale and the Rose' and then highlight one quotation that they thought summed up the story's main theme.

Identifying themes: exposing thinking

When the teacher gathered the groups together she gave a brief explanation of the different ways in which the question of what this story is about can be answered:

> **T:** We can describe the plot or we can talk about the 'big ideas' that underpin the story; we call them themes. What do you think the theme of 'The Nightingale and the Rose' is? I want you to highlight just one quotation from the story that you think sums up the main theme.

After about 15 minutes working in their own groups to complete this task, the class reassembled and the next step was explained. Each group was to create a statue of 'The Nightingale and the Rose' for Kensington Gardens. The statue would create a visual impression of the story's main theme and the quotation would be used as an epigram to help visitors understand the story. To illustrate the task, the children were shown a collection of literary statues and accompanying epigrams: Peter Pan in Kensington Gardens: 'The boy who never grew up'; Alice in Wonderland in Central Park: 'Twinkle twinkle little bat. How I wonder what you're at.'

The teacher chose the freeze-frame and quotation technique to support this task as it provided a quick visual image of the children's interpretation of the main themes of the story. It proved to be a good vehicle for initiating discussion between groups. They had to justify why they had selected their quotations and how these related to the themes of the story. By encouraging discussion between groups, the teacher arranged it so they had to defend their own ideas but also had to be open to the way others had interpreted the story.

Some of the quotations chosen by the groups were:

- 'Death is a great price to pay for a Red Rose.'
- 'Love is a Silly Thing.'
- 'Surely love is a wonderful thing. It is more precious than emeralds and diamonds and gold.'

One group said they thought 'Love is a Silly Thing' should have a question mark. The teacher asked whether there was a question mark in the text. They checked and confirmed that there was no question mark. The teacher said she was interested to find out why the group thought there might be one; she asked them if they thought there was a question mark in Oscar Wilde's mind when he wrote the story. In their opinion, did they think that Oscar Wilde was saying love is such a silly thing, or not? The children expressed uncertainty and this was left as an open question.

For the teacher this proved to be an important discussion. She had anticipated that this was one of the likely quotations that at least one of the groups would identify, but hadn't expected the comment about the question mark. In fact, this proved to be the most fruitful line of enquiry, taking the children further in their thinking. They had identified the potential in the quotation but were not fully aware of its significance, that is, how it related to the story's major themes.

Effective guided reading involves being able to pinpoint accurately what readers are able to achieve on their own and then identifying what they might be able to achieve with the structured guidance of the teacher. At this point the teacher knew that the next step would be to take that quotation and pose the question: 'Oscar Wilde thinks Love is a Silly Thing, do you agree or disagree?' The challenge was to work out how to lead the group to a consideration of this question without imposing her own thinking.

Lesson 4

Guided reading: building on ideas and taking thinking forward – one group – 45 mins

For this lesson, the teacher worked with one guided reading group, having decided from the previous lesson how she might build on their current understanding of the text. During this session, the rest of the class worked on other reading tasks relating to the two stories. These included working on vocabulary journals, writing alternative endings and creating a storyboard for a film version of 'The Nightingale and the Rose', set in space.

At the beginning of the lesson, the quotation 'Love is such a Silly Thing' was written on a card and placed in the centre of the table. The teacher asked the pupils whether they thought Oscar Wilde thought love was a silly thing. After taking a short time to scan the text, each child gave an opinion, which they had to support with evidence from the text. Unsurprisingly, they found it hard to distinguish between the voice of the narrator and the author.

In 'The Nightingale and the Rose' Wilde explicitly explores the concept of 'love' and there are two contrasting quotations, which would suggest that the author wants the reader to consider them together:

- 'Love is such a silly thing' is spoken by the student.
- 'Love is such a wonderful thing' is spoken by the nightingale.

At this point the teacher asked the children think about these quotations in relation to the characters speaking them and asked:

> **T:** Do you feel more empathy for one character than another?
> If so, which and why?

All of the children expressed an affinity with the nightingale. They expressed concern for the sacrifice and ultimate price that the bird had paid. They felt that the student wasn't worth the sacrifice because he so readily discarded the rose.

The next step was to look more closely at the words spoken by each character to see if they could identify the views each character expressed.

Their attention was drawn to two passages, one featuring the nightingale and the other the student.

> *'Death is a great price to pay for a red rose,' cried the Nightingale, 'and Life is very dear to all. It is pleasant to sit in the green wood, and to watch the Sun in his chariot of gold, and the Moon in her chariot of pearl. Sweet is the scent of the hawthorn, and sweet are the bluebells that hide in the valley, and the heather that blows on the hill. Yet Love is better than Life, and what is the heart of a bird compared to the heart of a man?'*

> *'She has form,' he said to himself, as he walked away through the grove – 'that cannot be denied to her; but has she got feeling? I am afraid not. In fact, she is like most artists; she is all style, without any sincerity. She would not sacrifice*

herself for others. She thinks merely of music, and everybody knows that the arts are selfish. Still, it must be admitted that she has some beautiful notes in her voice. What a pity it is that they do not mean anything, or do any practical good.' And he went into his room, and lay down on his little pallet-bed, and began to think of his love; and, after a time, he fell asleep.

Revisiting some themes encountered in the text

Using this focus on the characters of the nightingale and the student, the teacher asked the pupils to examine the theme of love, by clarifying what each character meant by it.

C1: The nightingale loves flowers, nature, and things like that.

T: What is the thing that she says she loves most?

C1: Life …

T: Where …?

C2: No, love, it says 'Love is better than life.'

T: Do you agree with the nightingale here?

C3: I think life must be most important because if you are not alive then you can't love anyone. So I think it's life.

Here, Child 3 takes a definite position that contradicts the position espoused by the nightingale. By analysing the nightingale's statement, Child 3 is beginning to understand how Wilde has characterized her. This developed further in the following interaction:

T: What do you think the nightingale means when she says 'What is the heart of a bird compared to the heart of a man?'

C4: It sounds as though the bird isn't as important.

T: **You** don't think the bird is as important?

C4: I do … but it doesn't sound as important. She's saying she isn't as important as the student. She has a kind heart and she thinks other people are more important than her.

T: What is the nightingale deciding to do here?

C5: To make a red rose and she knows she is going to die. She will die making the rose. It says 'Death is a great price to pay for a red rose'. So she KNOWS she's going to die.

Here we see Child 4 and Child 5 analysing a statement directly from the text, 'What is the heart of a bird, compared to the heart of a man?', and making some quite sophisticated inferences about the nightingale's character. Child 4 states that the nightingale considers people to be more important than birds – but also makes clear that she herself doesn't agree with this. Child 5 builds on this further, making the inference that the nightingale has made a conscious, reasoned choice to die for the student, again using evidence from the text. If this dialogue is related back to the first lesson in this sequence, we can see the benefits of the semantic mapping activity, where the teacher linked the idea of 'sacrifice' with 'love'. We can also see how the discussion of the ending in *Tadpole's Promise*, where the children considered how the frog might be feeling having just eaten the butterfly, links into this one.

T:	That's a difficult idea isn't it? It makes me feel a bit uncomfortable but sometimes people do decide that there are things worth dying for. What about the student, do you think he would make the same sacrifice?
(Lots of voices):	No!
T:	What attitude does he have towards the nightingale?
C3:	He's wrong about her.
T:	Wrong?
C4:	Doesn't understand her.
C3:	I agree with Child 4, because it says 'she would not sacrifice herself for others' but she has decided to die to make the red rose. I think the student doesn't really care.
T:	But he cares about dancing with his professor's daughter.
C3:	He doesn't care about the nightingale.

By asking the pupils to examine first the nightingale and then the student to explore the way Wilde has described them, the teacher pushes the pupils to develop their understanding of Wilde's portrayal of love. Having decided unanimously that the nightingale was definitely presented more positively than the student, they were further asked to consider the words spoken by the student and the words spoken by the nightingale. Could they tell which view of love Oscar Wilde is likely to have favoured, given his apparent preference for the nightingale over the student?

After reading

The group were invited to share their thoughts about what they thought they had learnt from rereading the story. Did they have a different understanding of the story now from when they first heard it?

Follow-up

- They could choose to reread the story.
- Make changes, additions, or amendments to the semantic maps.
- Compare 'The Nightingale and the Rose' with *Tadpole's Promise*, using 'double-bubble' thinking maps to plot their ideas. A completed example is shown opposite; a blank version of the double-bubble thinking map for teachers to use can be found on the website: www.guidingreaders.com/PDresources.

'Double bubble' map

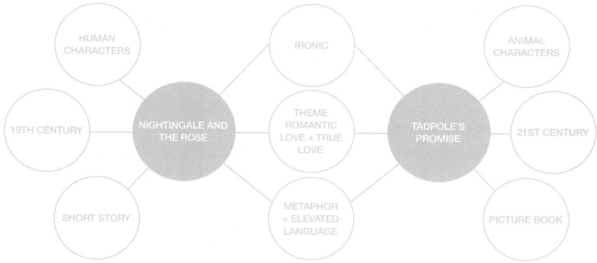

HUMAN CHARACTERS

IRONIC

ANIMAL CHARACTERS

19TH CENTURY

NIGHTINGALE AND THE ROSE

THEME ROMANTIC LOVE + TRUE LOVE

TADPOLE'S PROMISE

21ST CENTURY

SHORT STORY

METAPHOR + ELEVATED LANGUAGE

PICTURE BOOK

Teacher's reflections

Tadpole's Promise was an accessible starting point and the semantic mapping of 'love' provided a concrete activity that could be revisited later.

In the second lesson, as the class had little experience of nineteenth-century literature, other than simplified versions of *Oliver Twist* and *A Christmas Carol*, the teacher elected to read the story aloud while they listened and followed in their own copies of the text, because she wanted them to hear the tune and the cadences created by the unfamiliar syntax. She felt it was important that the first encounter with the text was a well-prepared reading by an experienced reader. There is a BBC recording of the story read by David Moffat, but hearing the text read by a person present in the room enables the students to make a personal connection; this can be more difficult with a recording. The pupils' initial reactions to the story were not all positive; getting them to focus on Wilde's literary language was a useful counter-balance to their emotional responses.

After this lesson, the teacher used the text potential diagram to map what the children had covered in their discussions and to identify gaps in their understanding. From this position she decided where it would be most productive to guide the subsequent discussion. While the children's ability to talk about the impact that vocabulary choices and phrases had on them when they read was satisfactory because they showed some awareness of literary features, the story's main themes had not yet been sufficiently explored.

In Lesson 3, close examination of the text was used to extract the main theme of love, getting the students to select just a single quotation to exemplify this theme. There was a lot of constructive discussion in this session.

In Lesson 4, the teacher wanted to explore authorial intention with the students, realizing that this is a tricky concept. In 'The Nightingale and the Rose', Wilde explicitly explores the concept of 'love', and the two contrasting quotations suggest that the author wants the reader to consider them together. A concrete way to enable the pupils to think about what the author was doing was to look closely at the characters associated with each of the quotations. 'Love is such a Silly Thing' is spoken by the student and 'Love is such a wonderful thing' is spoken by the nightingale. Through this approach, the teacher hoped that the pupils might get closer to what they thought Oscar Wilde's own position was.

In this lesson, the pupils made good progress, as they started to appreciate the way in which an author's point of view can intrude upon a text and how to examine the clues that might lead towards uncovering it, albeit provisionally.

Conclusion

When discussing this approach to classic texts with other teachers, some have felt that it required a considerable amount of subject knowledge, such as knowing about text features. However, the approach used here did not start by asking the pupils about features of text, but about what they felt. Starting with the pupils' own initial responses enables the teacher to gauge where to direct the subsequent teaching.

Reference

Wilde, O. (1888; republished 2008) *The Happy Prince and Other Stories*. Puffin (ISBN: 978-0-14-132779-2).

Willis, J. and Ross, T. (2003) *Tadpole's Promise*. Andersen Press (ISBN: 978-1-84-270069-3).

Memorial by Gary Crew

Context

This case study examines a sequence of three lessons given to a group of six high-attaining readers (five girls and one boy) in Year 6 (10–11 year olds) in a west London primary school; the lessons were taught by one of the authors. A similar series of lessons has also been successfully presented in a Year 7 class in a secondary school. In these three 40-minute sessions, the overarching aim was to encourage these children, who were perceived as successful readers, to read for deeper layers of meaning. This was to be achieved in two ways.

First, the text to be used was a picture book. Picture books had not previously featured in the reading material selected for this group and some resistance was anticipated from pupils who were keen to be seen reading chunky texts. A picture book was selected as a means of slowing their reading, and encouraging them both to pay attention to detail and to be more reflective in their reading generally.

Second, the pupils were going to be asked to generate questions about the text for themselves. Questioning has been a key strategy used by teachers in the case studies presented in this book, for accessing deeper layers of meaning; arguably, it is the most important strategy. However, in other case studies the questions have been generated by the teachers. The teacher believed that encouraging the readers to generate their own questions would enable them to read more slowly and to examine the text in greater detail.

Planning

Text selection

Memorial is a picture book for older readers written by Gary Crew and illustrated by Shaun Tan (2003). It has the potential to be used with pupils at the upper end of primary school and in lower secondary school. The title relates to two memorials – a tree planted and a statue erected after the First World War – in an Australian city. They are positioned side by side. As time passes, the council decides to take the tree down because its roots are destroying the road that now runs next to it.

The text is a first-person recollection that starts in the present tense: 'My great grandpa says they planted the tree on the day he came home from the war.' But it ends with a different person looking back at the rest of the book as though it were in the past: 'And now that I think about it, I know what he said is true.' At first, the voice is that of a young boy who hears the different generations of his family talking about their experiences of various wars – from the First World War to the Vietnam War – but at the end the voice is that of a more mature person. The shifts in time and speakers may be confusing for some readers, as there is no connecting narrative and minimal tagging to link the voices. In effect this creates a soundtrack of voices talking about their various memories connected with the old tree.

The painted illustrations are sophisticated. Textured effects make it look as though they are painted on wood, metal, or fabric, and these materials in turn have ageing qualities showing how the passage of time affects manufactured objects as well as human beings. There are also photograph-like images that capture images from the different time periods.

Double-page, wordless pages create reflective space. They invite the reader to stop and stare. These images focus on different aspects of the tree: the roots, a hollowed-out trunk, the large overarching canopy. Each of these spreads is juxtaposed against an aspect of the human story: the grizzled face of the great-grandfather, the internal scream of the father who can't talk about his Vietnam experience.

The language is generally accessible. There are a few context-specific words that provide evidence that the story is set in Australia, but pupils may not immediately realize this. In fact, readers often think the book is set in North America.

Thematically the book is very rich, and this makes it a particularly good choice for a group of readers who need to develop both depth and breadth in their reading, and to understand that developing as a reader means more than simply developing the stamina to read chunkier texts.

Text potential

Exploring what the text offers

Vocabulary

Context: 'Ypres', 'shrapnel', 'Moreton Bay fig', 'Vietnam', 'reveille'.

Possible unknown words: 'grizzled', 'hessian', 'trestle table', 'bitumen', 'intersection'.

Social context: 'hobo', 'tea service'.

Colloquial: 'Geez', 'breather'.

Language features

Informal conversational style.

Transitions from one speaker to another can be difficult to follow as no connecting narrative. This gives an authentic conversational feel to the text.

- Idiom: 'smart as paint'.

Subject

Four generations recall the wars they have fought in and the council's intention to take down a tree that was planted as a memorial after the First World War.

Literary features

- Narration, conversation.
- Point of view – child's perspective, though other voices heard.
- Retrospective (see final line) suggests this is a story that will continue through time and through dialogue.

Mapping text potential

Memorial by Gary Crew, illustrated by Shaun Tan

Text type, purpose, and intended readership

- Picture book – wide readership; timeless theme.
- Point of view – implied younger reader.
- Reflective text to encourage readers to think about repeated mistakes in history, the importance of memory and the perseverance and triumph of nature over humanity.

Coherence

Narrative features

Reminiscence/dialogue

Historical, social, and cultural context

Set in Australia, there are references that identify location: possums, Moreton Bay fig tree. There are references to the Vietnam War and the soldier wears an Anzac military costume. The children may not identify these references.

Grammar; Syntax

Past/present tense shifts. The story is told in the present but concludes in a present that looks back at the present of the rest of the text. This creates an immediate presence and at the same time underlies the passing of time that is central to the story. It may however be confusing for some readers.

Themes

- memories
- age and youth
- remembrance
- natural world vs human civilization
- endurance.

Visual features

- Images evoke a scrapbook/memory box.
- Techniques and media create wood-like and cloth-like textures.
- Small detail – insects and wildlife are important to the theme.
- Double-page spreads without words used to express psychological aspect.
- Images broaden the perspective offering multiple points of view.
- Use of light for literal depiction and symbolic depth.
- Pacing – double-page spreads offer reflective space.

Making links to background knowledge

- Study of Second World War in Year 5.
- War memorial in local high street.
- Remembrance Day.
- Australian context may not be familiar.

Lesson planning and organization

A review of the pupils' initial thoughts and questions, which were subsequently related to the text potential diagram, was followed by a planned sequence of work. Opportunities for group collaboration and dialogue were at the forefront of this planning.

Resources:

- copies of *Memorial*, one per pupil
- A1 sheets of paper
- thick marker pens
- whiteboards and markers
- a set of cards with the words 'TREE' and 'STATUE' written on them.

Lesson 1

First encounters

The pupils were given a copy of *Memorial* to take home and read, and they brought it back with them for the first lesson. The teacher gave them five minutes to look through the book and refresh their memories, and then asked them to make notes in their reading journals using the following prompts:

- first responses (thoughts and feeling about the book, likes, dislikes, etc.)
- connections (things the book reminded you of such as other books, memories, things on the news, films, and topics you have covered in school)
- puzzles (anything you found strange, unusual, puzzling, unclear)
- questions (any questions that you have about the book, would like to ask the author about, or need further information about).

They were asked to do this individually, without discussing their ideas with anyone, and this part of the lesson was therefore conducted in silence. The aim of working in this way was to encourage the pupils to develop a commitment to their own ideas before being exposed to the thinking of other members of the group. The pupils then shared their thoughts.

Child (C) 1: It's very differently set out to most books. Because when we learnt about the story mountain there's the opening, the build-up, the problem, the resolution, and the ending. But this one doesn't really do this. There's a lot of dialogue and pictures and the pictures say different things to the words. One of my questions is: did they chop down the tree? Because I noticed in the pictures it looks as though they chopped down the tree but the words don't actually say that they chopped down the tree.

C2: I didn't really like this book. I think this is just kind of like a report of a conversation they had as a family. I prefer a story that has lots of action and drama, rather than just a conversation in a book. I did like that they cut down the tree because that was a bit of action.

C3: The thing this book reminded me of was my great grandma because she talks about the war. And … um … the bit that confuses me is why there is so much dialogue, and also all the bits about the tree dying where it talks about the fumes killing the tree … My question is: why did they cut down the tree? I know it was pulling up the statue, but I think the tree was nice. I think it was set in Australia. I'm not really sure, but it mentions possums and I know they have possums in Australia.

C4:	I really quite like *Memorial*. It was a bit unusual and different to what I usually read, but I did like the storyline and how it was planned out. Nothing really puzzled me except I wasn't really looking at the pictures. I didn't realize they cut down the tree until I read it again just now, and then I realized that they had cut down the tree.
C5:	I really like this book. I felt that I was in the room with the people because it's laid out like a conversation. I do have some questions. I wondered how old the great grandpa was when he came home from the war. Where was it set?
C6:	I really liked the book. The tree isn't just a tree, it's really a memory, and even though the book has memories in it, the tree is a memory itself. I wonder if it was based on a true story.

Allowing the space for all of the children to speak their initial thoughts at length gave the teacher an insight into the way they were interpreting the story. From these observations, it was evident that some members of the group had identified some of the key features that were noted on the text potential diagram: for instance, the fact that this book does not have the conventional narrative structure of a story; that the way in which the dialogue is presented takes you straight into the scene, almost as if you were a witness to the conversation; that the tree is a potent symbol for memory; that the words and pictures tell different stories, and in the space between them a third story is told. In this case, Child 4 hadn't initially read the pictures and had therefore missed the irony that the tree is being cut down, even as in the text the boy asserts that he will stop the council from destroying it.

In this part of the process, the teacher must listen carefully in order to identify how the subsequent discussions might be structured to deepen the pupils' understanding. Possible questions to be followed up emerge: for instance, why isn't action an important aspect of this story? Can we identify with any certainty the setting for the story? Is dialogue the best way to tell this story? How would it have changed the story if a different way of narrating had been employed? By allowing time for the pre-reading and initial discussion, the teaching starts from a point relevant to the pupils' existing knowledge, experience, and interest rather than from a set of predetermined questions.

Generating questions

Before opening up the discussion, the teacher asked the children to map their questions on a question quadrant. A question quadrant allows children to reflect on the types of questions they can ask of a text, and where they are likely to find the answer. The one developed for this activity was as follows:

Questions to which there is only one answer, and the answer is likely to be found in the book	Questions to which there is only one answer, and the answer is not likely to be found in the book
Questions to which there is more than one answer, and the answers are likely to be found in the book	Questions to which there is more than one answer, and the answers are not likely to be found in the book

The children mapped their questions as a group. The teacher explained that they could start with the questions that they generated when they were taking notes, but if any further questions arose in the course of their discussion, they could add those as well. She explained that they didn't need to find the answers at this stage, although they were likely to start discussing possible answers. She also told them it didn't matter if they had blank boxes. It was more important that the questions were ones to which they wanted to find the answers – authentic questions. They also didn't need a long list of questions. The question quadrant they developed is presented below:

Questions to which there is only one answer, and the answer is likely to be found in the book	Questions to which there is only one answer, and the answer is not likely to be found in the book
Is the book set in Australia? *Did they chop down the tree?*	
Questions to which there is more than one answer, and the answers are likely to be found in the book	Questions to which there is more than one answer, and the answers are not likely to be found in the book
	Which is most fitting for a war memorial, a tree or a statue? *What inspired Gary Crew to write this story?*

The incidental talk while they were completing the task showed how they were constructing their understanding collaboratively. When one pupil noticed something, it was brought to the attention of the rest of the group. Examples of this are presented below in relation to specific questions.

Question: *Is the book set in Australia?*

C1: I think there's only one answer to C3's question. It's either 'yes' or 'no', but there can only be one answer.

C3: I think it is, because there's a sticker on the front and it says 'Children's Book Council of Australia'.

(Laughter)

C2: Oh yes … I didn't notice that.

C4 (quietly): It can't be Australia because they weren't in the First World War.

In this interaction, the children looked for evidence in the book to answer the question. However, Child 4 made a link to her background knowledge and suggested that it couldn't be set in Australia because Australia did not take part in the First World War. While this is incorrect, it showed how the knowledge we bring to a text can affect our understanding.

Question: *Did they chop down the tree?*

C3: There could be more than one answer.

C1: No there can't, it says they chopped down the tree.

C3: It doesn't say that; the pictures show that.

C4: I think it's in the book, and there's more than one possible answer.

C1: More than one answer?

C2: Yes, more than one answer.

This interaction shows that they were starting to look more closely at the text and, in particular, at the relationship between the written text and the pictures.

Question: *Which is most fitting for a war memorial, a tree or a statue?*

C3: That's a really good one.

C4: I think there's more than one answer to that.

C3: I think you could find that in the book.

C4: I don't think you could. They kept the statue because it was causing less chaos, but that doesn't mean it was more important to all the people.

C3:	Yes, but if you think about it, if the tree was more important they would have taken the statue away rather than the tree. So the statue was definitely more important.
C4:	If you think about it, they took down the tree because it says it was lifting the bitumen and it's dropping seeds on the cars.
C3:	It could be that some people say the tree is more important, but some people say the statue is more important, but the people who say the statue have got more power, and so they are the ones that are cutting down the tree.
C2:	The council.
C4:	Yes.
C1:	So it's more than one answer.

Child 3 described this as a 'good' question. Making a judgement of this nature suggested to the group that some questions we ask of a text were likely to be more important than others. Child 3 initially thought the answer could be found in the book, but through her interaction with Child 4, she realized the answer was not that straightforward, and reconsidered her position. The link Child 3 made to those with 'power' was a reasoned inference that Child 2 picked up on when he identified this as 'the council'. This also showed that Child 2 had been listening closely to the dialogue as it developed.

The pupils had started to develop a response to one of the major themes of the book (whose idea of importance counts?), but they passed over it quickly. The teacher made a mental note to come back to this later with a view to deepening the response.

Lesson 2

Reviewing the pupils' questions

In this lesson, the pupils reread the text in order to review their questions. The teacher felt that, through revisiting the text, the pupils were more likely to read it with greater care – and thus reach deeper layers of meaning – because they now had some relevant questions that they wanted to address.

The teacher then established some ground rules for peer-led, free-flowing discussion: they included an insistence that everyone stayed on the same page and worked through the text sequentially, rather than dipping into random pages. The teacher reminded them to pay attention to the words and the pictures, her reason being that an understanding of the text builds as the narrative develops. The pace was dictated by the group, so they paused for a lengthy discussion on some pages but moved more quickly through others.

The pupils began to engage with deeper layers of meaning as they attempted to answer their questions. Two examples of this are presented below.

1. Making inferences on author intent

C1: I like the way 'That's something I'll never forget' [read with emphasis] is by itself. It's much stronger there on its own.

C3: It's not so noticeable, but when you do see it then it makes you stop and think.

(They turn to the next page)

C1: I think these crosses look as though they have been washed out to sea.

C6: And have you noticed this picture here? It's a reflection, but where are the soldiers? There's only the reflection. I think it's because they have been killed and this is like the ghosts of the soldiers.

C1: The memory of the soldiers.

Here the pupils engaged with such things as layout and how the pictures communicate meaning. They built on each other's ideas, and the collaborative shaping of thinking was evident. When Child 6 said, 'like the ghosts of the soldiers', Child 1 took it one step further by relating this idea back to one of the major themes of the book: 'the memory of soldiers'. There were also misconceptions: Child 1, for example, thought the crosses looked as though they were out to sea, but the picture showed the mounds and hollows of no man's land, with the reflection of soldiers in the water that had accumulated in one of the shell craters. However, the poetic idea of the feeling that the image evokes is an effective one. Again, the teacher made a note to go back and look at this picture later.

2. Setting

C3: Have you seen this coin up here? It says 'one pound'. Actually it says 'Australia'. I REALLY think it's set in Australia now.

The children became more certain that the setting was in Australia, and so were finding answers to their own questions.

In revisiting the text, the pupils started to notice details that they had missed on the first reading. The page-by-page looking and discussion facilitated this as they picked up on relevant detail that connected with their questions. Completing the question quadrant at the outset had put the questions in the forefront of the children's minds as they read.

At the end of the lesson the teacher asked the group to review their question quadrant and decide whether there were any questions that they felt had been answered satisfactorily. These were crossed through. She also suggested that further questions might have occurred to them as they were discussing the book. Child 3 said that she had a further question: she wanted to know if Grandpa and Grandma knew each other when they were children. Were they childhood sweethearts who grew up together? This question was written on the grid in a contrasting colour. By marking the quadrant in this way, it was possible to see at a glance how the pupils' thinking was developing. The annotations showed what they were able to achieve on their own and where they would benefit from some extra support and guidance. The quadrant was therefore a useful piece of evidence that the teacher could use to plan the subsequent guided reading lesson.

Lesson 3

Guided reading with the teacher

After reviewing the question quadrant that the pupils had completed, the teacher decided to focus on one of the questions: Which is the most fitting for a war memorial: a tree or a statue?

She produced a set of pairs of cards, one with the word 'TREE' and the other with the word 'STATUE'. Each pupil was given a pair of cards:

TREE	STATUE

Later in the lesson, the pupils would be asked to choose which they thought was the more fitting memorial, and to hold up the relevant card. They would then be asked to justify their position.

However, to open up the dialogue, the teacher invited the children to discuss the nature and purpose of memorials. The pupils also noted a number of other things, such as medals and photographs, that helped the characters in the book to remember the war. The teacher then moved the discussion to consider the central question.

Teacher (T): Child 4 mentioned that when the soldiers came back from the war there was a lot of joy … I wonder which of the memorials, the tree or the statue, best represents that feeling?

C3: To some people that will probably be the tree because it was planted the day they came back from the war, but the Unknown Soldier might signify the joy and laughter of coming back to other people. Personally I think the tree is more joyful because it's a living thing. The monument is just a piece of brick and it's not alive. And also it shows a soldier which I think reminds them of the fighting and the war and the friends that they have lost.

C1:	Child 3's just given me an idea about the tree being a happy thing, and the soldier reminding them about a bad thing and that lots of people died.
C4:	But loads of soldiers died in World War I, and some of them weren't found so the Unknown Soldier represents those soldiers, so it's really important to have that memorial.
C3:	I disagree with that. I think it's making them remember their brother died, their son died, their father died, and reminds them of the bad things that happened.
C4:	Yes, but some of the soldiers wouldn't have been found. Being remembered is really important for them otherwise it's like they never existed. It's like a shared grave or tombstone for all of those soldiers who weren't recorded.
C3:	Yes, but it doesn't make any difference if they don't know who they were.
C4:	Well, they do know who they were because they didn't come back from the war. They just didn't find the bodies.

Here the pupils took quite distinct positions and were willing to justify their positions quite passionately.

At this point teacher then distributed the 'STATUE' and 'TREE' cards, one pair to each pupil. She asked them to decide which they thought would be the most fitting memorial at the end of a war. She asked them to select the card but not to show anyone else on the table. On the count of three everyone put their card face up on the table. Unsurprisingly there was a difference of opinion, which the teacher then sought to explore.

T:	That's interesting, there's a difference of opinion. Let's start with Child 2.
C2:	I think the tree because it was the soldiers themselves who chose the tree, the statue was just put there by the council because they thought it was a good idea. I was a bit in two minds because in some way the statue does represent the war more obviously. I think they feel that the tree is more part of them than the Unknown Soldier.
C1:	I chose the statue because you can write words on it and the names of the soldiers and it lasts for a very long time. It can also represent war better than anything else.
C3:	I chose the tree. It's more about life than death. I think the people who come back want to think about life. The tree is alive.

C2: The tree. They come back to the tree when they are happy. The tree lived on and they lived on.

C4: I think the statue. Child 3 said it doesn't really matter that some soldiers weren't remembered, but if you've ever been to see a memorial there are so many names written on the walls. I think you need somewhere for all the soldiers who weren't recorded but died.

The teacher drew the lesson to a close by asking the children to think of all the arguments that had been proposed in the lesson, to think about what others had said, and to say whether anyone had a compelling argument that might make them change their mind. Finally she asked the pupils to revisit the question quadrant, and to strike through any questions that they felt they had answered. She reminded them that if any new questions had emerged, they should write them on the quadrant using a different colour.

Teacher's reflections

The teacher felt that this was a very satisfying sequence of lessons, which achieved the primary aims. The pupils took more time to reflect during reading, instead of rushing from one thick novel to the next; they were learning how to question a text to reach deeper layers of meaning. In the reflective discussion afterwards the children expressed a new appreciation of the text. Some of them had been sceptical when they were given the book to read at home, and had been surprised at how much they had been able to gain from the rereading and the discussion. The teacher was particularly pleased that Child 2, who had expressed a dislike of the book at the beginning, said that she had found there was more to it, and that the discussion with the other pupils had helped her to see things that she had not initially noticed.

Conclusion

The process was designed to start with an open exploration of text; this had allowed the pupils to develop their ideas. Sometimes small changes in the way we teach can make big differences. For instance, not revealing our initial thoughts or commenting too quickly on pupils' ideas can develop an ethos of trust (not being judged too quickly); it can also give equal value to each participant in the group, which in turn makes them more forthcoming when expressing their ideas. Using the decision-making activity, where everyone turns a card at the same time, also allows pupils to develop a commitment to their own ideas without deferring to the most dominant view. The teacher can then guide the discussion by picking up the most fruitful lines of enquiry. The use of the graphic organizer (question quadrant) was a focal point for recording the pupils' ideas in this sequence of lessons, and served as a record of the work over the period of a week.

Reference

Crew, G. and Tan, S. (1999) *Memorial*. Lothian Books; Sydney, NSW: Hachette (ISBN 978-0-73-440545-6).

'For Forest' by Grace Nichols

Context

This sequence of three lessons was taught to a class of 32 children (aged 10–11) in a large, high-performing, four-form-entry junior school in south Essex. The pupils are largely white British, and are organized into sets for English; the set featured here is the lowest-attaining group.

The school has been reviewing its reading provision. Lesson planning used to be very tightly structured and units of work were designed to meet writing outcomes; the development of reading comprehension was not considered as a goal in itself. The school is now aiming to rectify this, with teachers developing a planning format that allows time for an open exploration of a text with a view to identifying which aspects to develop through explicit teaching. The class has a one-hour reading lesson four times a week. A mix of whole-class and group teaching is used, depending on the objectives of the lesson.

Planning

Prior to this lesson, the class teacher had been looking at ways of incorporating shorter texts into reading lessons so that the pupils could experience a complete text in one lesson. There had been a focus on picture-book fiction, but poetry had not hitherto been used. The teacher wanted to find a text that was connected with learning in other curriculum areas. As the class was working on a topic about rainforests, she searched various anthologies for a suitable poem on this topic. The first poem she selected was rejected after consulting her year group colleagues, who thought that it was too literal and did not afford the pupils any opportunity to work towards deeper understanding. Eventually, a poem by Grace Nichols, 'For Forest', was selected.

A sequence of three lessons was planned in collaboration with one of the authors of this book. As this was the first time that the pupils had encountered poetry in a reading lesson, there was an exploratory element to the work. The plan was to start with a 'think-aloud' strategy to gauge how the pupils were making meaning from the text, and to build on this in subsequent lessons. The teaching was spread over three lessons: the first lesson focused on context-building before the class read the poem; in the second lesson, the poem was introduced and the pupils were helped to understand any literary features they found difficult; and in the third lesson, the children revisited the poem and discussed it in groups to develop a deeper understanding. Only the first two lessons are described here. Each lesson lasted one hour.

Text selection

The selected text, 'For Forest,' is a short poem by the Guyanese-born poet Grace Nichols. Inspired by the author's childhood memories of the rainforest, it appeals to the reader to care for this precious, ancient, natural environment.

The Forest of the poem is personified as a woman who dreams, listens, and watches but does not speak. Forest is capitalized throughout the poem. This literary concept might be difficult for this group of readers as none of the texts they have read so far has used this device.

The non-standard constructions in Guyanese Creole might also be unfamiliar, and consequently a barrier to understanding for this largely mono-cultural group.

The repetition of phrases and key words is a poetic feature of Guyanese Creole, and adjectives are often repeated for emphasis.

The vocabulary is largely familiar, although 'teeming' may not be known to the group, 'roosting' may be unfamiliar in this context, and the poetic construction 'fast-eye' may prove confusing. Furthermore, the idiom 'let your hair down' may not be familiar, so the multiple meanings triggered for a more experienced reader may not be accessible to some children. Lastly, pupils may not have heard of El Dorado, or else they may associate it with references in popular culture, holiday destinations and the like.

The text

For Forest

Forest could keep secrets
Forest could keep secrets

Forest tune in every day
to watersound and birdsound
Forest letting hair down
to the teeming creeping of her forest-ground

But Forest don't broadcast her business
no Forest cover her business down
from sky and fast-eye sun
and when night come
and darkness wrap her like a gown
Forest is a bad dream woman

Forest dreaming about mountain
and when earth was young
Forest dreaming of the caress of gold
Forest roosting with mysterious Eldorado

and when howler monkey
wake her up with howl
Forest just stretch and stir
to a new day of sound

but coming back to secrets
Forest could keep secrets
Forest could keep secrets

And we must keep Forest.

Grace Nichols

Text potential

Exploring what the text offers

Vocabulary

Related words – words to do with sound: 'tune in', 'broadcast', 'watersound', 'birdsound', 'howl'.

Potential unfamiliar vocabulary: 'teeming', 'gown', 'caress'.

Language features

Non-standard English:

- 'darkness wrap her like a gown' (non-standard subject/verb agreement)
- 'howler monkey wake her up' (non-standard subject/verb agreement)
- 'letting hair down' (no pronoun).

Register: conversational/informal: 'but coming back to secrets'.

Coherence

Themes

Potential themes:

- care for the world's resources
- guardianship
- exploration and virgin territory.

Mapping text potential
'For Forest' by Grace Nichols

Subject

A poem about the ancient forest that has been around long before human beings inhabited the planet. It evokes a sense of guardianship. We are charged to take care of the forest as it has cared for the creatures that live below its canopy.

Grammar; Syntax

Non-standard constructions may be unfamiliar to the children.

Historical, social, and cultural context

The poet Grace Nichols was born in Guyana. This poem was inspired by her memories of the rainforest.

Making links to background knowledge

Contextualizing the poem may help children's understanding as some of the content may be unfamiliar.

Rainforests – location Guyana.

El Dorado – the mythical land that Raleigh searched for in Guyana.

Narrative features

Visual features

Literary features

Personification – rainforest as woman. This may be a difficult concept for this group:

- 'letting her hair down'
- 'darkness wrap her like a gown'
- 'dreaming about mountain'.

Title 'For Forest'.

Repetition of lines and words: 'Forest', 'secret', 'keep'.

'Fast-eye': literary construction, impatient?

Text type, purpose, and intended readership

A poem that awakens the reader to the beauty and longevity of the rainforest but holds within it the unstated threat of change. Very simply, the poet urges 'And we must keep Forest'.

Lesson planning and organization

Resources:

- copies of the poem for each pupil
- the text already prepared for the whiteboard and animated to reveal the poem line by line
- internet connection
- CD of Grace Nichols reading her own poetry, available from the Poetry Archive (www.poetryarchive.org/)
- short film about the rainforest
- BBC short video of Grace Nichols reading 'For Forest' (www.bbc.co.uk/education/clips/zmxrkqt)
- CLPE film of Grace Nichols reading 'For Forest', accompanied by John Agard (vimeo.com/34548833).

All of the lessons are whole-class lessons.

Lesson 1

Accessing and deepening contextual knowledge related to the poem

Given the pupils' lack of familiarity with Guyanese Creole, the teacher felt it would be beneficial for the children to listen to Grace Nichols reading some of her poetry before they encountered the poem 'For Forest'. The children listened to some of the more approachable poems from the Poetry Archive CD and talked about how listening to the poet helped to bring the poems to life. They discussed the way the poet sounded, and related this to their knowledge of Caribbean accents and dialects from television programmes.

As part of the Humanities scheme of work, an introductory mind map of 'Tropical Rainforest' was created. Pupils were asked to list all the things they associated with the rainforest and then group things together. One child had visited the Australian rainforest and was invited to give a short presentation to describe the experience. Some of the children had visited Kew Gardens and other botanical gardens with tropical greenhouses and were invited to recount their experiences. The teacher helped the group locate the rainforest regions on a globe and looked up some facts about the location of the rainforest; these were added to the mind map. The class then viewed a short film about the Guyana rainforest and Walter Raleigh's search for El Dorado.

Lesson 2

Introducing the poem – encouraging visualization

The pupils were first invited to listen to the poem. It was suggested that they might like to close their eyes and think about the images that were forming in their heads. This is an example of visualization as noted in Chapter 3, p. 41. In this instance the children were simply asked to create a mental picture without going a stage further and creating a physical visual representation, such as a picture or a map. After the first reading, they were given just one minute to write down anything that the poem had made them think or feel. The teacher then gathered the ideas together and listed them on the whiteboard without comment. In order to maintain interest, this was pacey and not laboured, as the teacher was focusing mainly on assessing how the children were responding to the poem. Most suggestions were about animals that they thought lived in the rainforest and the noises associated with those animals. The list was read aloud, again without comment.

Second reading – developing inference-making through reference to life experience

The children listened to the poem a second time, but on this occasion they also watched the accompanying video, which showed images of the rainforest. When the video had finished, the teacher posed the following question:

> **Teacher (T):** There's one line in this poem that is repeated four times, so it must be important to the poet: 'Forest could keep secrets'. What are the secrets that Forest keeps?

Boy (B) 1:	The things in the forest.
T:	Go on …
B1:	Like the monkeys.
T:	Anything else?
B1:	And the birds and that.
T:	And why do you think Forest would want to keep those things secret?
Girl (G) 2:	Perhaps it's to keep them safe.
T:	I wonder if anyone in this room has ever kept something secret because they wanted to keep it safe?
G3:	I've got a special box in my cupboard where I put all the things that I don't want my little sister to take because she breaks everything. She's SOOO annoying.
B2:	Sometimes I put a big sign on my bedroom door. 'Keep Out.'
T:	Last term do you remember we were reading Anne Frank's diary for our World War II topic? The annexe Anne lived in was kept secret so that her family would be safe. So yes, we do sometimes keep secrets to keep things safe.

Making inferences is critical to understanding poetry. This is because by their nature poems leave much unstated – there are 'gaps' that need to be filled if a deeper layer of meaning is to be achieved. With some poems it is more difficult to find 'clues' in the text itself because there are few words. In this instance, the teacher encourages the children to make links to their previous experience. Here, Girl 2 links the ideas of secrecy and safety, which allows Girl 3 to provide the example of her 'special box' as something that demonstrates this. The teacher then shows the children how making text-to-text links can also help to fill 'gaps' in understanding, when she refers to their previous work on Anne Frank. The children did not immediately make this text-to-text link so the teacher demonstrates how this can be achieved.

Clarifying word meanings through dialogue

After this short discussion about the reasons why people keep secrets, the teacher asked the pupils if there were any words that needed clarification. They offered 'gown', and there was a brief exchange of ideas around words that have the same root ('ball gown', 'dressing gown'); these were then related back to the image: 'darkness wrap her like a gown'.

G5:	What does 'caress' mean?
T:	Has anyone heard that word before?
GI:	I think it's when you kiss someone.

T: Those words do often go together: 'kiss' and 'caress'. To caress usually means to touch or to stroke something or someone in an affectionate way. So I wonder if we can work out what it means in the poem: 'Forest dreaming of the caress of gold'.

G2: Gold is stroking Forest?

B2: I don't get that. I mean gold can't really do that …

G1: It doesn't make sense.

In this section of dialogue we see children trying to make sense of individual words by sharing their thoughts. It is worth noting that this brief interaction between Girl 2, Boy 2, and Girl 1 did not require the teacher's involvement. The children are responding to each other directly and building on each other's ideas to come to a conclusion. They are working dialogically.

T: Has anyone ever heard the expression 'The sun caressed his skin …'? I don't think the sun can actually stroke your skin, so what could this mean?

G2: It's that you can feel the sun?

T: Mmm … [invites the pupil to carry on]

G2: I mean you can feel the sun on your skin like it's stroking you.

T: Would that make sense in the poem?

G2: I think so … I'm not sure.

T: Can anyone else help explain that line?

G2: B3.

B3: Forest is dreaming that she's covered in gold? [Rising intonation as the pupil expresses uncertainty.]

T: I think there's some information that might help you. Yesterday we looked at a film that explained how Walter Raleigh explored Guyana looking for the legendary land of El Dorado. One of the reasons that he went on that quest was because he had heard stories about the Golden King who covered himself from head to foot in gold dust. El Dorado means 'the Golden One' in Spanish. And we learnt yesterday that one of the places that he searched for in the land of El Dorado was Guyana, and this poem is written by Grace Nichols – who was born in Guyana.

B3: Perhaps it's one of the secrets that Forest is keeping. She's not letting anyone know where the gold is.

T: I wonder why she would want to keep that secret …

B3: Everyone would want it.

B4: Everyone would want it and they would steal her gold.

T:	There's another word in the next line that I just want to check that you understand: 'roosting'. What does that mean?
G6:	It's what chickens do.
T:	When?
G6:	At night, they go to sleep.
T:	Yes, they settle down and go to sleep.

The teacher then asked the children to reread the lines, 'Forest dreaming of the caress of gold/ Forest roosting with mysterious Eldorado' and share their interpretations. Through this discussion, the teacher was able to help pupils understand a passage that they had initially found difficult: (i) by clarifying the meaning of the words; (ii) by prompting them to think about their own experiences or occasions when they might actually have heard the words themselves; (iii) by providing additional information; and (iv) by relating their understanding back to bigger units of meaning in the poem.

Further clarification to deepen understanding

The teacher moved the lesson on:

T:	Is there anything that you found strange, unusual, or puzzling about this poem?
B3:	Is Forest a girl because it's got a capital letter and it says she's a woman?
T:	What do you think?
G1:	Yes, Forest is a girl.

There was general agreement that Forest was a real girl. When asked to explain why they thought that, pupils referred to her 'hair' and her 'gown'. They took this as evidence that the poem was about a real girl. The concept of personification is central to the poem, and the teacher realized that the children were having problems in seeing this in any way other than a literal interpretation. She decided to move away from the poem and did a quick internet search to find some images from Disney films.

She showed pictures from the 'Be Our Guest' scene in *Beauty and the Beast* and the more recent animation *Cars*. She asked the pupils if they had seen any of the films from which the pictures were taken, and then asked whether the characters were people. The pupils dismissed this emphatically.

B7:	That's a clock and a candlestick?
T:	Is it? It's got eyes and arms and it can sing and dance. I don't know any candlesticks that can sing and dance.
B7:	Yes, but they can in cartoons.
G1:	Yeah … they're like people but they are not people. The people are Beauty and that …

T:	Are there any other films where you have characters like people but they are not people?
G9:	Like the flying carpet in *Aladdin*.
T:	What's the carpet like in that film?
G9:	He's sort of shy because he's hiding, and then he makes friends with Aladdin.
T:	I notice that you used the pronoun 'he' to describe the carpet. But carpets aren't really 'he's or 'she's are they? It's just how they have been portrayed in the Disney film, as though they are people. Like Girl 1 said, 'they're like people but they are not people'. I wonder why they would make the film like that …
G9:	You can feel sorry for them. Like when the carpet is shy, you can feel sorry for him and you know what it feels like …
B1:	Sometimes they make you laugh. They make you laugh in *Beauty and the Beast*.

This was followed by discussion about the different character traits given to the objects in the images.

Revisiting the poem

As the lesson drew to a close, the teacher read the poem aloud and asked the pupils to consider whether the discussion had made them think differently about the poem. She told them that they would be revisiting the poem in the next lesson.

Teacher's reflections

This poem was quite challenging for the pupils on a number of levels. The choice of a challenging text enabled the children to reach for ideas that would not have been available to them had the teacher opted for a more straightforward poem about the rainforest. Even though the pupils struggled initially with the abstract concept of personification, when they began to relate it in a concrete way to something within their experience, this provided some 'penny drop' moments that were really exciting to witness. The children's understanding was still not secure by the end of the lesson, and they will need to return to the poem, and also look at other poems that use the same device in order to consolidate this new understanding. In particular, it would be helpful to ask them to think more about why the poet might have chosen to write the poem in this way, just as the Disney studios chose to give inanimate objects personalities in their films.

Conclusion

Poor choices in the selection of texts, especially if they are selected solely on the basis of cross-curricular connections, can limit the opportunities to stretch the pupils' thinking. The quality and potential of the text are paramount. Where possible, while it makes sense to have a text that supports learning in other areas of the curriculum, the quality of the text must not be sacrificed just so it can be used for 'curriculum spring-boarding'.

The compressed and allusive qualities of poetry allow a poem to be interpreted in many different ways, and the pupils' responses need not be limited to a received interpretation. Providing opportunities for pupils to voice their misunderstandings and to seek clarification is an important part of learning to monitor their own understanding. This needs to be supported and encouraged by the teacher

Reference

Nichols, Grace (1996) 'For Forest'. In Agard, John, and Nichols, Grace, *A Caribbean Dozen: Poems from Caribbean poets.* London: Walker Books (ISBN 978-0-074455-201-0).

Part 4

Developing guided reading through the school

Chapter 9: Building a reading school: opportunities for professional development

Chapter 10: Planning for provision across a year group

Building a reading school: opportunities for professional development

Introduction

This chapter is designed to be used to support professional development. It outlines six staff meetings of about 1¼ hours each, focused on developing reading comprehension through guided reading. These sessions are offered as a model that can be adapted to suit each school's circumstances. A school that is focused on improving reading practices will need to develop a sustained programme of professional development over time because teachers need ample opportunities to try out new approaches and embed them in their practice.

The first staff meeting focuses on the components of a comprehensive reading curriculum and the role of guided reading within that overall context.

The second meeting outlines a structure that can be used to audit the current reading resources available to support all areas within the reading curriculum. Taking stock of all the resources available in individual classrooms, as well as in the school library and hidden away in cupboards, can be illuminating. Getting a handle on the breadth and depth of reading material available in school as well as the gaps and what needs to be replaced, then organizing it for ease of access, is a good place to begin.

The third meeting focuses on planning: selecting texts with 'text potential', planning questions to support the development of comprehension through a focus on inference, with a range of planning structures, and finally some examples of productive follow-up activities to the guided lesson to embed learning.

The fourth and fifth meetings examine the effective talk that lies at the heart of good teaching and learning and shows how teachers can evaluate the success of the learning conversations that take place in guided reading lessons.

The sixth staff meeting focuses on how evidence collected during guided reading and follow-up activities can be used to support assessment.

It is recommended that one member of staff (probably the English subject leader) prepares and organizes as well as directs these INSET sessions. All the resources for these sessions can be found on the website: www.guidingreaders.com/PDresources.

Aims of professional development sessions

For participants to:

- discuss the components of a comprehensive approach to the reading curriculum (meeting 1)
- consider the place and role of guided reading within the reading curriculum (meeting 1)
- audit and discuss the range of texts that could form the basis of guided reading lessons (meeting 2)
- plan at least one guided reading lesson for a specific group of pupils in their class (meeting 3)
- carry out and evaluate the guided reading lessons planned (meeting 4)
- contribute to an action plan for the school for the further development of guided reading for pupils aged 7–12 (meeting 4)
- understand how the talk that takes place within a guided reading lesson is crucial in promoting learning and deepening pupils' responses (meeting 4)
- reflect on the talk that teachers and pupils use in a guided reading lesson through recording, transcribing, and analysing it (meeting 5)
- collect evidence to support assessment (meeting 6).

OUTLINE OF STAFF MEETING 1: The reading curriculum

Before the session

Collect together the following resources:

- copies of the 2014 National Curriculum Programmes of Study for Reading for Key Stage 2 (or any comparable local documents)
- enough copies of Handout 1: Reading opportunities, for all staff attending the training session (available on www.guidingreaders.com/PDresources).
- copy of this book.

Introduction

- Outline the aims of the INSET session (and whole programme, if appropriate). For participants to:
    - discuss the components of a comprehensive approach to the reading curriculum
    - consider the place and role of guided reading within the reading curriculum.
- Display or distribute the 2014 Programmes of Study for Reading (or local equivalent document) and Handout 1: Reading opportunities.

Activity 1

- Have participants, in pairs or year groups, use Handout 1 to brainstorm the opportunities they currently provide for the explicit teaching and practising of reading. They should also consider the different purposes that these opportunities provide in helping pupils develop as readers (*5–10 minutes*).
- Collate the current opportunities on a flipchart or IWB (interactive white board) under the two headings. Under 'Teaching reading', opportunities will generally include:
  - whole-class interactive reading
  - guided/small group reading.
- Ensure that participants understand the teacher's role in guiding reading, whether in whole class or small group contexts. Through discussion, ensure that the following points are covered to contrast the different situations:
  - *in the whole class setting,*
    - pupils sit so that they can all see the text clearly (this could either be reading from an IWB or from individual copies of the text);
    - the class will include pupils with a range of different levels of attainment working together, with the guidance of the teacher;
    - texts chosen are usually pitched at a level of difficulty just above the average attainment of the class.
  - *in guided and group reading lessons,* which typically involve the teacher working with small groups of pupils (usually 4–6) who have similar learning needs in reading,
    - the teaching is explicitly aimed at objectives that will move the pupils in that group towards independence (although if objectives are too narrowly defined this can be a hindrance rather than a help);
    - guided reading is a powerful teaching strategy that is much more closely targeted on the needs of specific groups of pupils.

Both strategies, whether with the whole class or with guided reading groups, are about explicit teaching.

  - Participants might also mention reading to children, which implicitly shows children what is involved in reading a wide range of texts and what more experienced readers do. It also allows them to hear the 'tune' of a text. This implicit awareness of rhythm, pitch and tone enables readers to develop an internal voice when they read quietly to themselves.
  - As children become increasingly proficient with their reading it is important that teachers continue to read increasingly challenging texts aloud. It is therefore important to have a clear understanding of the quality, challenge and range of books that are selected to be read aloud to children across a year and across their primary school years.
- Collate the opportunities for 'practising reading' that teachers organize for their pupils. These are likely to include many of the following:
  - partnered reading, where pupils read aloud to a peer and may then discuss what has been read

- group reading, where small groups read the same text, possibly as a preparation for guided work with the teacher, but always with the clear aim of thinking about the text
- paired reading, with an older child/adult; this would include 'hearing children read'
- reading at home, including home/school reading policies/programmes
- independent individual reading in class, including silent reading
- reading in other curriculum areas
- literature circles
- reading clubs
- library visits.

All of these are opportunities for pupils to practise and apply, in much more independent contexts, what has been taught or demonstrated to them. Usually pupils read materials that do not require them to be assisted by a more competent peer or adult, and there is a variety of texts, some chosen by the pupils themselves and some recommended by the teacher.

Activity 2

- Ask participants to look through the programmes of study and the areas of reading that should be covered within the reading curriculum planned by the school, and consider how well these areas are included in their planning.
- Outline the basic components of a reading curriculum, drawing on the examples generated by staff for illustration. A reading curriculum should include:
  - reading *with* – explicit teaching, using appropriate strategies as in guided reading
  - reading *to* – where teachers/more experienced readers read aloud good-quality texts to pupils and thus model the why and how of reading
  - reading *by* – where pupils have opportunities to practise and apply what they have learnt in more independent contexts.
- Have participants consider whether the current approach to reading ensures that these components are present, and if action points need to be noted.
- Conclude session by summarizing the above and informing staff that in the next session they will focus in much more depth on the strategy of guided reading, how it can be utilized to teach comprehension strategies, and how this book – *Guiding Readers: Layers of meaning* – can be a most helpful resource upon which to draw.

Handout 1: Reading opportunities

What opportunities do you plan or organize in your class for TEACHING and PRACTISING reading? What is the purpose of these different reading opportunities?

THE TEACHING OF READING	THE PRACTISING OF READING

OUTLINE OF STAFF MEETING 2: Text audit

This professional development session can be appended to session 1 or carried out as a separate session.

Before the session

1. Collect the summary of the main points arising from session 1.
2. Plan to carry out the staff meeting in the place where the majority of reading resources are kept (e.g. the school library or reading resource room).
3. Ensure teachers have access to the book lists (available online at www.guidingreaders.com) and have read the rationale for text selection contained in this book in Chapter 10, pp. 212–17.

Audit of reading resources

1. Outline the aims of the INSET session. For participants to:
   - audit and discuss the range of texts that could form the basis of guided reading lessons.
2. Summarize the three main areas of a reading curriculum as agreed in the last session: reading *with*, reading *to*, and reading *by*.
3. Ask participants to browse through and consider the reading resources available in the school library, their class library, and the reading resources room. Are there suitable resources for teaching reading in large and small groups? Participants should consider whether current resources include sufficient shorter texts, including picture books, poetry, short stories, non-fiction, and digital texts. If there are gaps for the year groups they teach, what needs to happen?
4. Have participants select some suitable texts for whole-class work, reading aloud, group guided lessons, and independent reading that they think would work or which have worked with different year groups.

Plenary

1. Participants share selected texts and explain why they have chosen them.
2. Participants discuss what the audit of texts has revealed and plan action to address any issues.

Before the session

1. Collect together the following resources:
   - copies of the 2014 National Curriculum Programmes of Study for Reading for Key Stage 2 (or local equivalent document)
   - copies of the text potential diagram (see p. 32)
   - examples of some of the texts mentioned in this book
   - copies of one or two case studies from Chapter 6, 7, or 8.
2. Ask participants to bring with them a text they would use for guided reading for a group in their class. This will be used as the basis for a planning activity. It would be useful for staff to bring the reading records for this group, showing the pupils' achievements in detail.

(The English subject leader may wish to supplement these with further examples of quality texts that the school has – see the lists of texts on the website www.guidingreaders.com.)

Introduction

- Outline the aims of this session. For participants to:
  - explore the potential of specific texts for teaching and learning
  - plan at least one guided reading lesson for a specific group of pupils in their class.

Activity 1

Areas for teaching: what does the text offer?

- Ask participants to consider NC Programmes of Study for Reading, and analyse the following: what are the main areas for development and teaching outlined in this document?
- Distribute copies of the text potential diagram (see page 32, also available at www.guidingreaders.com/PDresources). The facilitator explains the diagram. It illustrates schematically what needs to be taken into account when planning how to teach comprehension strategies, using a particular text.

Knowing what the text offers

On the diagram is a summary of the features that texts may contain, which potentially lend themselves to exploration for reading development, particularly comprehension. Teachers should consider every text, using this diagram to decide which areas of comprehension of the text would be most suitable for exploring with specific groups of pupils.

Teachers may quite legitimately decide to reject the book under consideration if they judge that it doesn't have sufficient qualities to make it worth selecting or, conversely, if its content is too challenging.

Choosing what to teach

Using the diagram, the teacher can decide on the specific areas on which to focus when teaching, taking into account the pupils' needs, the text, and the National Curriculum requirements with regard to comprehension. For example, Case study 10, *Memorial*, can be linked to the National Curriculum requirement to study the Second World War in Year 5.

Another text might have a range of vocabulary well worth analysing, so the teacher would then plan to teach or reinforce word-meaning strategies such as reading on and looking for clues in the surrounding sentence(s), finding related words with the same base morphemes, or drawing on knowledge of other texts.

The case studies included in the book show how teachers have decided on the most appropriate aspects of the text on which to focus.

* Ask participants to look at a text they will be using for guided reading and, using the diagram, discuss with a partner its text potential and the aspects of teaching for which it would be most suitable.

Activity 2

Planning: comprehension and inference-making

Explain that research suggests that the following strategies are powerful for developing comprehension and inference-making (see Chapter 3, p. 36):

* predicting
* questioning
* summarizing
* thinking aloud
* visualization (including graphic representation)
* seeking clarification, including attention to vocabulary.

All of the above strategies can be incorporated into a reading lesson. The presenter draws attention to the planning sheet: *The Lost Thing Session 2*. This is an example where a teacher has integrated all of the above strategies (except visualization) into a guided reading lesson. (These strategies are explained in Chapter 3, p. 36.) It is worth noting here that the teacher does not have to focus on all of the strategies in every session but can be selective.

Planning: questioning

A key strategy is questioning (see p. 38). Indeed the authors would argue that this is likely to be the most crucial strategy for developing inference-making.

As there are three levels of comprehension:

* literal
* inference
* evaluative/responsive

there are three types of question:

- literal – 'looking questions'
- inference/deduction – 'clue questions'
- evaluative/opinion – 'thinking questions'.

Example:

'Little Miss Muffet'

Little Miss Muffet

Sat on her tuffet,

Eating her curds and whey,

There came a big spider

Who sat down beside her,

And frightened Miss Muffet away.

- What frightened Miss Muffet? (*'looking'*)
- What would Miss Muffet do if she saw a minibeast running up her bedroom wall? (*'clue'*)
- Why do you think little children like this rhyme? *OR* 'Should we really be scared of spiders?' (*'thinking'*)

Planning: discussion

Participants consider the text they have chosen and devise three questions as above. Participants work in pairs to discuss and complete questions. (Further examples of these question-types can be seen in Case study 1: Advertisements; Case study 2: *The Lost Thing*; and Case study 5: Chocolate.)

Plenary

Ask participants to outline their teaching objectives and texts to another pair/whole staff.

After the session

Have teachers carry out planned lessons in class and evaluate them.

OUTLINE OF STAFF MEETING 4: Effective learning conversations and follow-up to Staff Meeting 3

Before the session

1. Remind staff to bring their questions and evaluations of the guided reading lesson that they planned at the last session.
2. Collect the following resources:
   - flipchart/large sheet of paper
   - flipchart pens
   - Handout 2: Transcript: 'At the Zoo' conversation (p. 207), for presentation on screen (also available at www.guidingreaders.com/PDresources).

Introduction

- Outline the aims of this session. For participants to:
  - evaluate the guided reading lessons planned in session 3
  - contribute to an action plan for the school for the further development of guided reading for pupils aged 7–12
  - understand how the talk that takes place within a guided reading lesson is crucial in promoting learning and deepening pupils' responses.
- Explain that this staff meeting will be in two parts: first, feedback from the between-session activity, then a focus on effective talk in guided reading sessions.

Activity 1

- Remind participants about the previous meeting. Explain that they are to get together now with two or three other members of staff to outline briefly what their experiences were when they used the texts and any questions they had planned. They should also note down key issues to be addressed.

Feedback discussions/plenary

Ask groups to provide feedback on key issues, which are collated on the flipchart or screen under suitable headings.

Effective interaction in guided reading sessions

- Draw out the key issues identified (or, if necessary, add to them) that demonstrate how the talk in guided reading lessons is crucial if learning is to take place. The second part of this staff meeting will focus on the practicalities of building effective learning conversations including:
  - the questions we ask that initiate the talk
  - the responses we make to the pupils' answers that build on and challenge their thinking.

The main point: it is essential that pupils move beyond literal comprehension, and develop the ability to infer, justify, and evaluate.

Therefore the questions we ask must focus on going beyond the literal and help to develop these abilities. However, the job is not over once the initial question is asked. The conversation/discussion that the teacher orchestrates *as a result of the initial question* is as important, if not more so, in moving the pupils' thinking on.

- Display Handout 2: Transcript: 'At the Zoo' conversation, and **uncover *only* the teacher's initial question**. Explain that the conversation they are about to look at is a good example of effective teaching talk in a guided reading lesson and that their task is to practise responding to what the pupil says in order to extend the child's understanding.
- Outline the context of the conversation:

<u>Before this session</u>, 7-year-old pupils had been asked to prepare by reading two short stories from the anthology *The Upside-Down Mice and Other Animal Stories,* edited by Jane Merer. The stories were: 'The Upside-Down Mice' by Roald Dahl and 'At the Zoo' by Brian Patten.

The children had also been asked to think about which of the two stories they preferred and to come up with one or two reasons to justify their choice.

The beginning of the session was devoted to a discussion about what makes one story 'better' than another, and a number of agreed criteria were written down. One of these criteria was 'easy to read'.

The dialogue below is from the end of the session, following the paired discussion within the group where the pupils had the opportunity to state and justify their preference with a partner.

Step 1

- Ask staff what kind of question is being asked here (i.e. evaluation with a reminder to justify).
- Uncover Jack's first response. Ask what they think about his response and what the teacher should say in reply.
- Uncover the response of the teacher. Is this what they expected? What do they notice about the teacher's reply?

Main points:

- She responds directly to the content of what he says rather than commenting on the quality of his answer.
- She makes a comment, then asks a further question, which encourages Jack to be more explicit and to clarify.

Step 2

- Uncover Jack's next response. Again, ask what they think about his response and what the teacher should say in reply.
- Uncover the next reply by the teacher. Again, ask if this is what they expected and what they notice about the teacher's reply.

Point out that the teacher has not yet praised Jack, by, for instance, saying 'well done' or 'excellent answer'. Discuss why this might be so, and the effect this kind of response might have. (For example: praise here would have the effect of evaluating Jack's answers rather than building on the content of what he has said; praise tends to indicate that the conversation is coming to an end and it is time to move on rather than having Jack say more to clarify his thinking; praise implies a right answer, not something to be further developed.)

Main points:

- She is building a conversation, again responding directly to what Jack says.
- There is an explicit challenge here to move Jack's thinking on. She draws attention to a contradiction.
- This is a statement, not a further question, but it still demands a reply.

Step 3

- Uncover Jack's next response. How has his understanding been moved on? What should the teacher say next?

Step 4

- Uncover the final part of this conversation.

Summary points:

- This is a conversation that has led to a change in thinking.
- It has encompassed three exchanges with the same pupil before moving on.
- Praise is not used, but feedback is implicit in the teacher's response.
- This is an example of dialogic teaching, defined as 'conversation with cognitive challenge' (Alexander, 2004) and is highly effective for teaching and learning. It should be an integral part of the talk that goes on in reading lessons, which aims to build comprehension.

Conclusion

- Ask teachers to consider whether the questions they asked in the guided reading lesson as discussed earlier gave rise to 'conversations with cognitive challenge'?
- Ask them to plan some further questions that they will use in their next guided reading lesson. (It may be useful for them to have a copy of the text they intend to use.)
- Ask teachers to make a video/audio recording of their next guided reading session and transcribe a short part of it (no more than 3–5 minutes) for discussion at the next staff meeting.

Handout 2: Transcript: 'At the Zoo' conversation

Teacher: Jack, please tell us which story you preferred, and why.

Jack: I preferred 'At the Zoo' because it was very mysterious and you didn't find out what was looking at what until the very end because when I first heard the story I thought there were some new arriving animals and the children were looking at them for a school project but at the end I found that these aliens were actually looking at humans at the zoo and the humans were the new arrivals.

Teacher: The story sounds very confusing. When did you understand that the children were in the cages?

Jack: Oh, not until the very end. In fact, the first time I read it I didn't get it at all. It took two readings and then I thought, 'Now I know what's going on!'

Teacher: But on our list of 'what makes a book worth reading' that we wrote earlier, we put 'Easy to read'. 'At the Zoo' doesn't sound like it was an easy story if you had to read it twice to understand it.

Jack: Yes, but the words were easy. The story wasn't. The story was a mystery, and I like mysteries, so that is why I like 'At the Zoo' better.

Teacher: So Jack prefers 'At the Zoo'. What about you, Karen?

OUTLINE OF STAFF MEETING 5: Reflecting

Before the session

1. Remind staff to bring the recordings and/or transcripts of a short segment of a guided reading lesson (as suggested at the end of the last meeting).
2. Collect together the following resources:
   - enough copies of Handout 3: Self-evaluation sheet: effective talk in a guided reading session (see p. 209), for each member of staff (available at www.guidingreaders.com/PDresources).

Introduction

- Outline the aims of the session. For participants to:
  - reflect on the talk that teachers and pupils use in a guided reading lesson through recording, transcribing, and analysing it (following meeting 4).
- Remind participants about the previous meeting. Explain that they are going to work in pairs to:
  - describe the context of the guided reading session
  - watch the video clip/consider the transcript they have brought along and use the questions on the handout to help structure their discussion
  - formulate one success and one issue to contribute to the plenary.

Activity 1: paired discussion

Plenary

- Have pairs feed back in turn the successes from their discussions.
- Facilitator summarizes and concludes by making the following points: in order for effective talk for teaching and learning to take place the teacher should:
  - ask genuine questions that go well beyond the recall of simple and predictable facts
  - expect pupils to provide extended answers in which they justify their ideas and responses
  - give pupils time to formulate ideas and views
  - respond to the content of what the children say, building chains of exchanges that move their thinking on, debating and telling children things rather than just asking questions
  - encourage pupils to speak directly to each other rather than always going through the teacher.

Activity 2: action planning

- Display list of issues from the last session and ask if more should be added as a result of this session's discussion.
- Have staff decide what the next steps should be in terms of action.
- Ask the English subject leader to formulate a clear action plan, building on whole-staff decisions.

HANDOUT 3: Self-evaluation: effective talk in a guided reading session

Year?

Group?

Text used?

Prompts for discussion:

- What question did you use to initiate this part of the guided reading session?

- Did the question give rise to thoughtful extended answers?

- Did you respond to the pupils' answers and build a conversation over more than one or two exchanges?

- Were your responses a mixture of questions, comments, and statements, some of which were designed to challenge the pupils' thinking?

- What will you try next, to develop talk for learning in guided reading lessons?

- What successes will you share in the plenary?

- What is the most important issue the school needs to address to develop this area?

OUTLINE OF STAFF MEETING 6: Assessment

Before the session

1. Ask staff to bring to the meeting some evidence of what the children did and said as a result of a guided reading lesson. This could include notes taken during the lesson, the recordings and/or transcripts of a short segment of a guided reading session used in professional development session 5 above, or any follow-up written or creative work by pupils.

2. Collect together the following resources:
   - enough copies of the annotated 'The Malfeasance' poem on pp. 103–04 in Case study 4 for each member of staff (available at www.guidingreaders.com/PDresources)
   - copies of the reading development continuum currently used by the school, whether that is the National Curriculum, a continuum such as 'First Steps', or the school's own version.

Introduction

- Outline the aims of the session. For participants to:
  - collect and analyse evidence to support assessment.
- Explain to participants that this session focuses on looking at evidence to make decisions about what children show they know, understand, and can do as readers, as a result of guided reading sessions. Explain that they are going to work in pairs to:
  - look at a piece of evidence based on one on the lessons in this book
  - consider evidence they have brought from their own class
  - relate the evidence to the reading development continuum currently used by the school.
- Hand out the annotated 'The Malfeasance' poem on pp. 103–04 in Case study 4:
  - describe the context of the session as set out in Case study 4 on p. 96.

Activity 1

- Arrange participants in pairs to look at the handout, and the relevant section of the reading continuum, and discuss:
  - What does this evidence show the children understand and can do?
- Encourage participants to summarize their conclusions in two sentences.

Plenary 1

- Have pairs feed back in turn their conclusions.
- Summarize conclusions and outline the next activity.

Activity 2: evidence from classes in the school

- Ask participants in pairs to take it in turns to share the evidence they have brought, referring to the relevant section of the reading continuum and discuss:
  - What does this evidence show the child/children understand and can do?
  - What evidence is useful in making judgements?
- Encourage participants to summarize their conclusions in two sentences.

Plenary 2

- Ask participants to share their conclusions and discuss how best to record the children's achievements based on the available evidence.
- Discuss what the above activity has revealed and plan action to address any issues.

Reference

Alexander, R. (2004) *Towards Dialogic Teaching: Rethinking classroom talk*. Thirsk: Dialogos.

Planning for provision across a year group

Our book lists

It will be clear from previous chapters that no simple formula using word count or sentence length can adequately assign a reading difficulty level to a text. Complexity is governed by a combination of features including familiarity with the subject, theme, plot structure, figurative language, voice, vocabulary, etc. However, a general gradient of texts will be useful to teachers who are planning guided reading. When creating our book lists, we have talked extensively about the ease and difficulty of specific texts. It is this collective wisdom that enables us to produce these lists, and we recommend it as a model that teachers should use in school. A staff development session devoted to how to organize texts in a suitable sequence for guided reading will help to encourage teachers to examine texts closely and discuss what makes reading easy and difficult, as well as raising awareness of how to identify multi-layered texts. While some texts could be suitable for different year groups, some agreement on assigning them to a year group will guard against children revisiting the same text and ensure they have exposure to a wide range of authors and texts.

Using short texts for group and guided reading

Guided reading is often made unwieldy because the texts chosen are simply too long. In some cases we have witnessed teachers trying to teach using a different long novel for each of their guided groups. Given that it is essential for teachers to know the texts they are using in guided reading, it is not surprising that this leads to dissatisfaction and an overwhelming feeling that guided reading cannot be managed. This can be avoided with thoughtful text selection.

Rich polysemic texts can be accessed by readers working at different levels of sophistication and can therefore be used with more than one group and in some cases can be used as a whole-class text, with supplementary texts chosen to provide additional challenge or support. For example, in Case study 9 (pp. 158–72), *Tadpole's Promise* was read with the whole class and some groups additionally read Oscar Wilde's 'The Nightingale and the Rose'. Reading Wilde's fairy tale aloud made it accessible to more pupils than would have been possible if they had been required to read it themselves. This integration of whole-class interactive teaching and guided reading using a limited number of texts makes it possible for teachers to have a good knowledge of the texts they are using and therefore to teach the guided reading sessions more successfully.

A teacher may have chosen a novel on the merits of some of the features described above but still not have planned how the reading will be covered across a number of lessons. One way in which we have observed teachers trying to tackle this problem involves using just extracts from the books and telling the group what happens in between, leaving lots of books unfinished in order to move on to something new because the momentum has been lost. Given that we build up our comprehension as we read a text, working with incomplete texts means that children are not given the full information on which to build deeper understandings.

There are ways in which longer novels can be more successfully taught in small groups, though it is best if they are not overly long. In order to do this, it is necessary to plan how the novel can be divided into manageable sections, with key episodes identified for the focus of teacher-directed guided reading and opportunities for independent and group reading built into a reading workshop. It may also be possible to use a text for guided work – a class novel that is read aloud – providing it can support the needs of different groups of readers.

Another solution is to use more short stories, which we find are generally underused. Not only is it more manageable for teachers to read and prepare lessons with short stories, but a good collection of short stories can potentially resource several teaching sequences.

Poetry

Our observations suggest that poetry is under-utilized in guided reading and yet poetry is richly allusive and its compressed language means that it affords capacious opportunities for interpretation and meaning-making.

A particular benefit of using poetry is that children can be introduced to texts that are not written especially for children. While it would be unusual for children to read a novel written for adults, except for the most precocious readers at the upper end of our age group, poetry does not have the same limitations. The implication of this is that the meanings subscribed within the poems are not limited to those that a writer or editor has deemed to be suitable for children and consequently reading poetry can be aspirational, as well as being readable and open to interpretation in more child-like ways. One of our case studies illustrates this (see 'The Malfeasance', pp. 96–110).

Picture books

Picture books are another great resource that can be used with readers beyond the initial stages of learning to read, as shown in a number of case studies in this book. Polysemic texts that derive meanings from the interplay of words and illustration provide a level of sophistication that could be difficult for readers to grasp purely from a prose text. Sometimes, this accessibility can be used as a means of creating a bridge into another challenging but less accessible text (see Case study 9, 'The Nightingale and the Rose', pp. 158–72). Furthermore, visual texts have their own structure and aesthetics, which allow readers to reflect on the different ways in which words and images carry meaning.

Wordless texts such as David Wiesner's *Flotsam* are no less challenging than prose texts. The pace required to read these texts is often slower than that required when reading words. Wordless picture books are useful for a number of reasons: (i) they can provide a level playing-field for readers who struggle to read words, but who can participate in groups alongside other readers, which creates important opportunities for nurturing their thinking and comprehension development; (ii) high-attaining readers have a tendency to read too quickly and therefore miss details, and the slower pace can attune them to looking for those vital clues that suggest alternative interpretations.

Non-fiction

Children are entitled to read non-fiction written by experts who are able to communicate their ideas to a young audience without patronizing them. Content should be accurate and targeted to the conceptual level of the reader.

It is useful to review how non-fiction is utilized in guided reading sessions across the school. Are real texts such as adverts, magazines, and newspapers used? (See Case study 1, Advertisements, pp. 58–71). Are readers introduced to different ways in which information can be presented through narrative, infographics, photographs, diagrams, drawn illustrations, etc. and do they explore the different ways in which the format impacts on the reader?

Non-fiction texts used in guided reading may include a comparison of information texts. An example of this can be seen in Case study 5, Chocolate (pp. 111–30). In this example the comparison of texts enables the readers to understand voice and authorial intention more easily than if the texts had been read independently.

Sequences of text

As well as identifying individual texts, it is useful to think about how one text relates to another in such a way that pupils' response and understanding can be deepened. The simplest way of doing this is to select texts that can be compared. For instance, P.J. Lynch's *The Snow Queen* might be read alongside the Disney book of the film *Frozen*; Rudyard Kipling's *The Jungle Book* might be read before reading Neil Gaiman's *The Graveyard Book*, which was in part inspired by Kipling's classic text. Comparison provides an opportunity for more than the reading of two related texts; the act of comparison lays bare for examination ideas such as authorial point of view and the treatment of a subject. In one of our case studies (Case study 7, 'The Wildman', see pp. 140–48) we show how, having read Kevin Crossley-Holland's *Beowulf*, the children went on to read a short story, 'The Wildman', by the same author. The story is written from Grendel's point of view, although he isn't named in the story. The interaction between the two stories created a new and deeper response to both texts as they were compared to each other.

There is a further way in which texts can be used together to build understanding. The selection of a simpler text prior to reading something that might appear daunting and inaccessible can pave the way for children to approach more complex texts and consequently more challenging ideas and language. For example, one of our case studies shows how *Tadpole's Promise*, by Jeanne Willis and Tony Ross, was read prior to a classic short story, 'The Nightingale and the Rose' by Oscar Wilde. The teacher's reflection was that the children would not have been able to tackle the classic text with the same confidence and insight without the bridge that was created by reading the other book first.

It is essential also to consider the balance of the familiar and the new in relation to content, style, language structures, cultural references, and appearance when assessing the level of a text. In general, learners can focus on what is new and challenging only within a context that is sufficiently familiar to enable them to orchestrate context, syntax, graphic, and phonic cues without undue difficulty.

Balanced reading provision

It has already been indicated that teachers need to make careful choices when choosing resources. In addition to the class teacher making a selection by thinking about the match of text to the readers, those responsible for literacy across the school will need to keep an overview of the repertoire of texts used within and across the years to ensure a balance of genres.

The selection of texts across a year might include a wordless book, a couple of picture books, a selection of stories from a short story collection, a selection of poems from a single poet's collection, a selection of poems from an anthology or a thematic collection, a magazine article, a comparison of two non-fiction books on the same topic, a short film clip, two short novels (read as a class text but incorporating guided reading sessions). The emphasis on shorter texts and the management of the novels through a mix of whole-class and group teaching makes the organization easier. The text selections in the reading lists are a good starting point.

On the next page is a table of the choices made by an upper primary (Year 5) teacher across one year, showing the breadth of text-type and subject as well as the emphasis on shorter but complete texts.

All of the books included in this list can be ordered direct from the website www.guidingreaders.com. You will also find free resources online, including teachers' notes and author interviews.

The website is updated regularly and newly published books that meet our criteria for selection will be added, so you can find the latest books to keep your collections refreshed and up-to-date. If you need any assistance or would like further information about any of these titles, you can contact us via the website.

Table 10.1: Texts selected by a Year 5 teacher

AUTHOR	TITLE	GENRE
David Wiesner	*Flotsam*	Wordless book
Shaun Tan	*The Lost Thing*	Picture book (science fiction)
Chris Van Allsburg	*The Wreck of the Zephyr*	Picture book (mystery)
Jamila Gavin	*Blackberry Blue*	Short story collection (fairy tales; several stories used over the year)
George Layton	*The Fib*	Short story collection, autobiographical, several stories used over the year
Malorie Blackman	*Cloud Busting*	Short verse novel
Chrissie Gittins	*Stars in Jars*	Single poet collection (selected poems read)
Michael Rosen	*A–Z*	Poetry anthology (poems by different poets; read across the year)
Frank Cottrell Boyce	*The Unforgotten Coat*	Short novel
Nicola Davies	*What's Eating You?*	Non-fiction (chatty style and cartoon illustrations); compared to *Pests, Plagues and Parasites*
Mick Gowar	*Pests, Plagues and Parasites*	Non-fiction (ORT reading scheme); compared to *What's Eating You?*

Conclusion

The aim of this book has been to show how teachers can support young readers to comprehend the text they read. It has done so by focusing on a number of specific issues of which teachers need to be aware. First, it considered the whole process of how readers make meaning from text. It described the complexity of the comprehension process because comprehension itself is not a single thing – it is composed of separate components that work interactively. Children will bring different types of knowledge and experience to the process of reading; this will affect the sense they make of the text and teachers need to take this into account.

Alongside this, the teacher needs to consider the text being read. All texts are located in a social and cultural context and for this reason we can't assume that all children will engage with the text in the same way. Each child will bring different expectations and their own unique experiences to the text they read. Teachers need to be aware of the challenges that a text might offer to individual readers – not just with regard to decoding the words. It is useful to consider texts both in terms of the hurdles they may present in reading the words as well as in terms of what they offer in rich ideas. What potential do they hold for expanding children's understanding? Unlocking the potential of texts provides the teacher with a focus or foci for their teaching.

This in turn leads us to consider what this teaching should look like. Guiding readers: why bother? Why is it necessary? These are questions teachers should ask as professionals who are developing their expertise in literacy.

We believe the need to guide readers is clear. Text comprehension is a complex process and is central to reading development. Comprehension itself cannot be taught; it is the outcome, the end result of the reading process. What we can teach are strategies to support comprehension. These strategies are well tested and well researched.

In England, as in many other countries, children are tested on their reading and the results are used to hold schools and teachers to account. Quite rightly, teachers will ask how our approach will enable children to perform well in tests. Although, within a culture of high-stakes testing, teaching children to do well in reading tests is fundamentally different from teaching for meaning, we would argue that, by providing children with strategies to support comprehension, they are more likely to have the embedded skills that they need to use when faced with tests. Without these strategies, they will never perform to a high level in tests, nor will they become engaged and critical readers in the fullest sense.

The process of guiding readers we are advocating here requires teachers to listen to what young comprehenders are saying and, through their responses explored via further questioning, deepen their understanding and engagement with a wide variety of texts. As such, the teacher provides access to layers of meaning that would not emerge if the children were simply involved in the age-old game of 'Guess what's in the teacher's head?'. In our approach, children are encouraged to reason, justify, speculate, and imagine through these co-constructed learning conversations. Children develop a clearer voice about the text; they engage with texts more readily and as a result their enjoyment and pleasure in reading is enhanced.

The case studies have illustrated this. Children were shown working with a range of texts including adverts, poetry, classic literature, picture books, and film. In all of these examples, children of different ages were seen using the same range of strategies to access the text, mediated through the dialogue encouraged by the teacher.

In these case studies we saw teachers opening up worlds for children. As teachers, is there anything more valuable we can do?

Acknowledgements

Many of the case studies reported here would not have been possible without the help of a number of teachers who gave us access to their classes and worked with us to plan and try out these lessons. We are grateful to them for their cooperation. In particular, we appreciate the assistance of:

Gareth Jukes and Carrie Cox, Marks Gate Junior School, Barking and Dagenham

Karyn Ballard, Valence Primary School, Barking and Dagenham

Hannah Birkett, Fullwood Primary School, Redbridge

Nevin Chinniah, Highlands Primary School, Redbridge

Áine Finnegan, Cranbrook Primary School, Redbridge